It is a deep blessing and an existential challenge that such a manuscript on the life and journey of the Christian Bible in the sociopolitical and cultural context of China is written with much careful research and thought. It is an awesome responsibility. The author narrated the wonderfully impossible "journey" of the Bible in China from various possible angles with concern for historical objectivity so that the "silent hand" of the Lord in the journey would not be mistaken.

As Scripture says, "The grass withers, the flower fades, but the word of our God will stand forever … so shall my word be that goes from my mouth; it shall not return to me empty, but it shall accomplish that which I purpose, and shall succeed in the thing for which I sent it" (Isa 40:8; 55:11).

Bishop John Chew
Archbishop, Province of the Anglican Church in South East Asia (2006–2012)

From Banned Book to Bestseller tells a story which is not widely known. A common narrative of Christianity in China is that it has been a persecuted church under the People's Republic and even now subject to tight control by the state. But why should such a state allow the Catholic Church in China to remain faithful to its teachings all these years? Why should it facilitate the establishment of a printing house in Nanjing which has made China by far the largest printer of Bibles in the world? Few Christians are aware that China is both the world's biggest market and the world's biggest exporter of Bibles.

This book helps to explain why the sinicization of Christianity is not merely a political requirement of the Communist Party of China. Sinicization is a long historical process through which the God of the Bible is gradually and progressively revealed to the Chinese people as their God, the God of their ancestors, and not a foreign God. For the Chinese, God must be Chinese. The early Jesuits like Matteo Ricci understood this. In their catechisms, Jesus, Mary, Joseph and the Apostles were Chinese.

Christian evangelism can only succeed in China if it is not seen as light brought in from outside to Chinese people living in darkness but as the nurturing of light already burning in the hearts of Chinese people from the beginning of its civilization. This spirit guided Protestants who came together in the early twentieth century to do a common translation of the Bible in Chinese. The sinicization of Christianity is a huge unfolding story. This book adds to our understanding of it.

George Yeo
Visiting Scholar, Lee Kuan Yew School of Public Policy
Former Minister, Foreign Affairs of Singapore
Former Member, Vatican Council for the Economy

We live in a post-pandemic world in a syndemic moment in history. Humanity's body, mind, and spirit have been affected. Against this very backdrop we are reminded of God's grand plan to redeem all people to see humanity flourish. Out of the darkness light breaks open. Cynthia's important piece of work picks up from those that have gone before her to remain faithful to the sacrificial lives and stories she encountered. Yet each one of those individual stories over time, place, and space points to God's story of unending love for the people of China—never abandoning them through the difficult years. It reminds us of God's people before who endured four hundred years of darkness before the bursting of light that caused angels in heaven to sing and celebrate. This book is a case study of hope. All people and all nations need hope. It is often said that the mark of a country's nationhood is its ability to provide for its people spiritual freedom to choose their spiritual destiny. China is today a nation of hope with all the birth pains that come with such a gestation. Yet in the midst of everything God has never abandoned the Chinese people. He will continue to be the voice even in the wilderness. Cynthia's writing captures pivotal moments in the journey taken by those whose sacrificial service led this banned book to be in the hearts and hands of so many both within and beyond China.

MICHAEL PERREAU
Director General, United Bible Societies (2011–2022)

This book by Cynthia Oh brings together a decade of personal experience in Bible missions in China, access to key archival material, and a passion to write mission history to produce a ground-breaking record of how the Bible grew from being a banned book into the bestselling book in China in the course of a few decades since the 1960s. In particular, the book traces the history of the Bible press (Amity Printing) in China that has produced millions of Bibles. In addition, readers will appreciate how the Bible has made inroads in various ways, through the promotion of Bible reading and application, into churches, society, and the lives of families and individuals. The personal stories gleaned from the ground offer a fuller picture of the effects of making the Bible available to a vast diversity of people who have been blessed by the Word of God that is able to bring about healing and transformation. This will be an invaluable resource for those interested in China, mission history, and Bible missions.

BISHOP EMERITUS DR. ROBERT SOLOMON
The Methodist Church in Singapore

One of the greatest untold stories in the remarkable saga of China's explosive church growth is this unique partnership, rooted in more than two centuries of international cooperation in Scripture translation and distribution, which has brought God's life-changing word to millions across China. One is struck by the patient, humble collaboration between UBS and Chinese church leaders, as well as their bold faith in believing in God for the impossible and the speed at which their partnership came to fruition, eventually resulting in the world's largest Communist country becoming the world's largest supplier of Bibles. Cynthia Oh's moving portrayal of Chinese Christians' sacrificial love of Scripture will deepen your own appreciation for God's Word and for those who have given their lives to bring the Bible to China.

BRENT FULTON, PHD
Founder, ChinaSource

Since the formation of the People's Republic of China in 1949, the Churches in China have experienced a wave of religious constraints. The last batch of the Bible was published in 1956 and had hitherto not been published in China again till 1979. However Chinese Christians carry a strong tradition of loving the Word of God as part of their spirituality. Even during the time of persecution such as the period of the Cultural Revolution (1966–1976) when almost all Bibles were destroyed, many Christians hid their Bibles, risking arrest and jail terms. Many memorized chapter after chapter of the Bible, some made handwritten copies to share with others in secret, others listened to gospel radio and transcribed passages and verses. The Word of God became the only source of hope for millions of Chinese Christians during this period of darkness.

As the church was allowed to resurface in 1979, the government facilitated the Official Church to print a few thousand Bibles and New Testaments using the printing press of the People's Liberation Army. Coming from this humble publication background, no one could ever dream that a few decades later China would become the largest Bible-producing country in the world with 162 million copies in more than two hundred languages for 160 countries and regions. It is in this context that Cynthia Oh has written this amazing story of the Bible in China—from a banned book into a bestseller, taking place in an atheistic country, China. She has the privilege to be a staff member of the United Bible Societies who was directly involved with and witnessed the Bible printing operation in China. Her story is nothing less than a miracle that has unfolded in our time, a story that is part of the matrix of God's might in our contemporary era. Her book is also a testimony of the ecumenical partnership of various Christians from different countries joining efforts to advance the kingdom of God through his words—a ministerial model that transcends traditional mission endeavors. This well-written volume is a must for any serious readers of contemporary Christianity.

Rev. Kim-Kwong Chan, PhD, DTh, Hong Kong
Author of *Understanding World Christianity: China*

Through meticulous research and compelling storytelling, Cynthia sheds light on the tumultuous history of the Bible in China, from its initial banishment to its eventual rise as a bestseller. From the Cultural Revolution to present-day China, this book takes us on a gripping expedition through the world of Chinese Christians who did everything to preserve and share the sacred text over the generations. It explores the transformative power of Scripture, the hope it instilled, and the courage it inspired in the face of challenges. Their unwavering devotion and unyielding resilience serve as a powerful reminder of the enduring relevance and universal appeal of the Scriptures. This book will leave you inspired, uplifted, and with a renewed appreciation for the profound impact of the Word of God.

Rev. Tony Yeo
Chairman, Evangelical Free Church of Singapore
Senior Pastor, Covenant Evangelical Free Church

This is a well-researched, in places first-hand, account of one of the most remarkable little-known stories of the last fifty years. Its author writes with both heart and discernment about the vision and work of the United Bible Societies. Her book is full of engaging stories about the influence of many ordinary Chinese Christians and amazing statistics about the Bible's impact in urban centers, regional areas, and marginal ethnic groups. She documents its influence not only on church growth but also the wider culture. Central to this was UBS leadership's close cooperation with the officially recognized churches and working relationship with the state religious authorities. This is definitely one of the must-read Christian books of the year!

Robert and Linda Banks
Authors, Biographies of Christian Women who Served in China

From Banned Book to Bestseller

The Bible Mission in Contemporary China

Cynthia Oh

Foreword by Kua Wee Seng

visit us at missionbooks.org

From Banned Book to Bestseller: The Bible Mission in Contemporary China

© 2024 by Cynthia Oh. All Rights Reserved.

No part of this book may be reproduced, stored in a retrieval system, or transmitted in any form or by any means—electronic, mechanical, photocopy, recording, or otherwise—without prior written permission from the publisher, except brief quotations used in connection with reviews. This manuscript may not be entered into AI, even for AI training. For permission, email permissions@wclbooks.com. For corrections, email editor@wclbooks.com.

William Carey Publishing (WCP) publishes resources to shape and advance the missiological conversation in the world. We publish a broad range of thought-provoking books and do not necessarily endorse all opinions set forth here or in works referenced within this book.

The URLs included in this workbook are provided for personal use only and are current as of the date of publication, but the publisher disclaims any obligation to update them after publication.

Unless otherwise indicated, all Scripture quotations are from the ESV® Bible (The Holy Bible, English Standard Version®), Copyright © 2001 by Crossway, a publishing ministry of Good News Publishers. Used by permission. All rights reserved.

Scripture quotations marked NASB are taken from the NASB® New American Bible®, Copyright © 1960, 1971, 1977, 1995 by The Lockman Foundation. Used by permission. All rights reserved. lockman.org.

Scripture quotations marked NIV are taken from the Holy Bible, New International Version®, NIV®. Copyright © 1973, 1978, 1984, 2011 by Biblica, Inc.™ Used by permission of Zondervan. All rights reserved worldwide. www.zondervan.com. The "NIV" and "New International Version" are trademarks registered in the United States Patent and Trademark Office by Biblica, Inc.™

Scripture quotations marked NJB are taken from The New Jerusalem Bible, published and copyright 1985 by Darton, Longman & Todd Ltd and Les Editions du Cerf, and used by permission of the publishers.

Scripture quotations marked GNT are taken from the Good News Translation® (Today's English Version, Second Edition). Copyright © 1992 American Bible Society. All rights reserved.

Published by William Carey Publishing
10 W. Dry Creek Cir
Littleton, CO 80120 | www.missionbooks.org

William Carey Publishing is a ministry of Frontier Ventures
Pasadena, CA | www.frontierventures.org

Cover and Interior Designer: Mike Riester

ISBNs: 978-1-64508-582-9 (paperback)
       978-1-64508-630-7 (color hardback)
       978-1-64508-584-3 (epub)

Printed Worldwide

28 27 26 25 24   1 2 3 4 5

Library of Congress Control Number: 2024941548

*To Chinese Christians whose testimonies
are the life of this book and to Bible men and women from UBS
whose love and labor for China have inspired me*

In honor of Marshall Broomhall whose work The Bible in China
has fired my imagination for this book

Contents

Foreword by Kua Wee Seng	xi
Preface	xiii
Introduction	xvii
1 Blazing the Trails: The Bible in China–The Seventh Century to the 1950s	1
2 Into the Dark Night: The Bible during the Cultural Revolution	13
3 Out of the Shadows: A Bible Press for China	25
4 Shining Forth I: Bible Distribution Work	37
5 Shining Forth II: Bibles for the Catholic Church in China	51
6 Fire of Revival: The Bible and Church Growth	65
7 True Vision: Braille Bibles for the Blind	77
8 Glows and Glitters in the Mountains I Bible Translation for Ethnic Minority People in China	89
9 Glows and Glitters in the Mountains II Bible Ministry to the Ethnic Minority People in China	101
10 A Light for Every Season: Scripture Portions, Selections, and Gospel Booklets	113
11 Fan into Flames: Scripture Literacy Classes and Discipleship Resources for Believers	125
12 Igniting Young Minds: Bible Ministry for the Family	135
13 In the Shadow of the Cross: Bible and Mental Well-Being	147
14 Fuel for the Fireplace: Bible Ministry to Seminary Teachers and Students	155
15 Oil for the Lamps: Bible Ministry to Pastors and Lay Preachers	165
16 Shine like Stars: The Bible Advocacy among Leaders of Society	175
17 In the Light of Scripture The Bible and the Contextualization and Inculturation of Christianity in China	189
18 Stellar Performance The Bible Printing Press in China: Milestones and Achievements	199
Epilogue–Light unto the Nations: The Unstoppable Word of God in and beyond China	211
Appendix–A Timeline of Bible Missions in China	213
Acknowledgments	219
About UBS	220
Bibliography	221
Index	225

Foreword

I first heard about Amity Printing Company, the Bible printing press in China, when I read the news of Rev. Dr. Billy Graham's visit to the press in Nanjing during his first trip to China in 1988. I did not quite believe the news about a Bible printing press in China. I knew about the Cultural Revolution years in the 1960s and 1970s when all churches were closed and Bibles were banned. How could the Chinese authorities allow Bibles to be printed again and permit a Bible press to be established in Mainland China?

I was skeptical about the Bible press in China till I visited it in March 1993 and saw for myself the printing of the Bibles at the press. I was invited by the United Bible Societies (UBS) in 1993 to help manage the press as the deputy general manager of the printing company. In 1996, I was appointed to the board of the company, and I served on the board for nearly three decades, retiring as the board vice chairman in November 2023.

Since 1993, I have had the blessings and joy of serving the Lord in the Bible mission in China through the UBS ministry. For the past three decades, I was privileged to serve and support the Churches in China in the whole range of their Bible ministry—Bible translation and publication, printing and distribution, sharing and outreach, literacy and studies, preaching and teaching, training and equipping, engagement and advocacy, etc.

The establishment and growth of the Amity Printing Company is an amazing miracle of God in modern mission history. God planted a Bible press in China in 1987, barely a decade after the end of the Cultural Revolution when Bibles were banned, confiscated, and destroyed. Once a banned book, the Bible became a bestselling book in China. More than 94 million copies of the Bible have been printed by Amity Printing Company and distributed by the Churches in China!

In response to the growing demands for Bibles, Amity Printing Company expanded its facility and production, becoming the largest Bible press in the world. By the end of 2023, more than 256 million copies of the Bible have been printed by the press since its establishment, including 162 million copies for export to more than 160 countries and regions in over two hundred different languages!

And the spread of the Word of God in China has contributed to the incredible growth and development of the Churches in China. As I reflected on the growth of Christianity in China over the past few decades, I'm reminded of the explosive growth of the early church in the Book of Acts, which St. Luke described as the spread and increase of the Word of God (Acts 6:7; 12:24; 13:49; 19:20).

Yet this amazing story of the Bible mission in China is not as well-known nor well-reported. Articles and books have been written about the phenomenal growth of Christianity in China, but not as much has been written about the miraculous story of the Bible ministry in China.

This inspiring story of the Bible mission in China needs to be told, the wonderful testimony of the impact of the Word of God in China needs to be shared, and the powerful work of God through his word in China needs to be proclaimed! We need to make known his deeds among the peoples and tell of all his wondrous works (Ps 105:1–2).

And what better person to tell the story and proclaim God's wonderful deeds in China Bible mission than Cynthia Oh! I have known and worked with Cynthia since she joined our UBS China ministry team as the communication manager in 2013.

She is gifted in writing, and she has used her gift to share many powerful and moving stories of the impact of the Word of God in China. She traveled to China many times over the decade, visiting local churches, meeting Chinese Christians, listening to their stories and testimonies, and sharing them through the UBS communication network.

She also has a keen interest in history, and she has done a lot of painstaking work and meticulous research into the archives, records, and reports of the UBS to piece together an inspiring and compelling story of how the Bible went from being a banned book to become a bestseller in China, spreading and impacting the lives of Chinese people throughout the land.

I have enjoyed reading her book, especially the many inspiring stories and testimonies. I was personally involved in most of the Bible ministries she has shared in her book, and I can vouch for them and their impact on the churches and Christians in China. I highly commend her book to all of you. You will be more informed of the Bible mission in China. You will be inspired by many testimonies and stories in the book. You will be encouraged by what God has done through his word in China. You will thank God and praise him for his miraculous work and wonderful deeds in China.

As you read this exciting story of the Bible mission in China, please pray and support the Bible ministry in China—that the Word of God will continue to spread and increase in China, despite the challenges and constraints. May his unstoppable word continue to increase and prevail mightily in China and all over the world!

So the word of the Lord continued to increase and prevail mightily.
—Acts 19:20

But the Word of God is not bound! —2 Timothy 2:9c

Kua Wee Seng
February 2024
Director, UBS China Partnership (1999–2021)
Amity Printing Company Management and Board (1993–2023)

Preface

> The light shines in the darkness, and the darkness has not overcome it.
> —John 1:5

This story came about partly out of a sense of curiosity while I served with the United Bible Societies China Partnership (UBS CP) as communication manager. During my first few years with the organization, two things intrigued and impacted me in particular, contributing to the creation of this book ten years later.

First, my visit to Amity Printing Company (APC) in Nanjing, China, in 2013 when I first joined the ministry. Under my director, Kua Wee Seng, all new staff had to visit the Bible printing press as part of orientation. He asked if I had known about the Bible printing press. I said, "No, I haven't heard of it." "Then, you must visit it," he said. So I made a trip there and toured the printing facility. I was impressed by its magnitude, but I had to confess I could not understand the full significance of the press.

In the course of my work, I interviewed Chinese Christians and church leaders who shared their experiences with the Bible—how they did not have Bibles during the Cultural Revolution, how it was so precious to them, how they rejoice at having Bibles now, and how God transformed their lives through his word. Many of them were telling me similar stories. Gradually, I realized I was entering into the middle of a story, the story of the Bible in China. I did not know what had happened at the beginning with the Bible, what happened along the way, and the significance of APC in the timeline of Christianity in China. Without an understanding of the past, I could not fully appreciate the current developments with the Bible in China.

So I began to research some of these questions on an ad hoc basis, like the story behind the translation of the beloved Chinese Union Version Bible and the circumstances leading to the establishment of the APC. But these were individual, stand-alone articles, and the full story still eluded me.

Along the way, the story became more multifaceted and compelling as I discovered more of God's work in China where his word was concerned—for example, ongoing Bible translations for ethnic minority groups in China, which early missionaries had started in the late 1800s, Braille Bibles for the blind, distribution of pictorial Bibles and Gospel portions to young people, and in recent years UBS's support of international seminars involving Chinese academia and overseas Christian scholars to talk about the Bible.

I began to wonder again: What is this story I am witnessing? From my visits to the local churches and interactions with the Chinese Christians and leaders, I sensed a beautiful story unfolding before my eyes, and I wished to capture it. The Word of God was spreading far and wide in China, and lives were being transformed, a Bible miracle no less. I also wished to know the story from the beginning so that I might capture it better. But who could point me to the beginning?

The answer lies in the second thing that inspired me to write this story—it was another book, *The Bible in China* by Marshall Broomhall, published in 1934 and currently out of print.[1] My colleague Yeo Tan Tan had passed it to me at the office one day, probably during my third or fourth year with the ministry. The book attempted to piece the story together from the beginning in the seventh century to the 1930s—how the Bible first arrived in China and spread in the big land thereafter. I was immediately enthralled by the book—you could say Broomhall swept me off my feet in my living hall (a pun on his last name)! Having written some stories about the Bible in China myself, I felt a sense of fraternity with him. The book, like a time machine with fiber optics, transmitted at superspeed inspiring stories and testimonies of old about the work of pioneering missionaries and Bible Societies in China before the formation of UBS and UBS CP.

It connected me with forerunners in the ministry of Bible mission in China. I felt tremendous gratitude that someone had written and recorded God's work, which gave perspective to the present. It "put me in my place" historically and deeply enriched my understanding and experience of the Bible ministry of which I was privileged to be a part. Subconsciously, while reading the book, I was inspired to do likewise one day by continuing the story where Broomhall had left off.

The final bit of this book's backstory is that it was written during the COVID-19 pandemic years from 2020 to 2023. I had just rejoined the UBS CP team after a nine-month mission internship overseas. The closure of international borders had prevented me from returning to the field, and I was grateful to be able to rejoin the team. However, like the rest of the world, we were not able to travel to China. I thought to myself, would this then be an opportune time to step back and look at the story as a whole?

Kua Wee Seng, the director of UBS CP (1999–2021), who had been involved in the Bible ministry in China for close to three decades, was about to retire. He was available to walk me through the recent history of UBS Bible ministry in China via a series of interviews, give me access to the China-related UBS archives that he has collected over the years, and point me to people who could help piece the story together. There was no reason not to write the story. It felt as if God had everything lined up for his story to be told!

In 2013, before joining UBS CP, I prayed that I might be able to serve God through writing. I was in the middle of my theological studies at East Asia School of Theology (EAST) in preparation for the mission field. But I was not yet ready to be sent, and the Lord in his love and providence led me to UBS CP. Interestingly, the recruitment process started from a water cooler conversation at EAST with Yeo Tan Tan, program manager of UBS CP at that time. She was taking a day course there.

Ten years later, I had not expected the Lord to answer my prayer again in ways unimaginable through the writing of this book. I am humbled to be given the chance to tell this amazing story; it is a merging of three of my interests—mission, history, and writing. What this book showcases is only a slice of the Bible mission of the registered churches in China carried out with the support of UBS. By choosing this focus, I am by no means disregarding the unregistered churches and Chinese Christians who worship in them.

---

1 Broomhall, *The Bible in China*.

I've read their stories in various articles and books, and I sympathize with the challenges they faced. I am also inspired by their sacrifices for the Lord. And I respect Christian organizations that serve the unregistered churches and seek to provide Bibles for them in their own ways. Books have been written on these subjects, but rarely are there books on the registered churches and what the Lord has done among them. Rarely do we hear about our brothers and sisters in Christ who worship at registered (often referred to as "Three-Self") churches. Rarely do we know how much they love God and his Word.

Thus, the bulk of this book aims to tell the journey of the Bible in China through a range of Bible missions the Lord has miraculously performed among the registered churches. This is the story that I believe needs to be told. Much of it is what I have witnessed this past decade in the course of my work with UBS. Admittedly, my story does not and cannot constitute the full picture of Christianity in China. Christianity in China is far more nuanced and complex than what one book can capture, but I believe my book is like a piece of the puzzle that provides a fuller understanding of Christianity and Bible mission in China: a facet of a dazzling diamond.

This book is based largely on firsthand accounts and testimonies from the archives, records, and reports of the UBS China ministry from 1985 to 2022, including interviews I conducted myself. I hope it will give you a glimpse into the lives of the Chinese Christians from the registered churches, their love and hunger for the Bible, and the spread and impact of God's Word among them.

I would be content if you feel half as inspired as I was when reading Broomhall and if you do not stop praising God as you turn these pages nor stop trusting God as you close the book.

Cynthia Oh
March 2024
Singapore

The author with a Tibetan believer, Qinghai Province, 2013.

Introduction

In 1987, Ronald Reagan, President of the United States visited West Berlin, and in a speech he appealed to Mikhail Gorbachev, the leader of the USSR, to "tear down this wall." He was referring to the divide between the world of democracy and communism resulting in the Cold War (1947–1991) and symbolized by the wall that divided the people of West and East Berlin.

In that same year, unbeknownst to many people around the world, an event happened where another barrier was being torn down for the people in China.

It was the opening of a Bible printing press in Nanjing, China, on December 5, 1987, set up with the support and donations of Christians all over the world through the United Bible Societies (UBS).

This was after nearly two decades of extreme scarcity and severe shortage of the Bible, which started during the Cultural Revolution (1966–1976). In the decade-long social and political turmoil, Bibles were seen by Christians as rare and precious as diamonds, but they were treated like pestilence by the authorities who sought to ban and burn them on a massive scale. To Chinese Christians who loved and cherished the Word of God, it was a period of much anguish and bitterness. Many thought the day would not come when they would see the Bible again.

When the Chinese Churches reopened in the 1980s, some Chinese Christian leaders, seeing the dire need, started printing Bibles at state-owned presses and even at the press belonging to the People's Liberation Army. From 1979 to 1987, slightly more than 3 million copies of Scripture were printed. However, Bibles were in such great demand that the needs of Chinese Christians could not be met.

Now with the Bible printing press, a wide door has been opened for the Word of God. Chinese Christians were again laying their hands freely on the book that had once brought suffering to its owners, even though many would not think twice about endangering their lives for it. It was an unfathomable and surreal experience. People from all walks of life—young and old, male and female, rural and urban people, pastors and preachers, teachers and students—flocked to church bookstores to buy Bibles. Chinese Christians began reading and studying, memorizing and meditating, quoting and teaching from the Bible once again.

Due to the vastness of the country, many Chinese Christians traveled on long journeys from the villages to buy and carry Bibles home—some carried them on their shoulders and wooden poles, some pulled ox carts and wheelbarrows, some transported using mules and horses, while others rode bicycles and motorbikes. To circulate the Bibles more widely, Chinese Protestant Churches under the umbrella organization of the China Christian Council / Three-Self Patriotic Movement (CCC/TSPM) lost no time in setting up distribution centers across China. By the 1990s, there were more than fifty such centers served by about one hundred staff and volunteers. In the 2000s, as demand for Bibles continued to climb, UBS supported the Chinese Churches with Bible distribution vans to accelerate the circulation of Bibles, especially in rural China. By 2015, there were more than eighty-five Bible distribution centers all over China and more than forty-five Bible distribution vans with some running the dirt roads of rural China bringing God's Word to Chinese people. While it did not mean that Bibles were in abundance, the Word of God was spreading rapidly and widely in different parts of China.

From the snowy mountains of Yunnan to the lush grassland of Inner Mongolia, the Bible was read; from the arid regions in the north to the tropical coastal lines in the south, the Bible was read; from the tranquil farmland in the countryside to the hustling and bustling cities, the Bible was read.

As the Bible was read and the Word of God obeyed in the lives of the Chinese Christians, it fueled an explosive growth of the Chinese Churches. Home-based Bible reading groups especially in rural China began to form and led to the mushrooming of many meeting points and churches. People were coming to faith as they joined home meetings, read the Bible, and witnessed the lives of Christians. It was estimated that the Christian population was increasing at an average growth rate of a million per year after the reopening of China in the 1980s. Based on official sources, from an estimated 700,000 believers in 1949, the Protestant population burgeoned to 40 million today worshiping in 60,000 churches and meeting points, served by 6,000 pastors and 190,000 lay preachers. The Catholic Church in China grew from 3 million in 1949 to 6 million in 2020. Unofficial estimates put the number of Chinese Christians at 100 million.

Meanwhile, the Bible press in Nanjing—Amity Printing Company (APC)—was kept busy. The Chinese Churches and UBS celebrated the printing of the first millionth copy of the Bible printed by APC in 1989. In 1999, the 20-millionth copy was celebrated! By the 1990s, APC was not only printing Bibles for Christians in China, but it was also exporting Bibles overseas, especially to churches in Africa. In 2008, APC moved to a new facility, which increased its printing capacity and raised its standards. In 2019, the 200-millionth copy of the Bible rolled off the press, of which more than 80 million copies have been distributed in China since 1987. The book that was once banned has become a bestseller!

With the advancement of technology over the decades, the Bible also appeared in various formats in China starting with the Bible on cassette tapes, CD-ROM, VCD, and DVD (the *Jesus* film), followed by the digital Bible app more recently. Different Bible editions were also created and published to cater to different segments of society in China—Bibles in simplified Chinese for the younger generation in the early 1990s, Braille and audio Bibles for the blind, *Pictorial Bible Stories* for the young, large-print Bibles for the elderly and those with failing eyesight, and the *Financial Stewardship Bible* for business people, to name a few.

Not only was the Bible available in Mandarin, but it was also produced in the mother tongues of the hill tribes in China, building upon the work done by past missionaries. UBS began supporting the churches in the 1980s by conducting translation workshops and later Bible translation for ethnic minority groups, such as the Big Flowery Miao, East Lisu, West Lisu, Black Yi, White Yi, Wa, and Ganyi, thus giving millions of China's ethnic minority people the opportunity to hear and respond to the life-changing message of Christ in their own language. Within the ethnic minority churches, the translated Bibles were transforming the way believers encountered and received the Word of God. So excited were they that Bible reading and study groups were quickly formed. Preachers using their mother tongues were able to give sermons that resonated deeply with the people's hearts.

Besides providing Bibles, UBS also supported the churches in providing Bible reference books in the early 2000s to help strengthen the theological foundation of the churches. These much-needed resources were given to the libraries of the theological seminaries and Bible training centers, as well as pastors, lay preachers, and seminary students. In addition, Bible training and equipping classes were conducted for pastors and lay preachers. Scripture literacy classes were held for those who longed to learn to read the Bible but had not gone to school or had limited schooling.

In 2010, UBS started to support Bible advocacy seminars and exhibitions in China to highlight the positive contributions of the Christian faith to society, engaging scholars and researchers from academia, church, and government. The year 2021 marked the tenth anniversary of the Bible advocacy seminar in China, a partnership between the UBS and the Shanghai Academy of Social Sciences. It is an initiative that has gained importance and urgency as the Chinese authorities continue to call for the sinicization of religions in China.

By the beginning of the twenty-first century, Churches in China were experiencing such unprecedented growth and expansion of Bible ministry that they were able to hold their first Bible exhibition in Hong Kong in 2004. The exhibition, which told the story of the Bible in China, continued to draw crowds when it was held in the United States in 2006, in Germany in 2007, and again in the United States in 2011. These Bible exhibitions were a testament to the spread of God's Word in China and the centrality of the Bible in the lives of the Christians in China. Visitors marveled at how the Word of God, which was once banned and had much difficulty taking root in China, is now so freely available in various formats, embraced and loved by millions of Chinese Christians, and continuing to transform lives in one of the most populous countries in the world—a story waiting to be told in this book.

The unfathomable had happened in a place where conditions were once harsh and unfavorable. How did the Word of God spread so rapidly in China, a country whose government is atheistic? And what is the story behind how Bible Societies got involved in the translation and publication, printing and distribution, engagement, and advocacy of the Bible in China after churches reopened in the 1980s? Before we delve into that, it is instructive that we look back at the trails left behind by pioneer Bible workers, missionaries, and Bible Societies, and their indefatigable zeal in carrying the light and giving it to China. Because it is on their shoulders that we stand.

*In terms of naming convention of places, I have used Hanyu Pinyin most of the time except for a few occasions where I used the form of romanization most commonly employed during the era of the narrative, such as "Peking" instead of "Beijing." For Chinese names of people, I used the Chinese system of putting the surname before the given name. Following the convention within UBS, I have used the term "Churches in China" and "Chinese Churches" to refer to both the Catholic and Protestant churches in China as a collective, while "churches in China" or "church in China" refer to some churches or an individual church in China.

1
Blazing the Trails

The Bible in China—The Seventh Century to the 1950s

> In the beginning was the Word, and the Word was with God,
> and the Word was God. —John 1:1

> He decided to carry the true Sutras (of the True Way) with him, and observing the course of the winds, he made his way (to China) through difficulties and perils.
> —An extract from the inscription on the Nestorian Stone Tablet

The Nestorians, Franciscans, and Jesuits

Who first brought Bibles into China, and how was the Word of God received? The Scripture was likely first carried into China in AD 635 by a group of Christians known as the Nestorians. This fascinating story is told through a historical artifact—a 2.8-meter-tall limestone tablet—standing today in the Beilin Museum in Xi'an, Shaanxi Province. Discovered in 1625, it takes us back to the seventh century when men arrived from the Church of the East during the reign of Emperor Tang Taizong.

It is worth reproducing a key excerpt inscribed in both Chinese and Syriac recording the Nestorian's missionary zeal, Bible translation work, and their exceptional reception by the emperor:

> And behold there was a highly virtuous man named A-lo-pen in the Kingdom of Ta-Chin. Auguring from the azure sky, he decided to carry the true Sutras (of the True Way) with him, and observing the course of the winds, he made his way (to China) through difficulties and perils. Thus, in the Ninth year of the period named Cheng-Kuan (A.D. 635), he arrived at Chang An. The Emperor dispatched his Minister Duke Fang Huan Ling, with a guard of honor, to the western suburb to meet the visitor and conduct him to the palace. The Sutras (Scripture) were translated at the Imperial Library. (His Majesty) investigated The Way in his own Forbidden apartment, and being convinced of its correctness and truth, he gave special orders for its propagation.[1]

It seems that the Nestorians were allowed to translate the Scripture and share the Christian faith in China during the Tang Dynasty. However, their work ended abruptly when the imperial edict of 845 snuffed out religious activities, affecting not only the Nestorian Christians but other religious groups as well.

---
1 Sweeny, "The Nestorian Stele Content."

In 986, a Christian monk from Najran (in modern-day Saudi Arabia) who had been sent to China by the Nestorian Patriarch in 982 was reported to have said, "Christianity is extinct in China; the native Christians have perished in one way or an-other; the church which they had has been destroyed and there is only one Christian left in the land."[2] While his observation may not be applied to the whole of China, one can sense the dismal state of the Nestorian Church at the time.

The skies seemed overcast at the close of the tenth century for Christianity and the Bible in China. The next attempt to bring the Word of God to China was made by John of Montecorvino, the first Roman Catholic missionary from the Order of Friars Minor, also known as the Franciscans. He reached Beijing in 1294, almost three centuries after Nestorian Christianity was last heard of after the fall of the Tang Dynasty.

John of Montecorvino translated the New Testament and Psalms into the Mongolian language, which was then the lingua franca of the Yuan Dynasty—a task seldom undertaken by the Catholics, who believed that the Bible should be kept in Latin. He inspired another Franciscan monk, Gabriele Allegra, who later in the twentieth century successfully translated the Chinese Catholic Bible, the Studium Biblicum Version, which is the de facto authorized Chinese Catholic Bible used today.

Under John of Montecorvino's leadership, the gospel spread to Fujian Province, a three-month's journey from Beijing. From his letters, it was reported that he baptized six thousand Mongols in Beijing. He was even appointed by the Vatican to be the archbishop of Beijing and primate of all the East in 1307. However, his ministry did not survive the fall of the Mongols in 1368.[3]

More than two centuries later, in 1582, the Jesuit missionary Matteo Ricci reached China. The light was rekindled. He and the early Jesuits saw the need for a basic Chinese Christian vocabulary. Hence, they translated Bible stories and Gospel readings for liturgical use. Subsequently, Jean Basset (1662–1707), a French priest, translated part of the New Testament into Chinese but died before he could complete it.

The eighteenth century closed with a complete Chinese Bible still not in sight and the future of Christianity in China uncertain.

Protestant Missionaries and Bible Societies (1800s to Mid-1900s)

In 1804, a group of Christians in England led by William Wilberforce captured the same vision of carrying the Scripture to different peoples and lands. They formed the British and Foreign Bible Society (BFBS). Interestingly, the manuscript by Jean Basset, which the BFBS had considered publishing in the same year the society was founded, was preserved in the British Museum.[4]

Robert Morrison, the first Protestant missionary to China, carried a copy of Basset's manuscript with him when he set sail from Britain in 1807. Because the East India Company had prohibited missionaries from entering China, Morrison, a British citizen, sought to sail via America. After arriving in New York, he had to obtain all the necessary documents and

---

2 "History of Early Christianity in China."
3 Moffett, "John of Montecorvino."
4 Cann, "UBS Bible Work in China: From Inception to 1959."

letters to ensure his safety and residence in the American quarters of Canton. On board the vessel, an American merchant asked if Morrison "really expected to make an impression on the idolatry of the Great Chinese Empire." Morrison replied, "No, sir, I expect God will."[5] It was this trust in God that saw Morrison through the coming challenges. As Broomhall put it, "His lot was maintained by a Higher Power than the world's most powerful monopoly."[6]

By the 1800s, the Bible had been translated into seventy-one languages of the world but not into Mandarin. But with Robert Morrison, this was about to change. Upon arriving in China, Morrison, who had started to learn Mandarin back in London, immediately embarked on Bible translation, using Basset's manuscript as a reference. In 1811, Morrison received the first grant from BFBS for his translation work. This marked the beginning of BFBS's support of the Bible mission in China, which continues to this day.

Under the hostile environment of the Qing Dynasty, challenges and opposition abounded in the Bible translation work. In secrecy, Morrison learned the Chinese language as locals were forbidden by the Qing government to teach the language to foreigners. This meant spending long hours without going out, cabin fever, and ill health during his initial years. These lines stand out from his letters home, "I feel the confinement a good deal," "I am under the continual dread of the oppressor," "The natives who assist me are hunted from place to place and sometimes seized." Later, printing blocks created for the printing of the New Testament were seized by the Chinese authorities and destroyed. Men who helped Morrison create the wooden blocks were also arrested. One can imagine the devastation Morrison felt.

In 1810, when the first Scripture portion was printed, it had to be camouflaged with a false cover page. As Scripture became more available throughout China, "the government decreed the death penalty for any European preparing or disseminating Christian literature and exile to northern Manchuria for any Chinese deluded by them."[7]

In 1813, Morrison was grateful to be joined by the second Protestant missionary to China, William Milnes, who assisted him in the Bible translation work. To understand the extent of the difficulty of language learning, one only need to turn to these famous lines by Milnes, "To acquire the Chinese language is a work for men with bodies of brass, lungs of steel, heads of oak, hearts of apostles, memories of angels, and lives of Methuselah."[8] Amid these challenges, Morrison and Milnes, together with their Chinese assistants, persisted in the long and formidable task of giving the Word of God to the Chinese in their language.

A copy of the first Chinese Bible, translated by Robert Morrison and published in 1823 by BFBS in several volumes.
Photo supplied by Cambridge University Library.

---

5 Hallihan, "Robert Morrison, Bible Translator of China, 1782–1834."
6 Broomhall, *Bible in China*, 55.
7 Nida, *The Book of a Thousand Tongues*, 71.
8 Doyle, "William Milnes."

A painting depicting Robert Morrison and his assistants working on the translation of the Bible into Chinese. Photo supplied by Cambridge University Library.

The Chinese Bible was finally completed in 1819 but was not published until 1823, sixteen years after Morrison arrived in China and started work on it. However, by this time he was the lone missionary to witness the first copy of the Chinese Bible rolling off the printing press in Malacca, a location chosen earlier by Milnes because the Chinese empire was still a closed land. Morrison had lost both his wife, Mary, who died of cholera in 1821, and his ministry partner, Milnes, who died of lung disease in 1822.[9] Milnes himself had lost his wife, Rachel, in 1819.[10] In the midst of these tragic losses, Morrison saw the fruition of a dream—the message of hope and salvation finally being made available for the first time in China.

Deeply aware of the limitations of his pioneering translation, Morrison himself began a revision process. Other and later Chinese Bible translations were also done with the support of BFBS and the American Bible Society (ABS), which started to support Bible missions in China in 1833. This support included the translation, publication, and distribution of various versions of the Chinese Bible translated by Joshua Marshman, Walter Medhurst, Karl Gützlaff, and the Board of Delegates (formed by a group of Protestant missionaries).[11]

Amazingly, by the late 1800s, there were about twenty-seven versions of the Chinese Bible done by missionaries sent by mission societies from different countries and church denominations. And this began to present a problem. Protestant missionaries in China saw that without a unified version of the Chinese Bible, without a common name for "God" and "Jesus," they were running the danger of "speaking of different deities" in the ears of the Chinese! However, due to translation and theological differences, discussion of a unified version had been fraught with difficulties.

1891 Chinese Old Testament by ABS.

---

9   Doyle, "William Milne."
10 Hallihan, "Robert Morrison, Bible Translator."
11 Cann, "UBS Bible Work."

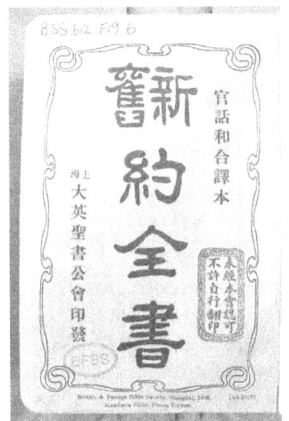

1919 CUV printed by BFBS.

A breakthrough came at the 1890 General Conference of the Protestant Missionaries of China held in Shanghai—a formal proposal for a unified version was approved as consensus was reached to translate the Mandarin Union Version of the Chinese Bible, later known as the Chinese Union Version (CUV). BFBS, ABS, and the National Bible Society of Scotland, which began contributing to the Bible missions in China in 1863, gladly came together to support the Bible translation.

The unified version saw the light of day three decades later in 1919, a translation project that survived the Boxer Rebellion (1899–1901), the collapse of the Qing Dynasty (1912) and World War I (1914–1918). Today, more than a century later, the CUV continues to be the de facto authorized version used by the Chinese Protestant Christians with its printing and distribution in China supported by the Bible Societies. More will be said about the CUV in chapter 17.

CUV Bible translators with their respective Chinese language assistants. L-R: Frederick W. Baller, Liu Dacheng, C. Goodrich, Zhang Xixin, Calvin Wilson Mateer, Wang Yuande, Spencer Lewis, and Li Chunfan.

Bibles in Local Dialects and Ethnic Minority Languages

Besides Mandarin, the Bible was also translated into Chinese dialects and ethnic minority languages by some missionaries and their local assistants. During this period, China still had millions of people who were not familiar with the Chinese language and needed the Scripture in their own dialects. Furthermore, contrary to popular assumptions, dialects were spoken by all classes of the community, not just the uneducated.

By the first three decades of 1900, several Scripture publications appeared for the first time with the support of the Bible Societies. This included some first portions of the Bible in twenty-six dialects. Between 1850 and 1933, the Bible Societies published full Bibles in Xiamen, Guangdong, Fuzhou, Shantou, Shanghai (1908), Soochow (1908), Taichow (1914), Ningpo (1901), Hinghua (1912), and Hakka (1916) dialects.[12] New Testaments were published in Jianming and Wenzhou dialects.

---

12 American Bible Society, "American Bible Society (ABS) in China 1931–1966, Pre-1930"; and Cann, "UBS Bible Work."

Similarly, full Bibles in Mongolian and Uighur and New Testaments in Kazah and Manchu were made available for non-Han Chinese people in the north and northwest. One of the greatest stories among the non-Han Chinese people in the early 1900s was the mass conversion of those residing in the southwest of China. Ethnic minorities who had no written literature were amazed to see their spoken language being given a written form by missionaries and to have the Bibles in their own tongue. These included the full Bible in Lisu, the New Testament in Eastern Lisu, Miao:He, Miao:Hwa, Yi, and portions of the Bible in Chung Chia, Kado, Keh-deo, Kopu, Laka, Miao:Chuan, Na-hsi, Shan:Yunnancsc, and Tai Ya.[13]

Shanghai language, recorded in *The Book of a Thousand Tongues*, a 1972 UBS publication, recorded the first Bible translations into languages all over the world including China.

For the island of Formosa, Scriptures were published in Taiwanese (derived from the Xiamen dialect), as well as in the indigenous Formosan languages of Amis, Bunun, Paiwan, Sediq, and Tayal, and the non-Formosan language of Yami.[14]

1912 New Testament in Hwa Miao printed by BFBS.

Bible Distribution and Impact of the Word of God

Concern for China's unreached millions was at the heart of the Bible Societies. In 1853, at the jubilee celebration of the BFBS, the *Chinese Million New Testament Fund* was set up. The goal was to provide and distribute a million Chinese New Testaments for the empire, which at that time made up one-third of the world's population. This included donating a press to print Scriptures.

Colporteurs at a covered stall selling Scriptures, Tientsin.

A whopping £52,000 was collected, way above the target of £18,000. Although sparked by the infamous Taiping Rebellion and hopes of heralding a Chinese Christian government, *Chinese Million New Testament Fund* was probably the largest Bible society project to be undertaken at that time.[15]

To circulate the Word of God, Bible Societies adopted a two-pronged approach. First, they strategically partnered with and supported both European and American mission organizations that were sending men and women to China to spread the

---

13 Cann, "UBS Bible Work."
14 Cann, "UBS Bible Work."
15 Cann, "UBS Bible Work."

gospel. These missionaries often purchased Scriptures from the Bible Societies for their ministry and evangelistic work.

Second, Bible Societies worked through colporteurs—men who promoted and sold Scriptures. After setting up an agency in Shanghai in 1836, BFBS employed local Chinese Protestants as colporteurs. They often accompanied the missionaries or Bible society agents to promote Scriptures or acted as forerunners with a tray of Scriptures tied over their necks, making contact with the locals in the cities, towns, remote villages, and even in the rural and mountainous regions of China.

Colporteur with a bike selling Scriptures in Peking.

The contributions of the colporteurs were not underestimated. Their importance to the Bible society's mission in China was often recognized and praised. The BFBS 1895 annual report said this about the colporteur:

> ... man who not only carry the Word of God in their hands but who has the Living Word in their hearts ... [usually] colportage work will go before preaching. [The colporteur] in his explanation of the Scriptures [can] better meet the prejudices, superstitions, hopes and fears of his purchasers. ... The twists and turns of a Chinese person's mind only a Chinese can understand and meet with effect. Over and over again, the colporteurs with his stocks of Gospels and his kindly pressure on the people to buy and hear, becomes the true pioneer of the Gospel itself.[16]

By the early 1900s, BFBS had an extensive colportage system with over three hundred colporteurs working with 180 missionaries representing thirty-two different mission organizations.[17] Chinese local women were also employed for the same purpose. Known as Bible Women, they were effective in reaching women and worked well with female missionaries.

What was the impact of God's Word upon the Chinese people during this period? Around 1887, a few years before the Boxer Rebellion, a colporteur said that "the brightest spot in their colportage work had been the conversion of a man, his nephew and two more of the same family in Long Tsuen through reading the Four Gospels."[18] The colporteur learned from the nephew that his uncle destroyed his idols at home upon reading the Scriptures and declared his intention to worship God. He did not know how, but he knew that God was in heaven. So each morning before breakfast, he went out to his doorstep to pray. So sincere was the man that though he did not know what to say, he knelt and kowtowed before God and prayed, "God, I truly worship Thee, God, I truly worship Thee."

Not only were the Chinese people coming to know God, but some were also willing to suffer for their faith. This testimony came not long after the Boxer Rebellion when anti-foreign

---

16 British and Foreign Bible Society annual report, 1895.
17 British and Foreign Bible Society report, "After a Hundred Years," 1905.
18 Broomhall, *Bible in China*, 161.

Two colporteurs working among the shipping population on the Chinese Bund of Shanghai.

sentiments were intense. A farmer staying not far from the city of Kwangchow removed idols at his home after reading a copy of the Gospel. But this so infuriated his family that they chained his hand and foot and blinded his right eye with needles. They even proceeded to put a chain around his neck and fastened him to the walls of the inner rooms of the farm compound. Day and night for over a month, the man held the Gospel to his bosom and cried to Jesus for deliverance, repeating the words of Bartimaeus, "Jesus of Nazareth, have mercy on me!" One day, torrential rain flooded both the city and the countryside. Houses collapsed and farms were swept away, including the one where the man was imprisoned. He then fled, chain and all, and went to a mission chapel. There he told his story to all he met that though the book that he kept had cost him the loss of one eye, Jesus his Savior had opened both eyes of his heart and given him peace.[19]

On the other hand, some colporteurs were met with setbacks, criticisms, and insults from their fellow countrymen. Christian missions had long been associated with Western imperialism. After the First Opium War of 1839–42 and a further conflict in 1858 leading to the ratification of a treaty in 1860, the whole of China was opened to Western influence. Some missionaries at that time had a negative view of Chinese culture, and local converts were compelled to renounce their own traditions. This resulted in some Chinese rejecting the Bible and Christianity. A colporteur reported in 1885, "I have been reviled as disloyal to my country for engaging in such a service. Many refused, with curses, to look at the books."[20]

The Work of Bible Societies in the 1920s–1930s

The 1920s and 1930s were a tumultuous period for China as she was ravaged by the competing armies of nationalists, Communists, and provincial warlords. But this period also saw an increase in Scripture circulation, church growth, and revival. When the Great Depression hit in 1929, ABS reported an all-time high of more than 5 million volumes of Scriptures (Bibles, New Testaments, and portions) distributed in a single year.[21] BFBS reported the same figure in 1930, while the National Bible Society of Scotland reported 3 million.

The 1930s continued with an unprecedented demand for Bibles, and Bible Societies were able to expand Bible ministry work extensively. Besides making Scriptures available to the villagers, a large number of Bibles were sold to university students (after ten years of student antagonism toward Christianity), and many copies were placed in hotel rooms and homes for the elderly in the larger cities. Several departmental stores were also supplied with Bibles to sell.[22]

---

19 Broomhall, 160.
20 Cann, "UBS Bible Work."
21 ABS report, "ABS in China, 1931–1966."
22 American Bible Society, "ABS in China, 1931–1966."

A Christian family at Luoding, China, 1934. This is a photograph of three generations of a Christian family. They all stand or sit in a doorway and are dressed in Chinese clothing. Used with permission from Maryknoll Mission Archives.

Distribution was facilitated by improved air and surface transportation (including the efficiency of the China Post) and the use of new technology. Bible trips were made to tribes of the northwest, and Scriptures were sent into Tibet by the West China Subagency. In East China, a gospel van (financed by the local Chinese) proclaimed the salvation message via radio, gramophone, and stereopticon, traveling many new roads and streets. Scripture portions were read on weekly radio programs along with stories and addresses about the Bible Societies' work.

During this period, challenges were faced. As the Communists were beginning to make inroads in western China, Bible work was disrupted in several parts of the country, and colportage work in some cities ceased. Other challenges include but are not limited to attacks by bandits, devastating floods (in the south and east), and invasion by the Japanese in the north (Manchuria). Reports of Scriptures being stolen or destroyed and local officials mistreating Bible society staff and colporteurs were submitted by the agencies to the Bible Societies.

Nonetheless, the Bible Societies continued the work whenever and wherever possible. They served on flood relief committees and donated Scriptures to flood refugees. They held several Bible study conferences (in Hong Kong and Canton) and Bible exhibitions (in Peiping). They directed colportage work, especially in prisons and military hospitals, and conducted Bible classes and Bible study campaigns, including recitations, reading and essay writing contests, preaching for soldiers, students, prisoners, and farmers (in East China). They printed portions of Scripture in the local newspapers (in Peiping and South China, also known as "newspaper evangelism") and spoke on Bible Societies' work at churches, etc.[23]

A Chinese minister in his house, 1937. Used with permission from SOAS Library.

China Bible House, 1937–1959

In the 1920s to 1930s, the BFBS and ABS attempted to coordinate and integrate their work in China starting at the subagency level. Both Bible Societies had set up agencies and subagencies in major cities, namely, Shanghai (Headquarters and East China Subagency), Peiping (North China Subagency), Hankow (Central China Subagency), Chengtu (West China Subagency), Canton (South China Subagency). Bible committees existed in important centers including Wuhan, Tsinan, Tientsin, and Peiping, in addition to Hankow and Canton.

---

23 American Bible Society, "ABS in China, 1931–1966."

Former staff and spouse of staff of China Bible House

In 1932, BFBS, ABS, and the National Bible Society of Scotland held a conference on China in London "with a view to encouraging the formation of a China Bible Society which, having the same basic principles as the cooperating Societies, shall share with them in the worldwide work of the distribution of Scriptures." An advisory council was formed in Shanghai in the following year to guide the process.

Finally, in 1937, a tentative constitution and procedures were agreed for the joint work of the China Bible House (中华圣经会) by BFBS and ABS for the very first time. In the spring of 1937, the China Bible House, located on Hong Kong Street, Shanghai, was inaugurated with high hopes to see the Word of God spread across the vast land of China.

Almost immediately the fledgling China Bible House met its first challenge. In the mid-summer of 1937, Japan invaded China, starting the Sino-Japanese War. Notwithstanding the conflict and the departure or internment of foreign Bible Societies' agents, China Bible House continued operation in a limited way and played an important role in the translation, publication, and distribution of the Bible as demand for Scriptures continued to rise in China.[24]

In 1938, Scripture reading and China Bible House news were heard daily on the radio. Colporteurs, though now smaller in number, continued their work traveling with certificates of appointment and Bible society armbands for identification. Sowing of the gospel went on with the Tibetans even though it was difficult and dangerous. Six thousand Tibetan Scripture portions were distributed along the Tibetan border in 1939 even though no missionaries were allowed while Bible work had to cease in Sinkiang in the same year.

In 1939, it was reported that China Bible House distributed Scriptures in thirty-nine dialects and thirty other languages in China. In that same year, it also held a colporteurs' training conference. Amazingly, from 1937 to 1940, China Bible House distributed a total of 16 million Bibles, Testaments, and portions.[25] After World War II in 1945, the National Bible Society of Scotland joined BFBS and ABS in the work of the China Bible House. Toward the end of the 1940s, China Bible House became more nationalized with the management coming under local Chinese Christians.[26] It had twenty-three staff working in the departments of accounting, publishing, sales, distribution, and stocktaking.

---

24 American Bible Society, Essay #15.
25 Mak, Lunchtime Talk on China.
26 Mak, Lunchtime Talk on China.

In some parts of northern China, Scriptures were distributed to students, soldiers in military hospitals, and refugees from Communist regions. In southwest China, Scriptures including the Hwa Miao Bible were distributed to the ethnic minority Christians during a three-day conference. However, restrictions were faced in other parts. In 1947, it was reported that the "Communists in Hunan Province prevented the Bible House from sending Bibles to the churches and schools" and in 1949, "Hunan Province was completely occupied by the Communists. Many churches were forced to close and Christians to burn their Bibles."

Mdm. Xu and Mr. Zhu Baoyuan.

In June 1949, China Bible House was elected to membership in the UBS, established in 1946. In December 1950, Dr. Li Pei'en, age eighty, was appointed as the first Chinese general secretary of the China Bible House. However, at the outbreak of the Korean War in 1950, China Bible House had to formally sever ties with UBS. The era of foreign missions work and missionaries ended as almost all of them were repatriated or expelled. In 1952, China Bible House withdrew its membership from UBS. Thereafter, Bible Societies set up an emergency office in Hong Kong. Dr. Li was imprisoned twice—in 1954 for two years and in 1958 when he passed away that year in prison.[27]

Zhu Baoyuan's name card. He served in the export department of the China Bible House.

In 1954, the Three-Self Patriotic Movement (TSPM), based on the principles of self-governing, self-supporting, and self-propagation of the churches in China, was formed by some local Chinese Protestants. The China Christian Council (CCC) was established later in 1980. Together, the TSPM and CCC became the umbrella organization that all registered Protestant churches in China would come under.

The next contact the China Bible House had with the Bible Societies was in 1956. A delegation from the Anglican Church in Australia led by the archbishop visited China. They were accompanied by Canon Herbert Arrowsmith, general secretary of BFBS, acting as the chaplain to the archbishop.

Plaque declaring the former China Bible House in Beijing as a protected historical and cultural building, 1984.

---

27 Cann, "UBS Bible Work."

It was a rare and unexpected visit after six years of silence. During the visit, China Bible House reported printing forty-three editions of Scripture since 1949 and had distributed about 3.5 million volumes of Scripture. The staff of the China Bible House eagerly heard updates about UBS and expressed a desire to be reconnected with UBS, although they had some reservations as to whether they would be able to maintain their independence.[28]

Two years after the visit, in 1958, China Bible House merged with three other publishing houses.[29] In May 1959, it was officially closed when the Chinese authorities took over the premises in Shanghai. Thereafter, it had a stock of Scriptures for distribution till the beginning of the Cultural Revolution in 1966 when all Bible work had to cease.[30] But did it really cease?

The former China Bible House in Shanghai, 3 Hong Kong Street, 2019.

Over the centuries, men and women of God who recognized the unsurpassed value of the Bible gave their lives to share it by translating, printing, and distributing it among the Chinese people. Whether in the imperial library as the Nestorians in the seventh century, being cooped up in a small room at the trading quarters as Morrison in the nineteenth century, or inventing writing scripts for ethnic minorities, each endeavored to give the Word of God to the people in China. Despite global economic depression, natural disasters, war, and political upheavals, we see faithful servants of God who continued to bring his word to the Chinese. They continued to do whatever was possible, blazing the trails for those who came after them. The light has never left but shines even brighter in the midst of darkness. We shall see this in the next chapter as the very lives of those who owned Bibles were threatened on a massive scale.

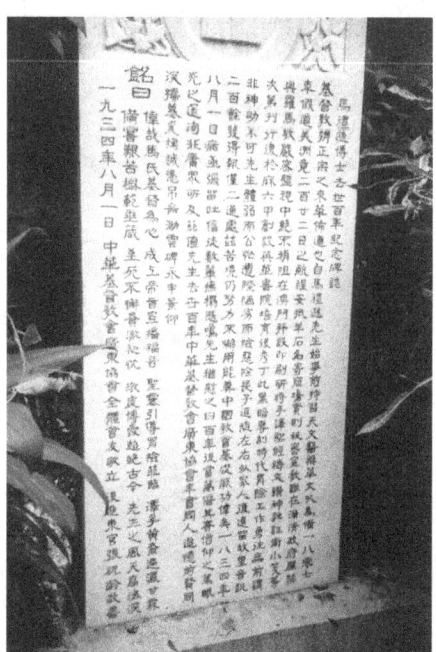

Memorial tablet of Robert Morrison's one hundredth anniversary of his death, Macau.

---

28 Cann, "UBS Bible Work."
29 John Erickson, "The UBS, China and Chinese Scripture," 1984.
30 Erickson, "UBS, China and Chinese Scripture."

2
Into the Dark Night

The Bible during the Cultural Revolution

Your word is a lamp to my feet and a light to my path.
—Psalm 119:105

The preacher would hold on to his precious Bible tightly. … He traveled to different places almost daily to share the gospel, risking his own life.
—An excerpt from a story during the Cultural Revolution

From 1966 to 1976, China was plunged into the dark years of the Cultural Revolution. This was seven years after the closure of the China Bible House in Shanghai. All Bible work had ceased. There was no longer any Bible printing or distribution, nor was there Bible teaching or preaching. Nobody was allowed to own a copy of the Bible. Nobody was allowed to engage in any religious activities. What happened to the Chinese believers and people who owned the Bible in such a tumultuous period in history? In 1949, the estimated number of Protestant Christians in China was 700,000. From the day of Morrison's Chinese Bible to the 1950s, at least a few hundred million Scriptures had been circulated in China.[1] These included full Bibles, New Testaments, and portions in Chinese, local dialects, and minority languages. What happened to these Scriptures, and did Bible work really cease?

Period of Trauma

To better understand what was happening to the Chinese Christians and their Bibles, it is important to catch a glimpse of what was happening to their country. In the early 1960s, China had just emerged from the trauma of the Great Leap Forward (1958–1962), where at least 20 million people died of starvation, famine, and forced labor in a social and economic campaign. Following the catastrophe, leaders of the Chinese Communists were split between continuing a pure form of communism or reversing some of these policies and adopting a more conservative approach. As criticism toward Chairman Mao Zedong mounted, Jiang Qing, Mao's wife, led the Gang of Four to stamp out criticism and purge those labeled anti-revolutionary. A revolution soon developed, with consequences that affected all levels of society.

---

1 Broomhall estimated 225 million Scriptures from 1814 to 1933 (*Bible in China*).

During this tumultuous and chaotic period, old cultures, habits, customs, and traditions were to be eradicated. The wild and violent operations were often carried out by the Red Guards, students and young people used by the Gang of Four under the banner of taking down feudal traditions. In this thoroughgoing revolution, besides unprecedented purges of the "bourgeois" and "revisionist" elements within the Chinese Communists, large swaths of the general population were identified as political enemies and terrorized. Landlords, rich peasants, teachers, scholars, intellectuals, artists, and religious groups were rounded up, interrogated, and tortured, while many government officials and party cadres were labeled as capitalists and sent to labor camps to undergo "reform."

Burnt Bible from the Cultural Revolution, Zhejiang. UBS multimedia database.

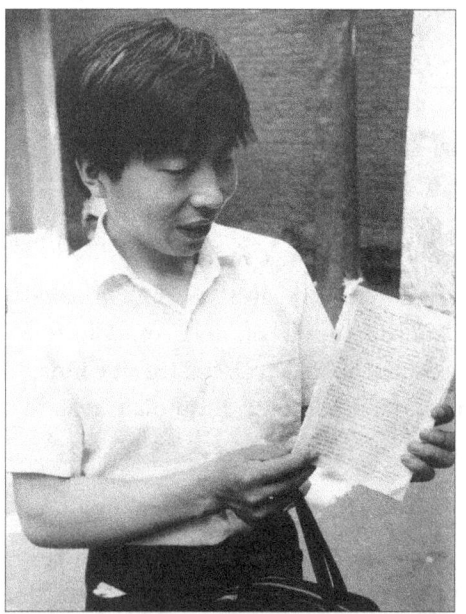

Wang Xu-Hen, a Nanjing Seminary student, with part of a Bible torn into sections when Bibles were scarce, Hefei, 1992.

Many Chinese at that time could neither fathom nor understand what was happening, and they were shocked and bewildered by the mayhem. According to official estimates, about 100 million people were affected by these political campaigns, and up to 2 million lost their lives. Among these were Christians. Their homes and churches were ransacked and destroyed, Christian meetings and activities forbidden, pastors and preachers sent to labor camps and prisons, and Bibles were confiscated, banned, and burned. Christians were forced to renounce their faith, and some were martyred, while others were publicly humiliated and tortured at struggle sessions as the Chinese Communist leadership claimed that religion was "poisoning" the people. Not able to withstand the trauma and suffering, stories were told of some Christians who lost their minds and committed suicide.

But some Christians continued to gather secretly—in homes, caves, and shacks. They continued to worship quietly, listening to gospel radios, reading the Bibles they had secretly stowed behind brick walls or buried in pigsties or stoves, passing around hand-copied loose scraps of Scripture as Bibles became more scarce. Some were memorizing and reciting God's Word when nobody was looking. sTheir stories give us a glimpse into what happened to some of the Christians and their Bibles during this period as their faith was put through the furnace and fiercely tested.

"We Are Just Going Home Sooner"

Wang Ziwen, a Miao Christian in Yunnan Province, was in his twenties during the Cultural Revolution. After his uncle Wang Zhiming, a Miao pastor, was martyred, the entire family was under the watchful eye of the Red Guards. Soon Wang Zhiming's two sons were brought to the struggle session[2] at Nujiang River, where they lost their lives. Wang Ziwen's two other uncles, his father, and his cousins were all imprisoned for their faith. Wang Ziwen described how he hid his Bible and his experience with his father on the way to a struggle session before his father's imprisonment.

> In 1973, after my uncle Wang Zhiming was executed, some guards came to my house. They were looking for some Bible reference books that my cousins had in possession. They hauled me up and forced me to lead them to my cousins. At that time, I had a copy of the Gospel of John hidden underneath my clothes. I was afraid that they would find out and so I kept praying silently to the Lord. On the journey, when they were not watching, I brought the book out to read. The words of the Lord in John 15:18 gave me strength, "If the world hates you, know that it has hated me before it hated you." By then, almost all our Bibles had been confiscated, what we had left were just a few rare copies. Besides the Gospel of John, I had also hidden a New Testament wrapped with cloth—by making a hole in the wall and sealing it with mud!

Tombstone of Miao Rev. Wang Zhiming, Yunnan. Rev. Wang's wife, Wang Ai, was buried with him.

> One night, my father and I were dragged to one of the struggle sessions. On the way there, my father encouraged me with these words, "We will all go home one day, sooner or later. If we need to go home sooner, that is a good thing!" We did not know what was going to happen, but with these words from my father, I was no longer afraid. At the struggle session, the Red Guards made a tall paper hat with the word "Jesus" and put it on my father's head. And they mocked us in front of a rowdy crowd. At the end of the session, they locked us up in a small cell. That night, I felt particularly close to my father as we gave thanks to the Lord and encouraged one another. Our love for the Lord was

---

2 According to Wang Youqin, "struggle sessions" were interrogations held in public to humiliate people thought to be anti-revolutionary (https://ywang.uchicago.edu/history/docs/2013_10_01.pdf).

burning strong. We were willing to die for our faith. Later, my father was sentenced to ten years of imprisonment. Thank God he was released two years later when our country's policies started to change. I wrote a letter to my father telling him, "Dear father, we can hear the birds singing. Winter is gone, spring has come!"

Singing in the Cesspool[3]

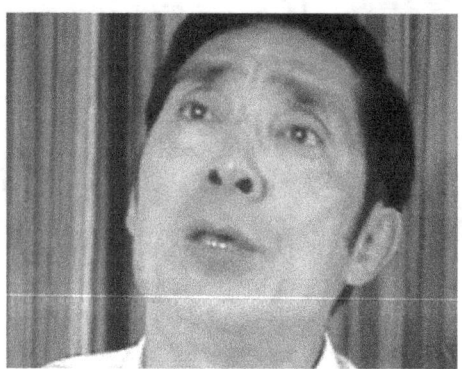

Rev. Chen, 1990s.

Rev. Chen was called home to be with the Lord in 2021 at eighty-nine years old.

Surely no one was looking at Chen now. He had been assigned to work in the cesspool of a labor camp, with his body submerged in the human waste of sixty thousand prisoners. How could he possibly stand another moment in it and even treat it like a garden? But during the Cultural Revolution, the cesspool was about the only place where you would be left alone, away from the watchful eyes of the Red Guards, the only place where you could be free to worship God out in the open.

"I could talk with God, praise his name at the top of my voice, and recite Scriptures that I had memorized. I had experienced how important it is for us Christians to memorize Scriptures," recalled Chen. He would sing, "I come to the garden alone, while the dew is still on the roses"—a Chinese hymn he had learned by heart. He was immersed in fellowship with God even while his body was submerged in the most unthinkable of places. The presence of God and the Word of God, which was hidden in him, helped him survive the extreme conditions and pressure he was put through.

Born into a wealthy family in the 1930s, Chen, who was an educated Christian, became an easy target for the ultra-leftist Communists during the Cultural Revolution. He was imprisoned in Shanghai City Jail for three and a half years, where he almost starved to death and wanted to eat his toothpaste. Later, he was sent to work in a labor camp and was assigned to the cesspool. He said, "This was a place avoided at all costs by the other prisoners, who were afraid of picking up diseases. But it turned out to be a blessing for me."

---

3 *UBS World Report,* January 2000. Adapted from an article by Dan Wooding.

During his eighteen years in the labor camp, Chen knew that it was the Lord who protected him: "Because he never left me nor forsake me, I was able to praise him. If the Lord had not been with me, I would have died on many occasions, but I never became ill." Chen even shared the Word of God with his fellow prisoners and saw several of them come to faith. Even when the guards punished him by sending him to confinement in small dark cells, he did not stop.

Chen reflected on those years with gratitude, "When I was released, I realized that many Christians had died. So, my being immersed in the labor camp actually saved me. Not only did I survive physically, mentally, and spiritually, I was able to forgive those that put me there."

After his release, the Lord used Chen to plant churches in China among the ethnic minority people in Yunnan Province, where he witnessed a significant growth in the Christian population among the Lisu, Lahu, and Miao tribes. He said, "The church in China today is really a wonder by God. The Holy Spirit has swept through China in a marvelous way."

Handwritten Bible verses and notes camouflaged as selected editorials from People's Daily, Red Flag and People's Liberation Army Daily during the Cultural Revolution, Zhejiang.

The inside pages of the handwritten camouflaged Bible verses and notes, Zhejiang.

Praise God that in the midst of the nightmarish upheaval, the Bible continued to speak, give hope, and challenge the hearts of Chinese Christians. Biblical truths that had been deposited in their hearts became the anchor of their souls. The Holy Spirit brought to mind these truths even as they went through unimaginable sufferings, helping them to draw strength from the promises of the Lord as seen in the life of Chen.

Still, many others experienced much anguish and pain as they were forced to surrender their Bibles and witness them being trampled and burned before their eyes. It was not an easy decision to make—to keep or not to keep their Bibles. Some felt that they had no choice but to secretly burn their Bibles, hymnals, and related literature. For others, they were prepared to endanger their lives to preserve their Bibles, come what may, as the following story tells us.

Saving My Bible at All Costs

"Down with the Cow Demons and Snake Spirits!" "Smash the Four Olds" and "Establish the Four News." These were the slogans and declarations that Lan Xin was familiar with growing up in the 1960s as a teenager in Liaoning Province. According to the authorities, the Bible belonged to one of the classes of the "Four Olds" and had to be "smashed." There was no question about it.

One day in the spring of 1967, a group of people descended upon a believer's home. They turned it upside down and searched it for a long time. When they finally emerged, some of them used a metal trowel to tap the walls of the courtyard surrounding the house. Lan recalled:

> I was standing outside the courtyard and was so scared that I broke out in a cold sweat. Just as I turned around to leave, I saw one of them using the trowel to dig in the spot where the believer's family had buried their Bibles. I was so anxious I bit my lips till it bled but I felt nothing and did nothing except pray. The person dug a while longer and then stopped without having found anything. Then the whole group left.

After this incident, fear began to grip the hearts of many Christians in Lan's village. Some began to secretly burn their Bibles and hymnals. Lan couldn't understand what was happening. But she remembered that her mother had told her they would never burn their Bibles. She viewed the Bible as more valuable than even her own life, more important than gold and silver.

Lan's mother loved the Bible. She read it every day after coming home from work. At night, while others were sleeping, she would read it well into the night. In those days, as Bibles were few and far between, Lan's mother separated her Bible into sections for her children to read. When Lan was able to read the Bible, she finally understood why her mother had ardently studied the Bible every day.

But now they had to make the difficult decision whether to keep their Bible. Lan and her mother had buried it under their kitchen stove. After the incident, they decided to send their Bible to a believer's home in the countryside to be buried in their back garden. However, not long after they sent their Bible away, the believer's son came knocking on their door. Lan said:

> He had brought a bag with him. My mind was buzzing, and my mother looked worried. As expected, the people in the countryside were afraid of being implicated, so they sent the Bibles and other books back to us. Moreover, they had added their own Bibles to the pile. So now we had three families' Bibles in our possession!

Lan and her mum were at a loss. Around the same time, a believer in their village was called up and hauled to a struggle session, where he was forced to reveal the names of other believers. Lan and her mum were then called in to explain themselves. All of this happened while they were in possession of a pile of Bibles and related books!

> We were in a dangerous situation, and we felt really scared as we hadn't the faintest idea what to do. If we went ahead and burned the Bibles, then all this trouble would disappear. But how could we ever bring ourselves to burn the Bibles we loved so much? We prayed hard and my mum's gaze fell on the beautiful bean flowers just opening up in abundance in front of our window. We could bury our Bibles there!

Lan and her mum had only a couple of weeks of peace before the next disturbance. The local neighborhood street committee suddenly carried out a scathing attack on religious believers. The head of the committee said, "All reactionary elements must be eliminated. Those who are believers should step forward, otherwise, we will drag them out by force."

After that, both mother and daughter knew that they could no longer hide the Bibles under the flowers. The following night, Lan secretly dug up the pile of wrapped Bibles, carried a trowel with her, made sure no one was looking, and ran off with the bag of Bibles over her shoulders like a thief.

> As I was running, I thought, "Where on earth shall I go? Where can I bury these books?" Tears ran down my face. "Lord! God! Is this what you've allowed to happen?"

Just then, a train whizzed past in front of Lan. She had reached the railway line without realizing it. She had an idea—bury the Bibles at the side of the track where long grass and weeds grew. In order to recognize the spot later on, she placed a fragment of brick there as a marker. By the time she finished, she was covered with sweat and tears. She recounted:

> I felt as if I had just lost something important in my life. I had to go but I just couldn't bear to leave immediately. I simply retreated slowly backward from that spot. A breath of cold air brushed my face and caused me to shiver—it was like waking up from a dream.

A week later, Lan had a nightmare. She dreamed that her Bibles were stolen. There was nothing left at the tracks. She was so affected that she couldn't go back to sleep. Early the next day, she hurried to the spot where she had buried the Bibles. When she saw that the grass on the ground was untouched and the piece of brick still lay in its place undisturbed, she heaved a great sigh of relief and shed tears of joy.

Sometime later, when the political storm had finally ended, Lan and her mum decided to retrieve the Bibles. Again, Lan went in the middle of the night at 3 a.m. She carefully dug out the wrapped Bibles and hurriedly carried them home. It was the last time Lan would need to dig the ground for her Bibles.[4]

Healed through the Bible

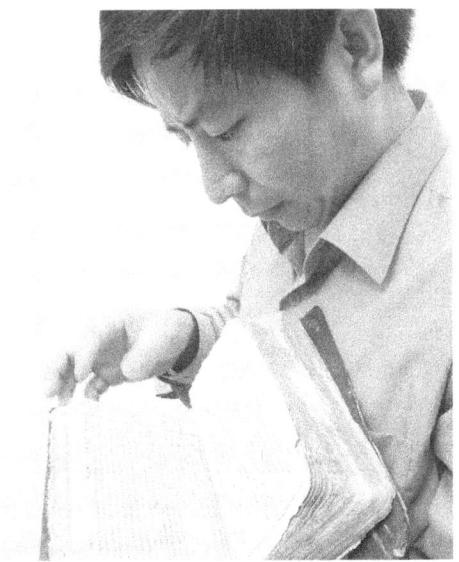

Jiang Yuchun with his former pastor's old Bible.

Even while the Bible was not allowed to see the light of day during those tumultuous years, it was still drawing people into the kingdom of God. One such person was Jiang, who lost his young wife to a tetanus infection after a terrible accident. Overcome with grief, he was losing sleep and soon was losing his mind. No medication or temple mediums, who were secretly operating, could heal him. One day, Jiang was so sad that he was wailing in an eatery. The owner who saw his condition invited him to a Christian gathering. Desperate, Jiang decided to visit, so he walked 20 kilometers with his ten-year-old son to the secret meeting place in the wee hours of the morning.

Upon arriving, they saw that about twenty Christians had already gathered. They heard

---

4 Adapted from Lan, "The Story of One Bible," translated from *Tian Feng* magazine.

portions of the Bible being read, sang hymns, and prayed—a sequence that repeated itself meeting after meeting. After attending the gathering for three weeks, Jiang began to feel better.

After a month, his health returned, and he could even work in the fields. Soon a passion began to burn in his heart to share the gospel. He began inviting his friends and relatives to the Christian meeting, doing so carefully and secretly. He did not forget to bring his ten-year-old son, Jiang Yuchun, who was impressed by the preacher of the Christian group. Jiang Yuchun recounted:

> The preacher would hold on to his precious Bible tightly. Ordinary believers were not allowed to touch it. He let me take a quick glance as I was an obedient child. At that moment, I was filled with awe and joy. The preacher traveled to different places almost daily to share the gospel, risking his own life.

Providentially, Jiang Yuchun grew up to become instrumental in Bible distribution in China when the tide turned and churches reopened in the 1980s. He served with the CCC/TSPM, the umbrella organization of the registered Protestant churches in China. Having a passion for the Word of God, he coordinated Bible distribution from the Bible printing press to the various Bible distribution centers across China. Today, Jiang Yuchun still has the Bible that belonged to the preacher, given to him as a keepsake thirty years later, and he too is holding on to this precious Bible that had weathered the storm of the revolution.

Converted through a Family of Christians and a Handwritten Bible

What can a family of physically challenged Christians do during the Cultural Revolution? In this next story, they were used by the Lord to lead a thirteen-year-old boy, Tang Weimin, to Christ. In his adulthood, he became a top Christian leader in Henan Province, chairman of the Henan TSPM, and one of the national leaders of the Protestant churches in China. He told us his story:

A stenciled Bible from the Cultural Revolution, Eternal Light Church, Zhejiang.

> Although the Bible was not legally available in China at that time, the Spirit of God was actively at work. The Holy Spirit used different ways to bring people to know God. I was one of the blessed ones brought to God by His Spirit through the only Christian family in my village. There were three members in this Christian family, and all of them, father, mother, and son, were physically disabled. The family was very poor, and they relied on the use of walking sticks to get around. They could not publicly demonstrate their Christian faith, but I knew that they always worshiped and sang hymns in their house.
>
> One day, they asked me to draw a cross for them. When I finished and passed them my drawing, I remembered the man's first words upon seeing the cross were "Praise God!" Then I noticed a small book on their table; it was handwritten. I asked the father what book it was, and he told me it was a copy of the New Testament (NT). He added, "We are illiterate. So, if you like, you can take the book home to read." I finished reading the NT

Hand-copied Scripture verses and hymns, which were cherished by Christians in Pai Kou village when Scriptures were hard to come by during the Cultural Revolution, Hunan.

within a week. During the first night of reading, I read until 3 a.m. I was an avid reader of books and had read many famous Chinese Classics like the *Romance of the Three Kingdoms*. But the New Testament really attracted me. The most interesting verse for me was John 3:16, "For God so loved the world, that he gave his only Son, that whoever believes in him should not perish but have eternal life."

When I returned the handwritten NT copy to the family after I had read it, the father asked me if I knew what the cross meant when I drew it the other day. "When I drew the picture at that time, I did not know what the cross meant. After reading the New Testament, I know what it means now: it symbolizes the cross which Jesus died on for our sins," I answered.

"Do you believe in Jesus?" he asked. I replied: "Yes, I believe but I don't know how to pray." The father of the family then replied, "Our family will pray for you. Let us kneel and pray." It really moved me to see this physically challenged family put their walking stick aside and get down on their knees with great difficulty to pray. That was how I received Christ.

Rev. Tang Weiming, a national leader of Protestant churches in China, 2013.

Sufferings of the Chinese Catholics

During the Cultural Revolution, Chinese Catholics saw their church buildings demolished, Bibles, missals, hymnals, and prayer books burned, and statues of venerated saints smashed to the ground. They were devastated, but many persevered, holding on to their convictions, and met secretly with priests who conducted masses for them. Bishop Aloysius Jin Luxian, a prominent Catholic Church leader in China, testified that it was the legacy of his forebears and the Word of God that kept him alive during those dark years:

> I come from a family who has been Catholics for many generations. Since I was young, I have been reading the Bible. I read it every day when I entered the seminary and the Society of Jesus. I love the Bible, especially the Gospel of John. I had memorized the whole Gospel of John, in Latin, when I was studying at the seminary. I was arrested and imprisoned in 1955, at thirty-nine years old. It was from memory that I was able to recite and reflect on God's Word from John's Gospel during my imprisonment when I had no access to the Bible. In 1982, I was released after a total of twenty-seven years of imprisonment and reeducation camp. God's Word is to me like the lamp unto my feet and the bread of my life; the Bible is the illuminating lamp that guides my life.

Bishop Aloysius Jin Luxian of the Catholic Diocese of Shanghai, 2006.

Another story told was not just of conducting masses in secret but of holding a funeral for a deceased Catholic. Yang was only six years old when the Cultural Revolution swept through China. Her grandfather, who was a believer, used his home as a gathering place for masses to be conducted secretly. She shared this story of how a priest suffered beatings for holding a funeral service:

> One day, a neighbor who was a fellow believer heard that a visiting priest was at our home conducting Mass. He ran frantically to our place to look for him. One of his family members had just passed away and he would like the priest to hold a funeral service. Such a thing was prohibited during those times and the priest would be prosecuted. Nevertheless, the priest was deeply moved by the sincerity of the believer and decided to help him. In the middle of the funeral service, some fierce-looking men barged into the house and dragged the priest away.
>
> The believers present were shocked and frightened. They ran to our place and informed us. Together with a few young men, my grandfather went out to look for the priest. But they could not find him. Just when we were getting very worried, the priest returned to our house, bruised, and beaten up. My grandparents cried when they saw his badly wounded body. I was very shaken. Instead of being upset with his tormentors, the priest said: "The wounds that I bore were nothing compared to those on Jesus. We should bear witness for him." After hearing what he said, I felt at peace because he helped me to understand my faith better. And my faith was greatly strengthened.

Inspired by the faith of Catholics around her, Yang grew up to be a nun, serving the Lord full time. When she faced difficulties, she would recall the testimony of the priest who suffered beatings and Philippians 2:6–7, "Who, being in the form of God, did not count equality with God something to be grasped. But he emptied himself, taking the form of a slave" (NJB).

Despite the ravages of the Cultural Revolution and suppression of all religious activities, some copies of the Bible survived and helped those who read it to survive the dark and diabolical years. Where there were no Bibles, Chinese Christians recited it from their memory. When persecuted, they produced fruit of the Spirit. When scourged, they counted it all joy. When mocked, they felt honored to be worthy to suffer for the Lord. What the enemy meant for evil God had turned for good. Many Chinese Christians experienced his intimate presence through the dark night and witnessed the fulfillment of his promises to them written in his word. And many inspiring stories can be told, as David said in Psalm 40:5,

> You have multiplied, O LORD my God,
>   your wondrous deeds and your thoughts toward us;
>   none can compare with you!
> I will proclaim and tell of them,
>   yet they are more than can be told.

Indeed, time would fail us if we were to recount all the wonders God did for the Chinese Christians during the Cultural Revolution. I think we can look forward to doing that in heaven! For now, we must turn now to another marvel of God after the Cultural Revolution, which is one of the main themes of this book.

Christian ladies who survived the Cultural Revolution now cared for at Wenzhou Christian Old People's Home, 1998.

Mdm. Fan with her old Bible printed in 1948, Yunnan, 2001.

Ninety-one-year-old Mdm. Wang and her old Bible preserved from the Cultural Revolution, 2015.

Yang Weizhen hid his father's 1934 New Testament behind brick walls for fourteen years during the Cultural Revolution, Yunnan, 2001.

Old worn-out Bibles collected from believers kept in a church in Henan. Each Bible has a story behind it yet untold! 2016.

3
Out of the Shadows

A Bible Press for China

> The grass withers, the flower fades,
> but the word of our God will stand forever. —Isaiah 40:8

> Twenty years ago, my Bible was taken from me. I've cried for twenty years … Now at last, God has brought me a Bible.
> —A seventy-six-year-old Chinese woman as she clutched her new copy of the Bible, 1985

During the Cultural Revolution, all religions were banned. Bibles were scarce and Chinese Christians had to worship in secret. The revolution ended around 1976, and in 1979 Chinese leader Deng Xiaoping launched the Reform and Open Door policy. Things began to change as the Chinese government initiated many broad reforms. Foreign investments were welcomed, and there was greater engagement with the international community. Most importantly, there was now some religious freedom. Churches reopened, and Bibles were allowed and could be printed again! The long night had ended, and morning had broken. But the churches in China soon realized that their own supply of Bibles was insufficient to meet the skyrocketing demands. How was the huge demand for Bibles in China going to be met?

A New Era

One of the first churches to reopen its doors was Centennial Church (百年堂) in Ningpo in 1979. Chinese Christians were once again able to gather freely; people were crowding to hear the gospel being preached.

According to *China News and Church Report* in November 1983:

> A 70-year-old pastor from Shandong Province reported that on a recent Sunday, he preached to 500 in the morning service, 600 at noon, and over 1,000 in the evening in a temporarily erected tent. "The fire of the gospel has been lit in China," he said, "and it is going to keep burning like a prairie fire."

The mood at that time was perhaps best captured in a Chinese hymn "冬天已往, 雨水已止." (Winter Is Past, the Rain Is Over), written by Weifan Fan and Lin Shengben in 1952, published in 1982. Inspired by and adapted from Song of Solomon 2:10–14, the lyrics express the hope of spring and Chinese Christians' deep desire for the Lord, to love and follow him wherever he goes, to belong to him. Here's the first stanza of the hymn:

冬天已往，雨水已止，百花开放，百鸟鸣啼，
何必等待，何必迟疑，
「我的佳偶，与我同去。」
耶稣我主，我爱所归，我身我灵永属於祢，
幽谷之中，思祢心切；
与祢同去，今又春回！

The winter is gone, the rain is over, the flowers in bloom, the birds are singing.
Why wait, why hesitate?
"My love, go with me."
Jesus, my Lord, my love, my body and soul are Thine.
In the valley of the shadow, I long for Thee.
I go with Thee, and now the spring returns!

A former missionary, H. R. Weber, visited China in the winter of 1984. He too witnessed the new face of China; churches reopening and filling up with worshipers:

> China today is like a meadow during the first warm week in spring: what seemed dead and destitute suddenly bursts out in flowers. Ten years ago, it would have been difficult to meet the Church at worship. ... [Now] wherever church buildings are restored to the Christians the assemblies become bigger and bigger. ... In greater Shanghai, there are now 32 Protestant and Catholic church buildings restored for Christian worship. ... In the whole of China, the number of Protestant church buildings used for worship is now about 1,000.[1]

What was once thought to be impossible was now happening. Chinese Christians were now gathering openly. They could sing. They could pray. But virtually none of them had Bibles. Without the Word of God, how could the church be nurtured and grow healthily? On the national level, the TSPM was reestablished, and the CCC was founded in 1980. Together they are known as *lianghui* (two organizations), CCC/TSPM, who serve the registered Protestant churches in China by providing resources to support church growth and development. Chinese church leaders serving at CCC/TSPM soon recognized that one of the most urgent tasks facing the church was to print Bibles for the believers, to replace the Scriptures that had been destroyed, and to bring the Word of God back to the center of the church.

Elder Ji Jianhong, a Chinese Christian leader, who recounted how some of the first Chinese Bibles published after the Cultural Revolution were printed on a press run by the People's Liberation Army, Nanjing.

However, all the printing plates were either lost or damaged. What could the church print with? By divine providence, a hidden Bible at the former Bible society office in Beijing was

---

1 Weber, "Impression on the Bible and Church Life in New China Feb 18–29."

retrieved! In a method known as photographic plating, the hidden Bible was used as the true copy to print Bibles (in the 1919 Chinese Union Version) in Shanghai, Fuzhou, and Nanjing at some state-owned presses. Amazingly, one of the printing companies that helped print Bibles was run by the People's Liberation Army (PLA) in Nanjing. Elder Ji Jianhong, one of the Chinese church leaders at that time, recounted how it happened:

> Nanjing had twenty printing companies but none of them could print Bibles. Finally, after much prayer, I approached the PLA press. I explained to the director of the press the need for Bibles, how the Bible is the source of spiritual life for the Christians. I asked them, "How can we say we have religious freedom if we don't have Bibles?" The director replied he knew that Bibles had been destroyed by the ultra-leftist of the Party and now the PLA had a responsibility to follow the Party's policy of restoration. And after some consideration, he agreed to print Bibles!

By the mid-1980s, the churches in China were able to produce some 1.8 million copies of Scripture. In November 1985, Bishop K. H. Ting, president of the CCC, said,

> Chinese Christians are Bible-loving, Bible-honoring and Bible-studying Christians. The period of the ultra-leftist Cultural Revolution when many Christians had their Bibles taken away from them by Red Guards was a time of testing and found the love for the Bible on the part of the Christians intensified. … In the last five years the China Christian Council in cooperation with the Christian Three-Self Movement has been producing Bibles. … Many Christians all over China gave money to their pastors months ahead so as to ensure that they get their Bibles as soon as they arrived. … In the last five years our production reached nearly 1.8 million, most were complete Bible, and some were New Testament with Psalms.

While this was no small achievement for the Chinese Churches to print Bibles, the supply of Scriptures during this period was not adequate to meet the huge demands of the burgeoning church. It was like giving a few drops of water to a severely dehydrated man. By 1986, the Christian population had grown to about 4 million according to CCC/TSPM.[2] More than four thousand churches were opened, several regional theological institutions were established, and many people were worshiping in homes. Christians everywhere, both in the rural villages and cities, young and old, were looking and asking for Bibles. There was a serious supply crunch.

The main reason for the shortage was that state-owned printing presses in a planned economy were allocated and assigned jobs by the state, and these jobs were given priority. The printing of Bibles was not the priority, and orders often took a long time to be fulfilled. Supply was lagging far behind demand. Millions of Christians in China were without a copy of the Bible.

How then would the growing demand for Bibles be satisfied? Could the Chinese Christians ever have a regular and reliable supply of Bibles? Would the Chinese authorities allow that to happen?

---

2 Unofficial estimates put the figure between 7 to 10 million.

"Chinese Bibles on Chinese Soil for Chinese Christians"

The Chinese proverb "A journey of a thousand miles begins with a single step" (千里之行, 始於足下) could encapsulate how a Bible printing press became a reality in China. Leaders of the registered Chinese Churches and UBS covered literally hundreds of thousands of miles in about twenty trips over seven years in mutual visits before the Bible press came to be. The result of the thousand-mile journey was the forging of a relationship, which bore the fruit of a continuous supply of the Word of God for China till today. It was a relationship based on mutual trust and respect.

The first step of the journey was taken in 1979 by the leaders of the Chinese Churches when a delegation from the CCC went to the US to attend the Third Assembly of the World Conference on Religion and Peace. They visited the Bible House in New York and were received warmly by the leaders of both UBS and the American Bible Society. Like in a dance, as the Chinese Churches stepped forward, leaders of UBS responded readily. In the subsequent years, the Chinese church leaders visited the German Bible Society, British Bible Society, and UBS Regional Centers in Hong Kong to learn more about the work of UBS, while the UBS leaders visited Nanjing, Shanghai, and Beijing.

At the same time, a personal friendship was built in the late 1970s between Dr. Eugene Nida, an eminent Bible translation consultant with the American Bible Society and Bishop K. H. Ting. Dr. Nida had been invited to teach at the universities and academic institutions in Nanjing, Beijing, and Guangzhou. During his visits, he had the opportunity to contact Bishop Ting and introduce the work of Bible Societies. Arrangements for UBS support of scholarly editions of biblical resources for Nanjing Theological Seminary were also made.

At the reception given by the Amity Foundation Committee for UBS Asia Pacific regional staff. Left to right (front): Han Wenzao, Chan Young Choi, Bishop Ting, Chen Zemin. Left to right (back): Han Bide, I-Jin Loh, Philip Wickeri, Zu Rulei, David Thorne, Zhang Birgduo. Nanjing, 1985.

A high point in the relationship came in January 1985 during a visit by UBS leaders to Nanjing. For the first time, discussions of a printing press that UBS might provide were held. Chinese church leaders had been sensing the dire need to print more Bibles. And the mission of UBS is to "enable Christians everywhere to fill the needs for the printed Word of God by their own efforts."[3] At a banquet held in honor of UBS leaders, Bishop Ting announced the idea of establishing a Bible printing press—to print Chinese Bibles on Chinese soil for Chinese Christians. In addition, the Chinese church leaders requested for UBS to support the printing of 100,000 Bibles at the PLA press as a start. This would mean one hundred tons of Bible paper support. The response from UBS was swift. The amount of USD$100,000 was raised, and Bible paper arrived in Nanjing three months later!

Around the same time, Chinese church leaders Bishop K. H. Ting and Dr. Han Wenzao, who were also leaders of the CCC, had a vision to contribute to Chinese society. They set up a social welfare charity organization known as the Amity Foundation in 1985. The foundation aims to "contribute to China's social development and efforts towards modernization, to make Christian involvement and participation more widely known to the Chinese people and serve as a channel for the international sharing of resources and people-to-people relationships."[4] Amity Foundation was the charity organization that would work with UBS to establish the printing press.

On March 1, 1985, a meeting was held in Hong Kong between leaders of UBS and the Chinese church to further discuss the possibility of setting up a Bible printing press in China. According to a report by John Erickson, "There were nine of us seated around the table and we had a 'talking document' prepared by David Thorne, the Production Consultant (from UBS). We had a very open, frank and congenial discussion which started with breakfast at 7.30 and then concluded at the Regional Center offices at 11.30."[5]

Signing of MOU between Amity Foundation and UBS on the intention to establish a Bible printing press in China, Hong Kong, 1985.

All the visits and meetings culminated in a landmark "Memorandum of Understanding" (MOU) signed on March 22, 1985, by Amity Foundation and UBS, announcing the intention to establish a Bible printing plant in Nanjing. It would prioritize printing Bibles and Testaments.

---

3 Address by Rev. Ulrich Fick at the opening of the APC in 1987.
4 Dr. Han Wenzao's official article on Amity Foundation, November 1985.
5 Dr. John Erickson's presentation to the UBS Executive Council Meeting at Vienna, March 6–9, 1985.

In the words of UBS General Secretary Rev. Ulrich Fick, the plan to build a Bible printing press in China was at that time the "most significant single project that the UBS has embarked upon in its forty-year history." Expressing his anticipation for the Bible printing press, Bishop Ting said, "It will relieve the need for Bibles in China."

The press was to be named Amity Printing Press, after the Amity Foundation. The two Chinese characters for Amity are "爱" (love) and "德" (virtue); 爱 and 德 highlight "love" as God's primary attribute and "virtue" as a dimension of Christian witness and involvement in society.

Amity Printing Press–"The Very Best of Its Kind in the Whole World"

The MOU set in motion the "Bible Press for China" project, launched by UBS, starting with a fundraising campaign among its fellowship. It was then the single-largest fundraising effort the Bible Societies had ever undertaken. Geoffrey Hill, UBS finance director wrote, "The Bible Societies see the invitation ... as a God-given challenge to which they want to respond in a way which is appropriate to the immensity of the need."

Preparing the ground for the construction of Amity Press, Nanjing, 1986.

Was there any opposition or concern? Some Christian groups had asked, "What about the unregistered churches in China? Would the Bible press end up printing Communist propaganda?" Other groups expressed skepticism and said that Bibles printed would just be kept at the storehouses; they would never reach the hands of the Christians. Rev. Dr. Chan Young Choi, the UBS Asia Pacific regional secretary at that time, recalled, "I could not promise them anything, but we could only trust God and trust the China Christian Council and the Chinese authorities."[6]

Laying the foundation stone for Amity Press, Nanjing, November, 1986.

It was estimated that the press would be able to produce at least 250,000 Bibles and 500,000 New Testament each year, plus hymn books and other Christian and educational literature. For more than two decades, a regular and adequate Bible supply had not been possible, and Bibles had to be smuggled into China. Now the opportunity had come for overseas Christians to share resources with the churches in China, to equip them with modern machinery fit for producing large quantities of Scriptures. Would they be willing to take the risk?

The foundation stone for Amity Press, Nanjing, 1986.

---

6 Rev. Chan quoted in an interview in 1995 at the celebration of the 10-millionth Bible printed by APC.

An early view of Amity Press, Nanjing, 1987.

Ceremony of the presentation of equipment by UBS to Amity, 1987.

They were. Within the next two years, thirty-six Bible Societies representing Christians and churches from all over the world contributed a total of USD$7.3 million. The donations went into the purchase of machinery and equipment as well as start-up capital for the press. The spirit of giving and fellowship in the body of Christ shone through.

Jiangning, a county with 750,000 inhabitants and a forty-minute drive from Nanjing City, was chosen as the location for the press. A historic moment came when Bishop Ting laid the foundation stone for the press in November 1986 in the presence of general secretaries and fundraisers from ten UBS member societies. It was a special moment for all of them. Soon, the blueprint for the building was drawn up. Construction began after the final harvest on the 36,000 square meter rice farm, where the press was to be built, and printing equipment arrived from different parts of the world to Nanjing.

In July 1987, a ceremony was held to present the printing equipment to the Amity Foundation as a gift. These included a state-of-the-art high-speed web press that could print on rolls of paper, sheet-fed presses, and automatic binding equipment that could handle both hardcover and paperback books. Typesetting of the thousands of characters needed for the Chinese text would now be done by computer instead of by hand, cutting the task of setting the Scripture text to a fraction of the original time. As Rev. Dr. Oswald Hoffman, then president of UBS put it, "The printing press is the best of its kind in the whole world."

Legal and regular Bible supply in China was becoming a reality. History was in the making. Less than a year after Bishop Ting laid the foundation stone, the printing facility was built and installed with shiny new equipment. All the work was completed in just over eight months, even though Western technical experts had said that it would likely take at least eighteen!

Installing a press machine at Amity Press, Nanjing, 1987.

Bishop Ting giving a speech at the opening ceremony of the Amity Press, 1987.

A view of a part of the APC, Nanjing, 1990.

An early scene from Amity Press, Nanjing, 1987.

A part of the Timson T32 Web Offset printing press at APC, Nanjing, 1995.

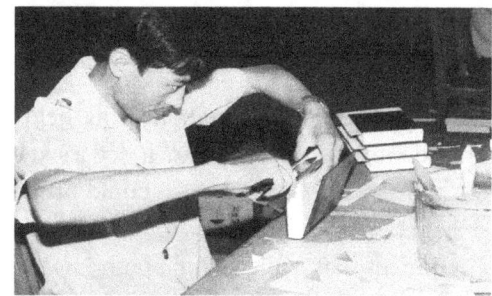
Checking Chinese Bibles at APC, Nanjing, 1992.

On October 14, 1987, the printing facility was abuzz with the whirring and rustling sound of machines and paper. Amid the smell of fresh ink, the workers at the press welcomed the first Bible that rolled off the press that day.

The official inauguration of the printing press was held on December 5, 1987, and was attended by both Christian leaders and government officials, dignitaries, and hundreds of overseas and local guests and Amity Press workers. In his address, Bishop Ting expressed his gratitude to the Chinese authorities, UBS, and Christians all over the world. He said that the press was the "product of prayers and efforts of people from within China and from overseas." He reiterated the purpose of the press, that it would "give priority to the printing of Bibles and other church literature."

Rev. Dr. Ulrich Fick in China on the opening of the Amity Press, 1987.

Rev. Dr. Ulrich Fick congratulated the Chinese Churches for making the Bible truly their own book, "not foreign or imported but printed and bound by Chinese here in China and circulated to Chinese." He remarked that "there is no book more important than the Bible. The Bible speaks to people wherever they are, across all cultures, and throughout the centuries. So, we trust that the Bible will give Christians here in China firm information about WHO they are, what they can HOPE for, and how they can SERVE both God and the society in which they live."

Impact of the Bible on APC Workers

One group of people the Bible spoke to was APC workers who spent hours producing this special Book, day in and day out. Be it typesetting, checking, printing, folding, binding, cutting, embossing, foiling, or laminating, each worker had a hand in producing every Bible that came out of the factory. Imagine the many pairs of hands needed to complete one Bible. In the process, some of the workers were drawn to its content and came to know its Author personally.

Li Wen joined APC in 1986 and came to faith in Christ in 1993, Nanjing, 2003.

One such person was Li Wen, who was among the first staff members to join APC in December 1986. Her job was to typeset the Bible. As an atheist, it was her first exposure to the Word of God. "Because of my work, I read the Bible for the first time," Li Wen recalled. At the same time, she was impressed by the conduct of the UBS staff with whom she worked, especially their patience. "When I made some mistakes, they did not scold or criticize me. Instead, they would affirm my work and patiently address the areas for improvement." When Li Wen learned that they were Christians, she became more curious about the Bible and wanted to know more about the faith. In 1993, she decided to put her trust in the Lord.

Li Wen continued to be instrumental in typesetting the Bible for the next two decades. In fact, she was responsible for helping to typeset the Chinese Bible into the Chinese simplified script in the horizontal format, which has blessed millions of Christians in China. When Li Wen was interviewed in 2019 at age fifty-two, she said, "I am filled with thanksgiving every time I think of my work at APC. I believe it was God who guided me into this work!"

Another staff member, Chen Chun, was also deeply influenced by her working environment at the press. After receiving Christ in 1994, she was not satisfied with merely producing Bibles. She wanted to study it and hence enrolled herself in a three-year correspondence Bible course at Nanjing Theological Seminary. In 2000, while reading the Scripture, she was deeply moved by Ezekiel 34:6, "[My sheep] wandered over all the mountains and on every high hill.

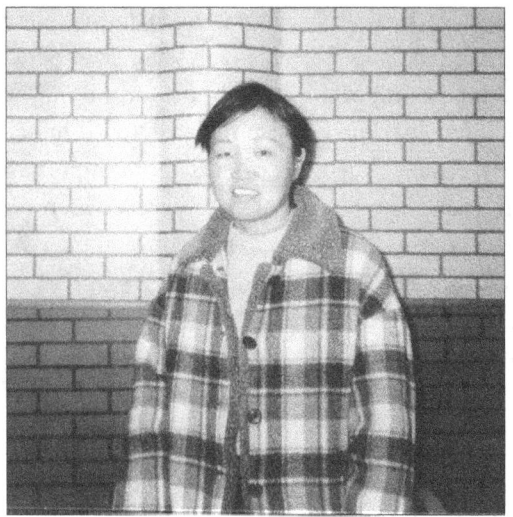
Testimony of Amity staff Chen Chun, 2004.

My sheep were scattered over all the face of the earth, with none to search or seek for them." She responded to this verse by committing her life to serve the Lord as a preacher. So, she began serving as a lay preacher at her church. Later, she quit her job at the press to become a full-time preacher. Praise the Lord for how he led an APC staff member from printing Bibles to studying the Bible to obeying and preaching the word! Additionally, in the later years, APC staff were also given the opportunity to attend seminars on the Bible conducted at Nanjing Theological Seminary to give them an appreciation of the meaning and importance of the book they were producing.

The First Chinese Simplified Script Bible, 1989

Within a year after the opening of APC, UBS and CCC/TSPM embarked on yet another Bible adventure—the Chinese Union Version simplified script Bible project. When Chinese Churches reopened in the 1980s, Chinese Bibles had been printed in traditional Chinese with a vertical layout. However, the younger population of the Chinese Churches were finding it challenging to read traditional Chinese script. This was because beginning in the 1950s and 1960s, the Chinese authorities had begun promoting simplified Chinese characters with fewer strokes for use in printed materials in an effort to increase literacy. There was hence a need to provide Chinese believers with Bibles in simplified Chinese script.

Back in 1984, CCC/TSPM had started to work on the conversion of the Chinese New Testament to a simplified script in a horizontal format. They did not yet have computers, so everything was done manually by a team of twenty-one staff and twenty volunteers. The work, led by Rev. Shen Chen'en, was completed in 1986, and the first CUV New Testament with Psalms in simplified script was published that year. But, what about the Old Testament?

In 1988, during a visit to the rural churches by some Chinese church and UBS leaders, the issue came to the fore. According to a report by Dr. Han, leader of the Chinese Churches, during a visit to a thousand-strong church, local believers came up to him successively to express their need for simplified script Bibles. They cited reasons like the low education level in the rural areas and difficulty reading the Bible in traditional script. Dr. Han was "deeply moved by their genuine thirst for God's Word." On the way back, he shared what he felt with UBS delegates who were on that trip. "Suddenly, a word here and a word

Dr. Han giving the Chinese simplified script Bible to a rural lay leader, 1989.

Large crowd attempting to buy new Chinese simplified script Bible at Community Church, Shanghai, March 1989.

there, we started holding a meeting in the car. Our friends from UBS promised to provide technical assistance."[7]

Shortly, UBS shared a box of computer disks, which aided in the conversion of the Chinese Bible from traditional to simplified script. The process seemed quick and easy enough till the issue of modern punctuation came up. Dr. Han wrote, "It was very difficult to apply modern punctuation to the Chinese which was used 70 years ago." Thankfully, the Lord provided help from several Christians from Shanghai who were experts in the Chinese language to solve the difficulty. Proofreading, both a voluminous and laborious task, was another hurdle. Duan Yuzhen, staff member of CCC, and Ruth Li, staff member of UBS Asia Opportunity, courageously took up the arduous task!

Launched on Easter Day, March 26, 1989, at various church services in Shanghai, the CUV simplified script Bible was a historic moment for Chinese Christians. It is worth repeating here two points highlighted by Bishop Shen Yifan on the power of resurrection in his sermon at Community Church in Shanghai at the launch. First was the fact that the church, which suffered many hardships during the Cultural Revolution, had not only survived but reemerged and grown at least fivefold. The other was the printing of Scriptures. The CCC had printed more than 3 million copies since 1979, and now the complete Bible was available in simplified script. For the first time, the Word of God could speak to everyone, including young people, attesting to the power of resurrection and hope for the future.

Dr. Loh I-Jin, a UBS leader who worked closely with Dr. Han on the project, echoed Bishop Shen when he wrote in his report, "There couldn't be a better way to celebrate the resurrection of Christ than to openly distribute an edition of the whole Bible which can speak intelligently and meaningfully to everyone for the first time in that vast country."[8]

People attempting to buy the Chinese simplified script Bible, 1989.

---

7 Adapted and translated from Wenzao, "How Bountiful Is God's Grace—A Report on the Publication of the Bible in Simplified Script."

8 I-Jin, *UBS Asia Opportunity News Update*, No. 2.

People with the Chinese simplified script Bible, 1989.

Young woman with newly purchased Chinese simplified script Bible, Jiang Pu Meeting Point Church, 1989.

Indeed, the reemergence of the Chinese Churches after the Cultural Revolution and the printing of Scriptures on Chinese soil point to the power of resurrection. Within about two decades, China went from being a place where Bibles were confiscated, banned, and burned, to being a place where Bibles are now printed legally and openly. Since its inception in 1987, APC has not stopped producing Bibles. True to its mission and promise, priority was given to the printing of Bibles and Christian literature. But what about distribution and accessibility? Were Bibles kept in storehouses and left to grow moldy? How was this enormous task of distributing and spreading God's Word in the vast land of China carried out? Would people living in the remote parts of China deep in the cold mountains or far away in the scorching desert lands be able to get a copy of the Bible too?

4
Shining Forth I

Bible Distribution Work

Man shall not live by bread alone, but by every word that comes from the mouth of God.

—Matthew 4:4

I can live without food for days, but I cannot survive a single day without the Word of God.

—A flood survivor from northern China who used government aid of sixteen yuan to buy a Bible costing twelve yuan, 1998

The decade following the opening of the APC in 1987 was no less tumultuous than before. On the global front, the Gulf War (1990–1991) erupted in the Middle East; the USSR collapsed in December 1991, bringing the Cold War to an end; genocide and civil conflicts in Rwanda and other African countries claimed half a million lives in 1994; and Asian countries suffered a financial crisis in 1997.

As for China, it went through international isolation and strained relations after the June Fourth Incident at Tiananmen Square in 1989. Besides political challenges, there were also natural disasters. In 1996, 1998, and 1999, China was hit with floods. The flood in 1998 was the worst in forty years, affecting twenty-four provinces, killing three thousand people, and displacing 220 million.[1] How did the fledgling Chinese Churches do amid these challenges? Was Bible work affected, and how did UBS continue to serve and support the Chinese Churches, especially in Bible distribution?

Bible Printing Continued without Interruption

One of the worries after the June Fourth Incident was the authorities' reaction to religious activities. Even as the authorities assured the Chinese people that conditions were returning to normal after the June Fourth Incident and that there would be no change in its policy of reform and opening up to the outside world, many chose to lie low. Naturally, one key area of concern to the Chinese Churches was the printing and distribution of Bibles.

The work at Amity Foundation, the parent organization of APC, was adjusted and reduced, particularly in its education division. But Bible printing at APC did not cease. According to a newsletter by Dr. Philip Wickeri, the overseas coordinator of Amity Foundation, "the Amity Printing Company has continued its work without interruption. …

---
1 *South China Morning Post*, July 6, 2016.

On June 12th, the UBS issued a press release announcing that it was 'business as usual' at the APC and that there was 'a stable mood' among the workers."

UBS continued to donate Bible paper throughout the 1990s. About 750,000 Bibles and Testaments were produced at APC in 1989 and 1.4 million the following year. In 1999, the total volume of Bibles printed by APC since 1987 stood at 20.2 million copies. The total amount of paper required for 20 million Bibles was thirteen metric tons with an estimated value of USD$25 million, which UBS donated over an eleven-year period![2]

The resolve to provide the Chinese Christians and China with the Word of God was clearly seen on the part of the CCC/TSPM leaders. As early as November 1989, they formed the Bible Commission (literally "The Chinese Christian Bible Publication Committee" in Chinese) to look into Bible ministry work. The chairperson of the commission was Professor Jiang Peifen from Nanjing Seminary, and the executive secretary was Rev. Bao Jiayuan. A standing subcommittee was also set up consisting of leaders from both CCC/TSPM and the seminaries. Two working groups were formed, "Checking and Revising" and "Publishing and Distributing." Systems and infrastructure were put in place. This commission grew in the following decades to include several working groups as Bible ministry expanded. Despite daunting challenges domestically and internationally in the '90s, God's Word was set to spread in China, where one-fifth of the world's population resided.

Countrywide Network of Bible Distribution Centers

A worker at the distribution center in Nanjing, China, stacks Scriptures in preparation for a shipment to churches around the country, 1992.

Preparing parcels of Scriptures for posting to other distribution points and churches at the Nanjing Distribution Center, 1993.

One of the strategies to spread God's Word in the vast and diverse landscape of China was to set up a network of Bible distribution centers across the country. With the support of UBS, these were first opened in the capital of provinces where infrastructure was more developed. By the late 1990s, all provinces (except Tibet) had at least one Bible distribution center, with some having two to three centers receiving truckloads and cartons of Bibles from APC.

From these distribution centers, the Word of God went out all over China. From the pristine Qinghai Lake in Xining to the multi-ethnic Kunming, the word was read; in the arid desert region in Hohhot to the azure beaches of coastal Xiamen, the word was read; from the historical city of Xi'an to the technological hub in Shenzhen, the word was read; amid the lush grassland of Baotou to the bustling cities of Shanghai and Beijing,

---

2 Kua, UBS Asia Opportunity report, 1999.

Shining Forth I

Bibles loaded onto hand carts at the Hefei Distribution Center begin their journey to churches and Christians in Anhui, 1991.

Delivering Bibles to a church in Suzhou, near Hefei, Anhui, 2006.

Bibles packed high on a bicycle outside the distribution point in Zhengzhou, China; these were carried 90 kilometers to the rural churches where they were needed, 1993.

People crowding round the Bible distribution point window in Zhengzhou, Henan, 1993.

A donor trying out carrying Bibles on poles, 2004.

People queuing to buy Bibles, Nanjing, Jiangsu, 1999.

A young man browsing through the Scriptures available at Wenzhou Bible Distribution Center, Zhejiang, 1998.

the word was read; from icy Harbin to hilly Nanning, the word was read; from the industrial base in Taiyuan to the railway hub in Nanchang, the word was read.

Henan Province, which has one of the largest Christian populations, had five distribution centers, and Fujian Province had six. Some regional centers like the ones located at Nanjing Theological Seminary and Jiangsu Province serve multiple provinces. Bible distribution centers usually located at the office buildings of the Provincial Christian Council / TSPM, city churches, and theological seminaries were managed and served by staff and volunteers. In 1998, a decade after the setting up of APC, there were fifty-nine centers and more than one hundred staff and volunteers. To improve on their work and gather feedback from on the ground, annual meetings were held with distribution center staff and leaders of the CCC/TSPM, where UBS leaders were also invited to attend.

Testimonies from the Bible Distribution Centers

At these annual meetings, stories and testimonies were shared. Here are some stories that capture the deep joy of the Chinese Christians as they bought the Bibles from the distribution centers.

Liaoning Province, 1993

Two ladies set off from their village at 4 a.m. on bicycles so that they could reach the distribution center located at Shenyang Theological Seminary at 9 a.m., just as the center opened. They entered the center full of enthusiasm to buy Bibles. Upon hearing that the Bibles were sold out, they were in a total daze. One of them protested, saying that they had cycled five hours from their homes, suffered some leg injuries on the way, and had been tasked by fellow Christians in their hometown to buy Bibles. How were they supposed to face their fellow Christians if they were to return without the Bibles?

Then they saw a few cartons of Bibles on the floor and wanted to pay for them. But the center manager told them those cartons were designated to be delivered by train to another place in the province, already registered to be shipped out. When they heard this, they sat down on the floor and cried, saying that they would sit and wait for the Bibles. The acting production manager of APC, who was at the center, was moved by them and requested the center manager to release the Bibles to them first,

People buying Bibles, Nanjing, Jiangsu, 1999.

promising to dispatch more Bibles to the other place later. So, the two ladies immediately got up from the floor and paid for the Bibles. They were grateful for the cartons of Bibles, carefully strapping them to their bicycles. As they started their five-hour bicycle journey home, they prayed, "Lord, bless us and protect us on our journey home."

Xinjiang Province, 1993

One often has to travel a long distance in order to arrive at a Bible distribution center. Once, two ladies traveled for two days to get to the distribution center at Urumqi. As soon as they arrived, they were told that all the Bibles had been sold out. On hearing that, the two ladies started crying. One of them said, "We live far away, and it took us two days to get here. We just built a small church and none of us have the Bible." She insisted, "We will not go home without a Bible!" Moved by their earnestness and determination, the minister gave them his personal copy. Then the two ladies wrapped the Bible carefully and went home with great joy and thanksgiving, even though what they got was only one copy of the Bible!

Bible distribution by the British and Foreign Bible Society and Scottish Bible Society to Miao Church in Yunnan Province, 2003.

Hebei Province, 1997

Bible distribution was deemed so important and urgent that a Christian man who worked as an engineer earning RMB 700 a month decided to quit his job. He became a full-time distribution center manager, earning only one-third of what he used to. When asked how he copes with supporting his wife and child, he said, "We eat at our parents' place!" Even the parents chipped in!

Shanxi Province, 2003

Zhang was a volunteer at the Taiyuan Bible distribution center. Her health was not good, and her family opposed her volunteering work. Her husband and eighty-year-old mother, who were unbelievers, said, "You don't earn a cent from doing volunteer work at the church, so why waste your time! Furthermore, your elderly mother has to cook and do the household chores when you are away." But as she pressed on, Zhang's health gradually improved. After volunteering for eight years, not only has her husband stopped objecting to her work but her mother has also come to believe in the Lord. At eighty-eight years old, her mother was still able to help with the cooking and household chores. Zhang said, "Thanks be to the Lord for his grace is not just sufficient but far surpassing what we can ask for or imagine."

Bible distribution centers serve Christians almost round the clock with their most urgent needs. Although there are stipulated opening hours, center staff and volunteers, who usually live near the center, still serve people who arrive late. One of the center managers shared at the annual meeting in 1998 that he had to open the center at night on many occasions because many Christians came from faraway places to buy Bibles and often arrived at night. On one occasion, a Christian arrived with just enough money to buy one copy of the Bible. He did not have any money left to go home. So the center manager bought a train ticket for him out of his own pocket.

Inner Mongolia, 1998

Another story was told of a distribution center at Hohhot, the capital of Inner Mongolia. An elderly lady who traveled on horseback for four days to reach the city. As soon as she reached the church and saw the minister, she knelt, clinging to the minister's leg and crying out of despair. She said, "I just won some friends to Christ. I desperately need your help in teaching me how to explain the Christian faith to them, and they need Bibles!"

UBS groups also visited the Bible distribution centers to hear how the Word of God was being circulated throughout China. In 1995, a visit was made to Hefei, Anhui Province, which saw a growth of a hundredfold, from an estimated ten thousand believers before 1949 to one million in 1995. The local church leader shared how the demand for Bibles was outpacing supply:

> Not only churches need Bibles, but government officials also want Bibles too. Many of the Communist Party members have Bibles. We share with local believers that Bible paper is donated by our friends abroad. Here at the distribution center, it costs twenty yuan. At a commercial bookstore it will probably cost one hundred yuan. The Bible might be the most affordable book in China, but it is the most precious book. We never put a price on the Bible because it is a priceless treasure. The biggest problem for this distribution center is that we do not have enough Bibles to meet the demand. Every day, we receive phone calls from all over the province asking for Bibles. People need Bibles just like people need water.

Perhaps the words of another Bible distribution center manager in Xi'an, Shaanxi Province, Ms. Wang, best sums up the demand for Bibles and the importance of Bible distribution, "Our center sells about a thousand Bibles a week. … When I eat, when I sleep, at any time people come to ask for a Bible. This is a sacred position; I'm helping to deliver spiritual food."

"Project Light" (光的计划)–Bibles for Unregistered Churches

Project Light booklet produced by EGMI circa, 1992.

The story of Bible distribution in China in the 1990s would not be complete without an account of how Bibles were also provided for unregistered churches. How this came about through a partnership between CCC/TSPM and East Gates Ministries International (EGMI) is our next focus.

At the end of the Cultural Revolution, due to the severe shortage of Scriptures, Bibles were smuggled into China from overseas to meet the spiritual needs of Chinese Christians. In 1981, it was reported that Project Pearl, a clandestine delivery of one million Bibles by Open Doors, a UK-based Christian organization, was conducted at the port in Shantou. However, as these Bibles were illegally brought in, some were confiscated by the authorities and consequently owners of these contraband Bibles often got into trouble.

With the establishment of Amity Press in 1987, Chinese Christians can now obtain a copy of God's Word from church bookstores legally and openly. This includes Christians who belong to the unregistered churches. However, due to historical reasons, some Christians from unregistered churches preferred not to buy Bibles from registered churches.[3] There remained an acute need for Bibles among them as more Chinese came to know the Lord and as old and worn-out Bibles needed to be replaced.

In 1991, a plea came from some key leaders of unregistered churches to EGMI, a US-based Christian organization led by Rev. Nelson Graham, the son of Rev. Billy Graham (who visited APC in 1988), requesting one million Bibles legally printed in China for safe and secure distribution throughout their networks. They told EGMI that times are different now. It is much safer for people to own Bibles that are printed in China. EGMI had been involved in supporting the churches in China. The plea resonated with EGMI,

Left to right: Rev. Franklin Graham, Rev. Billy Graham, Dr. Han Wenzao, and David Thorn at APC, 1988.

who then approached the American Bible Society and UBS. With the help of the UBS regional office in Hong Kong, leaders of EGMI were introduced to CCC/TSPM, which was the only legal publisher of the Protestant Bible in China. They met with CCC leaders Dr. Han Wenzao and Rev. Bao Jiayuan.

The intent of EGMI was conveyed—they wanted to support the printing of one million Bibles at APC with the goal of giving them for free to "Christians wherever they may meet with the emphasis to those meeting in homes." It was providential that all parties saw the importance of providing Bibles legally printed in China to Chinese Christians wherever they may worship. Leaders of CCC/TSPM understood that there were Chinese Christians who did not particularly feel close to the registered churches and preferred to meet in homes. In the early '90s, it was estimated that 10 million Christians were worshiping in registered churches while about 15–20 million were worshiping in homes. Other unofficial estimates put the total number of Christians in China at sixty million in the early 1990s.[4]

There was an initial concern about coping with the huge quantity proposed by EGMI. The chilly political climate after the collapse of the USSR certainly did not help. But the leaders of CCC/TSPM saw the importance and urgency of meeting the needs of the Chinese Christians as well as making Bibles available to seekers. They took the step of faith to partner with EGMI to meet the needs of Chinese Christians. Amazingly, the Chinese authorities gave the green light. With that, the joint agreement, which took eight months to negotiate, was reached to allow EGMI to fund the printing of one million Bibles over five years, from 1992 to

---

3 For further reading on the background, readers may wish to consult works by Brent Fulton (Chinasource.org), Philip Wickeri, and Paul Hattaway.
4 China News and Church Report quoting State Statistics Bureau Survey, 1992.

1996. Rev. Nelson Graham said, "We thought it would take several years to reach this kind of agreement and are so grateful to God for the spirit of partnership and understanding that He has brought about in such a short time. Every day we wake up and realize that God is much bigger than we thought He was the day before."

Notably, Rev. Doug Sutphen, one of the founding presidents of EGMI involved in the meetings with CCC/TSPM, was formerly from Open Doors and had coordinated Project Pearl. A former missionary to China in the 1970s to the 1980s, he said that the "era of Bible smuggling is now past and the era of communication, cooperation and trust has now begun." According to Rev. Bao Jiayuan, who coordinated Bible distribution for the CCC, anyone can request Bibles at the CCC Bible distribution centers. "There are no pre-conditions, such as previous connection with the local or provincial Christian Council."

This new endeavor to spread the Word of God in China through legal means was aptly called "Project Light." Inside the EGMI newsletter, Rev. Billy Graham was quoted as saying, "Project Light is an historic and remarkable opportunity and one that I fully support. The greatest tool of evangelism for anyone is the Bible!"

One of the home meeting points that received Bibles in 1992 through Project Light was the Damazhan House Church in Guangzhou, led by well-known minister Samuel Lam. Letters from this church show appreciation for the CCC's effort to give all Christians in China access to the Word of God.[5]

In 1995, as CCC and EGMI completed the distribution of the one million Bibles ahead of schedule, the two parties signed another agreement in May to distribute up to 5 million Bibles within the next five years, from 1996 to 2000. According to EGMI's twentieth-anniversary magazine, they distributed 3.5 million copies of Bibles in China under Project Light, highlighting that "delivering millions of Bibles to unregistered churches could not have been accomplished without the Chinese authorities' approval as well as the permission and assistance from the CCC/TSPM."

It is inspiring to see that when the body of Christ united, a greater good was brought forth for the people in China. Praise God!

Bibles for Victims Caught in the Century's Worst Flood

Another important Bible distribution work in China in the late 1990s was for flood victims. In June 1998, the Yangtze River burst its banks and swallowed a large part of eastern China, including the provinces of Jiangxi, Fujian, and Henan, and its waters spread as far north as Inner Mongolia.

A story was told of an old believer who used the last few precious moments as the waters surged to find his Bible and put it into a plastic bag before he was evacuated. When asked why he didn't reach for jewelry, family photos, or cash, he simply answered, "Money and material goods you can always get, but the Word of God is the most valuable thing we have."

One of the badly hit areas, Nanping City in Fujian, saw the worst flooding in centuries. Torrential rain caused landslides on hills and mountains, which claimed the lives of many people, injured many others, and left tens of thousands of people homeless. People's livelihoods

---

5 *Amity News Service*, May 8, 1993.

Rev. Fergus Macdonald, general secretary of UBS, presenting Chinese Bibles to villagers who were affected by the flood in Fujian, 1998.

were destroyed as whole villages, fields, and fishponds were submerged and crops devastated. The Nanping Municipal Christian Council reported that three church buildings had collapsed in that area and many of the remaining churches were damaged and unsafe. In addition, twenty thousand Bibles and hymnals were lost in the flood waters. And the council pleaded for Bibles.

Following the report, the China Christian Council/TSPM launched a free distribution program to give fifty thousand Bibles to Christians who had lost their Bibles. The total cost was estimated at USD$73,000. In response to an urgent need for Bibles, UBS allocated funds to support the project.

Thank-you letters written by churches and recipients of the Bibles once again reveal how precious the Word of God was to the Chinese Christians. A church in Fuquan City, Nanping wrote:

> Many of our brothers and sisters in Christ are migrant workers from other provinces. They are poor and have difficulties even with their daily meals. So they were moved to tears upon receiving the Bibles saying, "This is the great love of God to us. If not for His love, how would these precious books have reached us? How would the pastors and leaders know of our financial difficulties? We are ever grateful. This is the work of Christ on the cross." We have not met. You do not know us but you know God. And I do not know you but I know the Father, Son and Holy Spirit. The Lord bless you in all that you do.

A church in Yizhou, Guangxi Province, wrote:

> We can only express our thanks and the great current of warmth and love we feel in our hearts on this piece of paper. Thank God and thank you our benefactors! When the brothers and sisters in Christ here received the Bibles, there were many tears of gratitude. The floods had destroyed our crops, affecting hundreds of families in our area. We were thinking to ourselves, what shall we eat tomorrow? But the Lord Jesus taught us, "Man shall not live by bread alone but by every word that proceeds from the mouth of God" (Matt 4:4) and He said, "I am the bread of life, whoever comes to me shall not hunger, those who believe in me will never thirst" (John 6:35). Thanks be to God!

A believer from Henan, Fangcheng, wrote:

> Since receiving the Bibles you've sent us, my heart has not stopped beating with joy and gratitude and I've come before the Lord several times to thank Him for I owe it to Him all that I have and to the body of Christ who has given us this offering of love. We are moved to offer up ourselves, our all, our entire being to the Lord for His use. And we also ask the Lord to bless your work.

Bible distribution in Henan Province where eight thousand from different villages turned up, 2004.

Seizing the Twenty-First-Century Opportunity–Gospel Wagons for China

At the turn of the new millennium, as millions of Chinese were turning to Christ and thousands of churches were built, demand for Bibles was outpacing supply. By the early 2000s, the CCC/TSPM, with the support of UBS, had printed and distributed about 25 million copies of the Bible, and there were already seventy Bible distribution centers across the country, but not every Chinese Christian had a copy of the Bible. This was especially so in rural China, where most of the Christians were found and churches were growing rapidly.

Moreover, Bible distribution centers were mostly located in urban areas, and supplies were usually snapped up before Christians from the villages could lay their hands on a copy. CCC/TSPM received reports that in some remote mountain churches, one hundred people were sharing one Bible. In some villages, ten families on average were sharing one Bible and one hymnal.[6] There was thus a cry from the rural Christians for more Bibles.

Bible distribution van on the way to the villages in Jiangsu, 2001.

---

6 *UBS Asia Opportunity News Update*, July 2000.

At the same time, God was moving the hearts of UBS leaders to close the large gap in global Scripture access. Nations that were once closed to the gospel were now opening their doors and seeing phenomenal church growth. As the UBS Fellowship entered the twenty-first century, the task of making God's Word available to all nations remained unfinished and ever more urgent. To fulfill its mission, UBS embarked on a four-year campaign known as Opportunity 21 to expand global Scripture distribution, outreach, and engagement. It was to be one of the most significant programs of outreach ever enacted by the fellowship.

Supporting churches in China in Scripture distribution was one of the top priorities of the Opportunity 21 campaign. In response to the need for Bibles in rural and remote areas in China, funds were raised not just to print more Bibles but also to purchase Bible distribution vans to transport Scriptures. Funds poured in from the various Bible Societies, and forty-six vans were purchased and donated to the churches in China over the years, even after the campaign ended.

The first Bible distribution trip by van was to the northern part of Jiangsu Province in February 2001. This was a poorer region compared to the south, and many of the Christians in northern Jiangsu were subsistence farmers. During that maiden trip, a team from Jiangsu Christian Council / TSPM traveled 700 kilometers in three days, visiting churches in four districts and distributing three thousand copies of Bibles and hymnals. Church workers and members in these districts received them with applause saying, "You have not only the Word of God but also your love and care for the village churches." It was acknowledged by the local churches that the van was no ordinary vehicle but a gospel wagon—one that brings the gospel of Christ wherever it goes.

With these Bible vans, it was reported that rural pastors who used to travel days to the distribution centers, with some carrying boxes of Bibles on their backs or on poles over their shoulders, were now freed up for their pastoral ministry. And churches in remote areas that used to wait one to two weeks for the Bibles to be sent by public transport can now expect to receive their Bibles in a matter of days.

On another trip in 2003, Kua Wee Seng, UBS CP director (1999–2021), accompanied a UBS donor to Liaoning Province, northeast China, to distribute Bibles using the distribution van. Over two days, a total of fifteen thousand copies of Bibles were donated and distributed for free to the poorer Christians in the counties and villages. A retired government official, Xing Suqin, who was serving as a volunteer at the Liaoning Christian Council shared,

Bible distribution in Sichuan, 2004.

> The number of believers here has increased greatly. This is mainly because Christians are sharing the gospel. Whether they are at home, in the fields, on the bus, or even just taking a walk along the street, they are willing and ready to share the good news in their hearts. The believers share their faith whenever there is an opportunity to do so, right where they are!

Ms. Xing Suqin was a department head of the Liaoning Religious Affairs Bureau, 2003.

The need in Liaoning was so great that another Bible distribution trip was organized in October of the following year with some Bible Societies' donors, led by the president of Liaoning Christian Council, Rev. Sheng Guangwei. The group went to the district of Chaoyang and thoroughly enjoyed the fellowship they shared with the local brothers and sisters in Christ.

Bible Distribution at Xinjiang, 2006.

Bible distribution at Meijia, a village near Hefei, Anhui, 2006.

Bible distribution in Henan, 2009.

Bible Distribution in Yunnan, 2014.

Bible distribution in Hunan, 2014.

Mdm. Wu Qiang Jin started a rural church at her village in Hunan. She is seen here with lay preacher Tong Xin Jun carrying Bibles supported by UBS, 2014.

Bible Distribution in Henan, 2016.

Bible Distribution in Shandong, 2018.

Bible Distribution in Shandong, 2018.

It is astounding as we reflect on how God's Word was spreading and shining forth in China after the end of the Cultural Revolution. Through the Bible distribution centers, vans, and other means of distribution, millions in China heard the message of hope and salvation. Many Chinese who were once dwelling in darkness have seen a great light, and for those dwelling in the region and shadow of death, on them a light has dawned (Isa 9:2). As we close this chapter, here are two stanzas of a song written by Rev. Shen Guangwei from Liaoning Province, who was moved by the Holy Spirit to compose it to praise God and mark the wonderful experience of the Bible distribution mission:

> Bible, Bible, Bible
> Salvaging many souls and breaths
> Afraid not of the long travels
> Fear not the hilly, bumpy and uneven paths
> Testimonies spread throughout the land like fire
> Laughter and praises filling the passage
> Peace with you the entire road
> Wishing you a fruitful voyage

5
Shining Forth II

Bibles for the Catholic Church in China

Ignorance of Scripture is ignorance of Christ.
—St Jerome, born ca. 342, translator of Latin Vulgate, ordained priest, and biblical scholar

More than twenty years ago (in the 1980s), we had no more than twenty Catholic Bibles for five to six hundred parish members. One church member would read the Bible aloud through the amplifier for the rest of the congregation to listen to God's Word.
—Father Wang Yuliang, Shandong Province

Located in Beijing, the Cathedral of the Immaculate Conception, commonly known as Nantang ("southern church"), is China's oldest Catholic church. Its foundation was first laid in 1605 by Jesuit missionary Matteo Ricci who had won the favor of Emperor Wanli. When the cathedral was rebuilt in 1657 during the reign of Emperor Shunzhi of the Qing Dynasty, a stone tablet was inscribed with the words "Cathedral Built by Imperial Order." Amazingly, the tablet still stands in the churchyard today.

A Catholic church in Shaanxi Province during Mass, 2010.

The current building, the fourth church on the site, dates to 1904 with a statue of Matteo Ricci standing within its compound. It might be a surprise to some that about five thousand Chinese Catholics come to this historical cathedral each week for Masses.

In 1949, when China came under Communist rule, there were about 3 million Catholics in China. Today, the number has risen to 6 million. They worship in 6,400 churches under ninety-eight dioceses and are served by sixty-six bishops, 3,800 priests, and 6,100 nuns. Unofficial sources put the number of Chinese Catholics as high as 12 million, including those in the unregistered churches. How great was the need for Bibles among the Chinese Catholics? How did the Bible ministry partnership with UBS start? And what was the effect of God's Word in the lives of the Chinese Catholics? We shall attempt to answer these questions in this chapter.

The Need for Bibles after the Cultural Revolution

After the Cultural Revolution in 1976, the Chinese Catholic Patriotic Association (CCPA), originally established in 1957, was restored. In 1980, the Bishops' Conference of the Catholic Church in China was formed. Together they formed the twin organization that registered Catholic churches come under. During this period, there was a great scarcity of Catholic Bibles and liturgy books as these were destroyed during the Cultural Revolution. The spiritual needs of the believers were obviously great. Priests and nuns needed to be trained, Bibles and liturgy books needed to be printed. The twin organization thus looked into alleviating these challenges.

Thankfully, in 1982, the Sheshan Seminary in Shanghai reopened, where priests and nuns could be trained to serve in the parishes and shepherd the flock. It was the first to reopen after the Cultural Revolution. Bishop Aloysius Jin Luxian, who was released from imprisonment after the Cultural Revolution, was appointed as the rector. The following year, the Catholic Church in China set up Guang Qi Publishing in 1983, the first press to be set up by the Catholics in China to start printing Bibles and liturgy books to meet the urgent needs of the Chinese Catholics.

Bishop Aloysius Jin Luxian of the Catholic diocese of Shanghai with Ruth Li and Kua Wee Seng, 2006.

According to Bishop Jin, the Catholic Church had traditionally emphasized theology and liturgy more than the reading or study of the Bible for the laity. But a ground-breaking change came in 1968 after the Second Vatican Council (Vatican II), initiated by Pope John XXIII and later carried on by Pope Paul VI. One significant outcome of Vatican II was Dei Verbum, a dogmatic constitution, which affirmed the centrality of the Bible in the life of the church and called for it to be made available in the languages of the people. Vatican II also opened the door for other languages besides Latin to be used during Mass, hence making Bible translation essential.

When Vatican II took place, China was in the throes of the Cultural Revolution, and the country had already cut off diplomatic ties with the Vatican in 1951 to prevent undue foreign influence. Even though the Catholics in China were not able to participate in Vatican II, the Word of God played a central role in the lives of many Chinese Catholics.

The need for the Word of God can be seen in this recollection by Father Wang Yuliang from Shandong Province, "More than twenty years ago (in the 1980s), there were not more than twenty Catholic Bibles shared among the five to six hundred parish members. In those days, church members would read the Bible aloud through the amplifiers for the rest of the congregation to listen to God's Word. A Bible, to me, was a rare and precious commodity." Chinese Catholics are Bible-reading and Bible-believing people. How then would this need be met?

Partnership with UBS

As with the partnership with the Protestant churches in China, UBS's relationship with the Catholic Church in China also started from friendships. The first is the friendship between

Bishop K. H. Ting of the CCC/TSPM and Bishop Aloysius Jin Luxian, both from Shanghai. Bishop Ting, knowing the needs of the Catholic Church in China, introduced Bishop Jin to UBS.

The first contact was made in 1983 when UBS leaders visited Bishop Jin at the Shanghai Sheshan Seminary. Recalling the meeting during an interview in 2003, Bishop Jin said:

> UBS leaders Rev. Chan Choi and Dr. I-Jin Loh took the initiative to visit me. They came to me with such humility and sincerity. They told me, "The purpose of UBS is to share the gospel with the whole world, bringing God's Word to every person." As I was then translating the Jerusalem Bible into contemporary Chinese, I requested Bible paper support from them. They agreed without hesitation. This impressed me tremendously because at that time we had not been able to secure any support from any organization. UBS was the first to stretch out their hand to us.

In addition, Bible translation consultation was given, and Bible resources were shared with Bishop Jin. In 1985, Bishop Jin completed the Chinese translation of the four Gospels of the Jerusalem New Testament and printed them with the support of UBS. On the need for a new Bible translation, Bishop Jin said in the same interview, "Our mission is to share the gospel. The word of the Lord is the gospel. With the passage of time, language has changed and there are also new discoveries in the original text of the Bible as well as advancements in the research of archaeologists and biblical scholars. Hence, there is a need for fresh Bible translation."

Two other publications followed. First was a revised version of the New Testament published in 1996. Bishop Jin revised his Chinese translation of the Jerusalem New Testament using the New Jerusalem Bible as a reference. Second was the English-Chinese diglot of the New Jerusalem New Testament published in 1999. UBS was privileged to support the Catholic Church at the Shanghai Diocese to print and distribute one million copies of the New Jerusalem New Testament. The Old Testament was not translated because Bishop Jin later suffered from failing eyesight and ill health, passing away at age ninety-six in 2013.

In 1994, following the goodwill that had been established between Bishop Jin and UBS, and with the help of Dr. Han Wenzao, China Protestant church leader Kua Wee Seng, representing UBS Asia Opportunity, reached out to national Chinese Catholic leader Liu Bainian, to explore UBS's partnership with the Chinese Catholic Church in their Bible ministry. They spoke over the phone, and by the providence of God, an agreement was reached for UBS to begin to support the Chinese Catholic Church in Bible printing and distribution.

Liu Bainian with UBS leader Miller Milloy, 2005.

It was a faith venture for both parties. UBS was trusting God for funding to support the printing of Catholic Bibles. The Catholic Church in China was also trusting God for the same.

Praise God that he provided! UBS was able to fund the Bible paper and arranged for the printing of the first fifty thousand copies of the Bible at APC for the Chinese Catholic Church. Since then, about 2.6 million Catholic Bibles and 1.1 million New Testament have been printed and distributed to the Chinese Catholic Church. Most of the Bibles were printed with Bible paper support from UBS. Today, UBS continues to support the mission of the Chinese Catholic Church to spread the Word of God in China through Bible printing and distribution.

Bibles for Survivors of the 2008 Sichuan Earthquake

The year 2008 was a significant one for China. It had emerged from the global financial crisis relatively unscathed and was poised to host the Olympics for the first time. But in May 2008, three months shy of the Olympics, it was hit with one of the worst earthquakes in the nation's history. The magnitude-8.0 earthquake struck Wenchuan City, Sichuan Province, in the southwestern part of China, with tremors felt as far away as Thailand and Vietnam. It left 87,000 people dead, 370,000 injured, and 5 million homeless.

Bible distribution to survivors of Sichuan earthquake, 2008.

The earthquake's epicenter at Wenchuan made the counties of Beichuan, Wenchuan, Pengzhou, Dujiangyan, Mianzhu, and Shifang the most severely hit counties in the region.

One can only try to imagine the degree of devastation and depth of pain experienced by the survivors. In Mianzhu County alone, which has a total land area of 1,245.3 square kilometers and a population of 520,000, it was estimated that more than thirty thousand were injured, 6,805 lost their lives, and countless people were missing at that time.

Notably, in many rural areas, village infrastructure, including roads and water systems sustained severe damage. More than 90 percent of the homes had been destroyed, and people were living on subsistence. Churches in Sichuan were badly affected by the disaster. Believers lost their loved ones and their homes, while many church buildings were damaged irreparably and deemed structurally dangerous. The majority of the Mianzhu Christians were poor and living in rural and mountainous areas, and they were among the hardest hit.

Mianzhu Catholic church staff erected temporary tents to sleep in and used a nearby area as a place of worship. Despite its structural constraints, the church acted as a local distribution point for rice, oil, clothes, and even Bibles. Through the efforts of the

Buildings damaged by the 2008 earthquake in Sichuan.

local church workers together with some church volunteers, more than seven hundred people attended the worship service in tents at the church grounds. This was a marked increase from its two-hundred-strong membership prior to the earthquake. Amid grief and loss, people were seeking something that would last.

Never was there a greater need for Bibles and other Christian materials that would comfort the grieving. A local priest shared God's Words of encouragement to the congregation as some questioned the sovereignty of God amid the calamity. Believers old and new needed the assurance that God is good and that he has not forgotten them. In response to the need for Bibles amid such devastation, UBS donated thirty thousand copies of the Catholic Bible to China. Father Li of Chengdu Catholic Diocese shared how the Bibles made a difference to them:

> Out of 100,000 members in the diocese, nearly 60,000 of our members' families suffered damages from the earthquake. The Bibles gave believers much joy and gratitude as they took them home. The priests, sisters and volunteers who were involved in giving out the Bibles were deeply encouraged by our believers' response. Up to that time, they had no idea they had such great love toward the Bible. Many of the locals who had heard about the Bible distribution enquired at the distribution points hoping to get a copy for themselves. The Bibles provide so much comfort to the survivors, helping them in this unique moment to ponder upon God's Word and serving as an instrument of prayer.

In 2016, my colleague and I visited Father Jiang of Xiushui Catholic Church in Beichuan County, who shared with us his experiences—the need to live with unanswered questions and to cling to God's Word in the midst of suffering and pain. He recalled spending weeks walking the ruins after the earthquake, counseling and praying for his parish members who lost their loved ones. One of them was a crippled woman who survived the earthquake but lost her son and daughter-in-law. He shared: "She couldn't talk the first three times I visited her. On the fourth visit, she finally spoke and said she wanted to die. But she couldn't jump since she was crippled and didn't have the means to buy pesticide. No words were adequate to describe her loss. It was heart-breaking."

"It is especially hard when we look at the thousands of children who died in the earthquake. What wrong have they done? Isn't it unfair? We felt helpless and were bewildered by what God had allowed to happen. I have no answers and I need to live without having answers. I know I can't overrule God's will, so I submit to his sovereign will even though I do not understand. Going back to God in submission is the only way," he shared candidly.

What stayed with me was Father Jiang's reflection on the tragedy eight years later. He said, "Man's life is vulnerable and transient. This world is not our destination; we are sojourners. So rejoice always and give thanks. The verse from 1 Thessalonians 5:18 helps me to move on."

In 2008, a total of 230,000 Bibles and New Testaments were printed and distributed to the Chinese Catholic Church. In times of darkness, God's Word points to Jesus as our eternal hope and comfort. When there are no answers to suffering, Christians look to Jesus, their suffering Lord who will one day return as King. What was required of the Catholic Church in China was to be faithful in her mission to spread the word of hope.

The One Million Scripture Project!

One high point of the Bible mission in the Chinese Catholic Church took place in 2009, the year after the earthquake in Sichuan. During this period, the Chinese Catholic Church was reporting an average growth rate of 100,000 annually. Chinese people were coming to faith in droves, especially in the rural areas of China, and needed Bibles. But most of them were subsistence farmers who could not afford a copy of the Bible. According to a priest

New Testaments in Studium Biblicum Version published by the China Catholic Bishops' Conference, printed at Nanjing APC.

serving in the Shanghai Catholic Diocese in 2009, parishes were encouraging Catholics to read their Bibles more regularly. The diocese launched a "read and study the Bible daily" campaign. They also encouraged congregational reading of Scripture passages before and after Mass. "Unfortunately, not all the believers in China own a Bible, especially the rural folks who are too poor to own one."

Therefore, in response to the spiritual needs of the Chinese Catholics, the Taizé Community and UBS co-funded the printing and distribution of one million copies of the Bible and New Testament for the Catholic Church in China in 2009. It was an unprecedented initiative. Annual Bible production for the Catholic Church thus far had hovered between 50,000 and 100,000. From 1994 to 2008, a period of fourteen years, the cumulative total production of Catholic Bibles and New Testaments was 1.1 million. Now, just within a year, the Catholic Church was going to receive one million Bibles and New Testaments. Never had such a large volume of Catholic Bibles and New Testaments ever been distributed for free in China!

What was the response of the Chinese Catholics to the free Bibles? In Beijing and Hebei Province, where some of the free Bibles were distributed, many Catholics were overjoyed to own it for the first time! During masses, Bible passages were recited aloud for believers to follow along. Now, with their own Bible, parishioners, some of whom were semiliterate, said they could practice reading God's Word at home with their children or grandchildren. One of the parishioners who could not read said she liked listening to and learning the Bible at masses and Bible reading sessions. When she got the Bible, she began learning the Chinese characters because she wanted to be able to read the Bible on her own soon!

Catholics reading the free Bibles they received, Hebei, 2009.

A Catholic priest of a parish in Beijing shared happily that they were now able to give a free Bible to newly baptized Catholics. "More Catholic believers are beginning to see the importance and value of reading Scriptures, so they are in fact reading the Bible on their own. We also conduct Bible study for our parishioners and laity training classes."

These free Bibles were proving to be popular among the Chinese Catholics also because it was in the Chinese simplified script typeset in the horizontal format—a change that was done by APC with help and funding from UBS in the 1990s. Older believers were delighted with the new Bible's horizontal format and larger character size, while younger Catholics liked the new format and simplified script as it conformed to current school textbooks.

Notably, out of the one million copies of Scripture, 800,000 were New Testaments (with Psalms and Ecclesiasticus). At that time, the Catholic Church had a greater need for New Testaments for the nurturing of faith of new believers as well as for seekers of the faith. Hence, the decision was made to print more New Testaments than Old Testaments. In an interview with UBS in 2009, Father Anthony Chen of the Diocese of Shanghai, director of Guangqi Research Center and Publication, alluded to the same need. He said that in Shanghai, many Catholics were "first-generation Catholics" adding to the municipality's total of close to 300,000 Catholic believers. One main reason, cited by Father Anthony Chen, was that the Diocese of Shanghai had an outreach program for young people. "We have been organizing and running young people's camps for a few years during school holidays for both believers and unbelievers. These camps have been very well-received by the public."

Word of God Is Active and Alive

As Bibles were printed and distributed, the Word of God was read and heard in churches, chapels, seminaries, and the homes of believers and seekers across China. Hearts were encouraged and strengthened with the teachings from the holy gospel, which pointed them to salvation and eternal hope in Jesus. Selected here are stories from four different places in China—Gansu Province, Shandong Province, Shanghai, and Sichuan Province—that show the transformational power of the Word of God.

One such person is Guo Jiangyun, a lady in her forties from Gansu Province, western China, whom I had the privilege to meet in 2016. A teacher by profession, Guo was plagued by depression and suicidal thoughts. Before her conversion, she had felt inferior and ashamed because both her mother and grandmother were mentally unsound. All their relatives shunned them, the talk being that insanity ran in their family. Praise God that an elderly Catholic friend reached out to her, and she felt the warmth of God's love. She received the faith and testified how the Word of God has changed her:

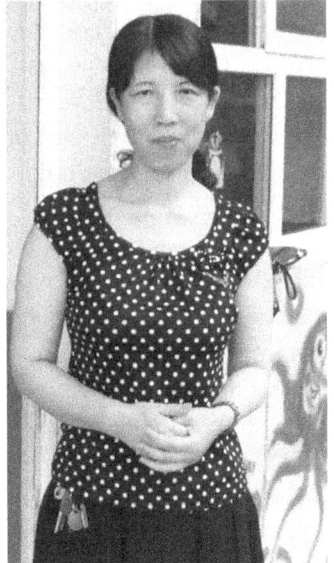

Guo Jiangyun, Gansu, 2016.

> After my baptism, I started reading the Bible more regularly. Scripture did not change me overnight, but I noticed I was desiring God's Word more and more. In fact, if I did not read the Bible or pray for a day, I would feel something amiss. As a teacher, I strive to do well and that makes me full of myself. But through the lenses of the Bible, I saw my own sinfulness. Coming face to face with my weaknesses humbled me. I realized I could only overcome them with divine help. Slowly, God enabled me to love, forgive and show empathy towards others. Every word I read has life and I understand now why the Bible teaches us to feed on his word. It is really food for my soul. I am very moved each time I read the Scriptures. It is like passing from death into life.

Guo Jiangyun felt so liberated and strengthened that she started leading a Bible reading group in her parish and saw the blessings multiplied. One of the members of the group was Lu

Fuhua, age fifty-one. She testified how the Word of God was real and active in her life and how coming to know Jesus through the Bible has helped change her mindset:

> Before coming to the Christian faith, I was always unhappy. Having two daughters and no sons made me feel inferior to others and I was miserable most of the time. Knowing my situation, a friend invited me to attend Mass. All my life I had felt wronged because of the discrimination my daughters and I received from a traditional Chinese society that values males more. It has made me miserable for so many years. But now I realize, Jesus has suffered even greater injustice. He did no wrong and yet was cruelly nailed to the cross for our sins!

Not only were the Chinese Catholics reading the Bible for themselves, but they were also buying it to bless their family and friends—sometimes out of their own poverty like the old widow offering her two small copper coins to the Lord (Mark 12:41–44). They gave sacrificially so that others could also share in the eternal hope that Jesus offers. Liu Fengqin, a Catholic faithful from Shandong Province is a shining example.

Lu Fuhua attended Bible reading led by Guo Jiangyun, Gansu, 2016.

Despite being a poor farmer, Liu saved up to buy a Bible from her parish bookstore. She spends half an hour each day reading the Bible. Whenever she is feeling down, she turns to God's Word to look for answers and comfort. One night while sleeping she heard the words "The Glorious Cross," and some days later she received the vision of a burning candle in the dark. Liu believed that the Lord was urging her to share the good news with others. She then began to be part of her parish's outreach team visiting the poor and disabled in her village, giving them Bibles, and reading God's Word together with them. In total, she has bought fifteen Bibles for her family and friends using her own savings. "I consider it important that everyone who yearns for God and desires to read his word owns a Bible," Liu said.

Donors from UBS were so encouraged by Liu's testimony that they donated free Bibles to her parish through the Catholic Church so that Liu and the outreach team could bless more people in her village. One of the free Bible recipients was Liu's friend Zhang Pengpeng. It was his first Bible, and he has been reading it every day enthusiastically. Though paralyzed from the waist down since he was eighteen years old, Zhang was full of joy because he knew that God remembered him and saved the poor (Ps 113:7).

Zhang Pengpeng with his Bible from Liu Fengqin, 2018.

Another Catholic who received a free Bible from Liu was Zhang Yaodong, fifty-five years old. Zhang hurt his spine in a work accident and has been wheelchair-bound for five years. He owned a traditional script Chinese Bible previously and was delighted to receive a simplified script Bible, which made it easier for him to read the word. He also joined a Bible-reading group via WeChat, a Chinese social media app. Praise God for Catholics like Liu who answered his call to be a light in the darkness for her village!

As Catholics were faithfully reading their Bibles, the Lord used them to lead people to him. This was what happened to Shen Cheng, a twenty-seven-year-old believer from Shanghai, who shared his testimony in 2009. Shen had a habit of reading the Bible wherever he went and whenever he could find time. For a period, he was reading

Zhang Yaodong (in wheelchair) receiving a Bible from Liu Fengqin, 2018.

his Bible at McDonald's. This caught the eye of Lu Xiaochen, a twenty-five-year-old university student working part-time at the same fast-food joint. Lu became curious when he saw Shen sitting alone, day after day, reading a big book with a crucifix in front of him. His curiosity got the better of him, and he initiated a conversation with Shen, who then shared his faith. Shen's sincerity in answering all of Lu's questions and his love for God made a huge impression on the younger man.

As the days progressed, a spiritual friendship was forged at the most unlikely place—McDonald's. Shen never forced his faith on Lu. When Lu decided to be baptized as a Catholic, no one had doubts about Lu's seriousness with his new-found faith. In fact, on the day of his baptism, Lu had a scheduled surgery at the hospital. Against the doctors' advice, Lu left the hospital that morning for his baptism ceremony and returned just in time for his surgery. He said what sustained him was Philippians 3:8, "Yes, I will go further: because of the supreme advantage of knowing Christ Jesus my Lord, I count everything else as loss. For him I have accepted the loss of all other things and look on them all as filth if only I can gain Christ" (NJB).

The Bible was also bringing the Catholic community closer together, and through the community, unbelievers were being drawn to

Father Anthony Chen (middle) with Shen Cheng (left) and Lu Xiaochen (right), 2009.

Christ as this next story shows. In 2016, I met Sister Meng Jiumei, who served in Longci village parish in Sichuan Province. She impressed me with her dynamism and liveliness.

Believers at Longchi Church with Sister Meng Jiumei (second row, first person on the left), Sichuan, 2017.

She told me that, besides attending Masses, the believers here also come to church for fellowship, where they have a time of sharing, singing, dancing, and Bible reading every evening. "I believe that the Word of God is very important in the lives of believers," shared Sister Meng, who has read through the Bible seven times. "Coming together for fellowship and Bible reading is therefore important as it bonds us as a community."

One such participant at the daily session was Jing Wei, thirty-four years old, previously an unbeliever, who came from Hebei Province and married a Catholic from the village of Longci. She has since learned more about the Christian faith from Sister Meng, who hailed from the same province as her. Jing shared, "Bible reading sessions have helped me a lot. Things are livelier now with our singing and dancing sessions. I look forward to my baptism as well as that of my two sons', this Christmas!"

A Catholic with his Bible study notes, Gansu, 2016.

The Need for More Catholic Bibles Today

Chinese Catholics' love and need for the Bible is evident in the fact that, even in the early 2010s, more than twenty years after Bibles became more available and accessible for the Catholic Church in China, Sister Han from Shandong Province reported that there were only three Bibles left in the church book room and none in the storeroom during one of UBS's visits. Bibles delivered to her parish quickly sold out. She said, "There are not enough Bibles. In some village fellowship groups, five to six believers have to share one Bible."

The situation was the same for Sister Meng Jiumei's parish, whose story we read above. She shared in 2016, "We need Bibles both for adults as well as youths. The majority of the believers here are farmers. From my estimate, only one out of five believers here have a Bible.

The need for Bibles is great here. Please remember us!" With the kind donation of Christians via the Bible Societies, Bibles were subsequently delivered to her area through the provincial Catholic diocese.

In 2018, a thank-you letter from Huzhuang parish, Shandong Province talked about the pressing need for Bibles:

> As our parish covers quite a big area and the number of parishioners is big, our current stock of Bibles is not enough. Now that we have received the seven boxes of Bibles from you, it will meet a pressing need here including for use during Mass, in reading and learning the Bible together, thereby helping us to grow in our knowledge of God and receiving his help. We want to thank you once again for your donation and we will use the Bible diligently to know the word and experience God, preparing for the spread of the gospel.

In 2020, at a Bible distribution in Leshan diocese, Sichuan Province, Father Zhang Zhenglin said, "Parishes in counties like Pengshan and Mingshan are hard to reach. Parishioners in counties like Luding, Baoxing and Hanyuan are impoverished, and many cannot afford a Bible. At the same time, we are seeing a steady average growth of one thousand new members each year, hence supply does not meet demand." When one thinks about the mountainous and hilly regions that account for 80 percent of Leshan's total land, the challenge to the distribution of Bibles is unimaginable. The Chinese Catholics in these regions continue to need the Word of God today.

In 2021, something memorable happened at the Shaanxi diocese. Bibles supported by UBS arrived on World Mission Sunday, October 24. According

Bible distribution at Inner Mongolia, 2020.

Catholic Bibles arriving at Jilin, 2021.

to Father Zhang Suwen, "In the past decade or so, churches all over China have set off a wave of Bible reading and study, and many Catholics are sharing their faith, and the churches have changed greatly due to the deepening of Catholics' understanding and knowledge of the Bible." With the arrival of the Bibles, he looked forward to "helping more parishioners to understand and live out the Word of God, and bear witness for the Lord in their respective positions and lives and bring Jesus Christ to their friends who have not yet known him."

Sanctuary of a Catholic church in northern China with a globe behind the cross and words at the side: "The Blood of Christ Saves All, the Light of Christ Shines to All Nations."

Expansion of Bible Ministry

Over the years, the Bible ministry of the Catholic Church in China has gone beyond printing and distributing Bibles, New Testaments, and Scripture portions. UBS has been privileged to support the Catholic Church in China in other areas of Bible ministries, including setting up a Bible resource center at the national seminary of the Catholic Church in China, supporting provincial seminaries with Bible reference materials, conducting Bible equipping classes for seminarians, donating Bible medical vans, supporting Scripture literacy classes and biblical parenting classes, and inviting Catholic church leaders to participate in Bible advocacy seminars. Each of these will be featured as the rest of the chapters unfold. Praise God for the work he has done in the Catholic Church in China and for the support of Christians all over the world given via the Bible Societies that made this wide range of Bible ministry possible!

Church volunteers carrying medical supplies from a Bible medical van at Haixing Village church, 2010.

Bible medical van going up a muddy road to a village church in Yunnan, 2010

UBS leaders visiting CCPA/BCCCC in Beijing.
L-R: Daniel Loh (UBS CP Co-Director), Bishop Shen Bin (President of BCCCC),
Rev Dirk Gevers (UBS Secretary General), Dr. Bernard Low (UBS CP Co-Director), 2023.

Praise God that today, on an annual average, Catholic Bibles are being distributed to over three hundred church locations, while Protestant Bibles are being distributed via more than eighty designated distribution centers, reaching Christians in more than sixty thousand churches across China. Over the years, with a more developed infrastructure and logistics capability in China, more people have been able to have easy access to God's Word. We shall see in the next chapter how the availability and spread of God's Word fueled one of the world's fastest-growing churches as the Bible was read, memorized, and obeyed in the lives of the Chinese Christians. We shall see how fires of revival were sweeping across China.

6
Fire of Revival

The Bible and Church Growth

As for what was sown on good soil, this is the one who hears the word and understands it. He indeed bears fruit and yields, in one case a hundredfold, in another sixty, and in another thirty.
—Matthew 13:23

The growth of the church depends upon the growth of Christians. The growth of Christians depends upon being fed with the Word of God.
—Rev. Luo Zhenfang, presenting at a conference in Hong Kong on "The Role of the Bible in the Growth of the Church in China," 1997

Let Numbers Tell the Story

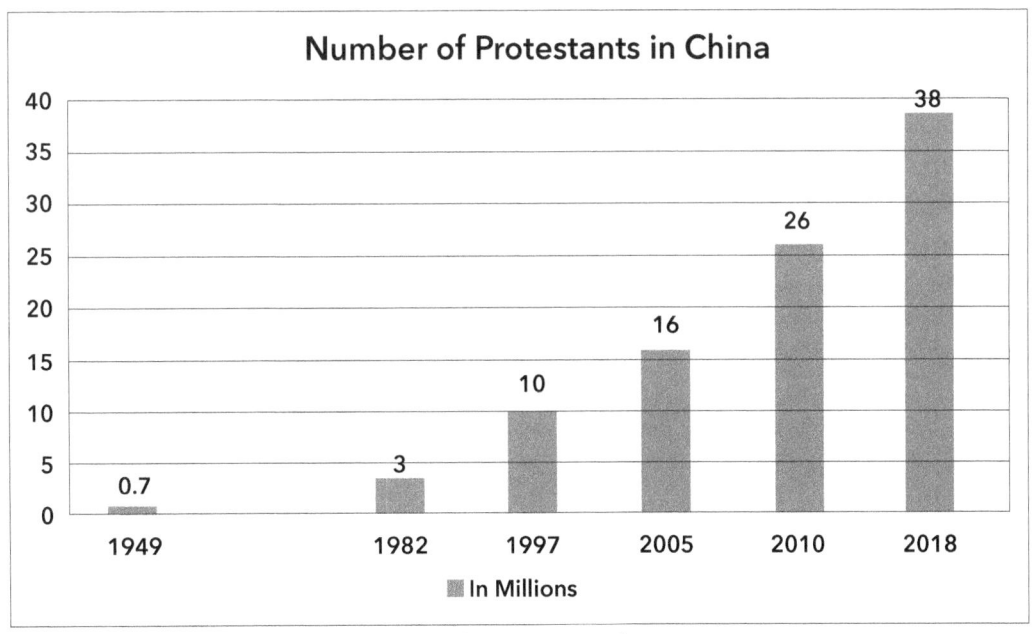

Growth of Christianity in China.

The phenomenal growth of the Churches in China in recent decades is a modern-day miracle. One could say it is a continuation of the Book of Acts, where people who believed in the Lord Jesus were added daily to the church, as the fire of revival swept through China. According to China's official sources, the Protestants numbered 700,000 in 1949. After the Cultural

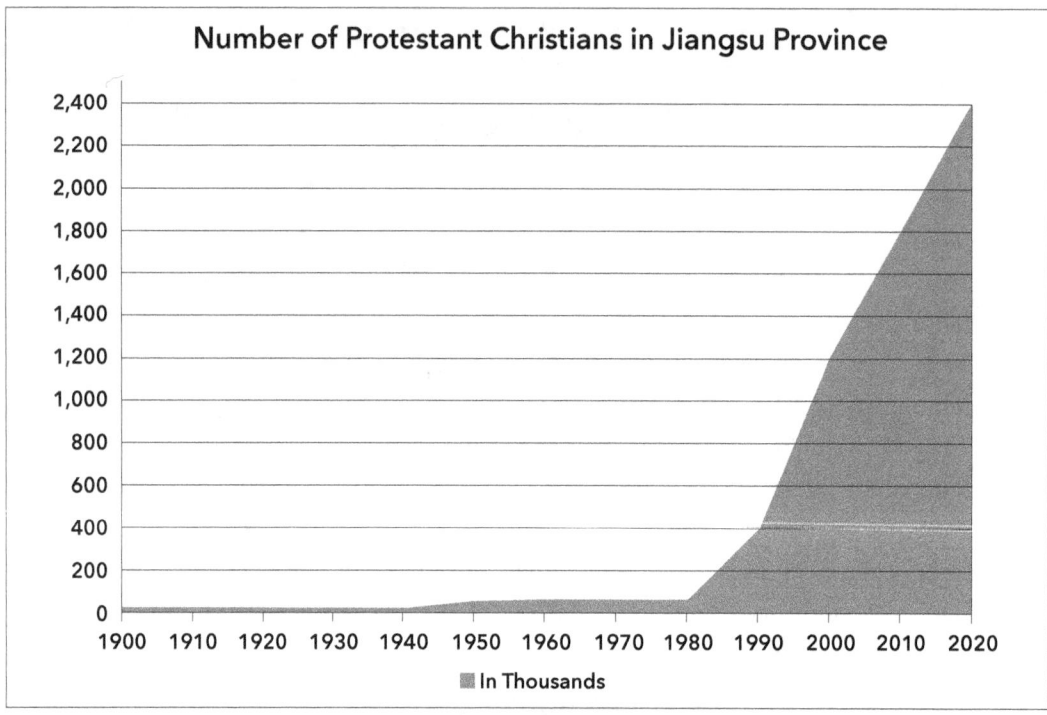

Growth of Christianity in Jiangsu.

Revolution when many thought that the Chinese church was moribund, many believers had, in fact, continued to cling to their faith while others found faith. By the mid-1990s, the Christian population had increased to 12.5 million. In 2020, the official figure reported by CCC/TSPM was 38 million, a fifty-four-fold increase from 1949. If we include believers worshiping in unregistered churches, the total number of Protestants and Catholics could be about 100 million, more than a hundredfold increase!

Believers overflowed and seated outside the church and along the streets during a church Sunday service, Anhui, 1995.

At a Bible distribution in a church in Anhui, 2006.

On the provincial level, Anhui Province saw its Christian population increase from 38,000 in 1949 to 800,000 in the early 1990s—a twenty-fold increase. Jiangsu Province, a coastal area, had about 50,000 believers in 1949. In 2020, the number has soared to 2.5 million, yielding a fifty-fold increase.

In terms of registered churches and meeting points, the numbers tell the same amazing story. With Deng's Reform and Open Door policy in place, church buildings repurposed during the Cultural Revolution were now returned to Christians for worship, and an average of three churches reopened or were erected every two days. The first to reopen was the Ningpo Centennial Church (百年堂) in 1979 in April. This was followed by Xinjie Church (新街堂) in Gulangyu, Fujian Province, and Mu'en Church (沐恩堂) in Shanghai, in the same year. In 1986, more than four thousand Protestant churches had opened for worship and religious activities in China. This number tripled in 1996 to twelve thousand churches and another twenty-five thousand meeting points. By the early 2000s, there were an estimated fifty thousand churches and meeting points. And this number rose to sixty thousand in 2020, according to CCC/TSPM. Undeniably, the Word of God, like the seed planted in good soil, was taking root and bearing fruit in the land of China, yielding a hundred-fold and beyond.

Exponential growth seen in a church in Luhe, Nanjing, Jiangsu, 2016.

Church Growth Anchored upon the Word of God

What has led to the unprecedented exponential growth of the Churches in China in recent decades? When I read through the testimonies and stories gathered over the years, it became clear to me that one key reason was the way Chinese Christians loved and valued the Bible.

Culturally and historically, the Chinese are a people with a great reverence for literature. Respect for the printed word is "almost a religion to the Chinese and the man of letters

The congregation overflowing to the staircase area of the church, Anhui, 2006.

holds the highest rank in society."[1] A few Chinese proverbs will flesh this out for us. "When you read a book for the first time, you get to know a friend; read it for a second time and you meet an old friend" (初读好书, 如获良友; 重读好书, 如逢故友), "Words convey truth, Truth nurtures people" (文以载道, 以道育人), and "He who teaches me for a day is my father for a lifetime" (一日为师, 终身为父). To the Chinese, books are friends, the written word carries weight, and teachers are highly esteemed.

---

1 Broomhall, *Bible in China*, introduction.

When it comes to the Bible, Chinese Christians' sense of reverence is even deeper for the Bible is not any other literature but God's Word. And being God's Word, the Bible is authoritative in their lives (2 Tim 3:16–17); it tells them who they are, who God is, and where salvation is found. The Bible informs their worldview, value system, and outlook in life. Some will kneel while reading the Bible as an expression of their coming under the authority of the Scripture. From it, they know who holds their future and where their eternal destiny lies. It is a lamp unto their feet and a light unto their path (Ps 119:105). Therefore, they esteem and love the Bible.

The cost of a Bible was equivalent to about twenty eggs, Anhui, 2006.

Chinese Christians were so well-known for their love for God's Word that when Bishop K. H. Ting was asked in the 1990s if the Bibles printed in China had missing chapters or books, he said, "Chinese Christians love the Word of God. They would be the first to tell me if there are any missing parts in the Bible!"

As we shall see in the following testimonies, Chinese Christians were reading and memorizing the Bible, copying and obeying it, and as a result, their lives were transformed by it. They were also spreading the word to others and passing down their

Xiaonan Jie Church in Hohhot City. About five thousand people attend the church, Inner Mongolia, 2018.

faith to their children and grandchildren. We shall see that, as the Bible was made available and as Chinese Christians fed on the spiritual food given by God (1 Pet 2:2), the Holy Spirit was causing the fire of revival to sweep through China. Millions repented of their sins and came to faith in Christ. Praise God that the Bible has fueled the growth of the Chinese Churches numerically and spiritually in the past few decades!

Reading and Memorizing the Word

Many older Chinese Christians shared that it was the Word of God memorized by heart that sustained them through the dark night of the Cultural Revolution. When the Bible was declared to be poisonous literature, they secretly hand-copied portions of Scripture and memorized them. We are reminded of what the prophet Jeremiah said, "Your words were found, and I ate them, and your words became to me a joy and the delight of my heart, for I am called by your name, O LORD, God of hosts" (Jer 15:16). The Chinese Christians took and ingested God's Word into their being.

Chinese believers love the Word of God. A man reading his Bible in Wenzhou, Zhejiang, 1998.

According to a former missionary, H. R. Weber, who visited China in the early 1980s, "the Bible was during that time a memorized Scripture." In Shanghai in 1984, he interviewed an eighty-five-year-old Christian, Rev. Koo, and asked how he kept his faith during those dark years. He replied, "I had no Bible, but I read it from my memory."

Rev. Chen Yiping from Fujian Province, whom my colleague and I had the wonderful opportunity to interview at his home in Gulangyu in 2017, had a similar experience with the Bible. He was called up by the leftists during the Cultural Revolution because of his Christian faith. Recalling the scene when he was made to parade on the streets, he said:

Rev. Chen Yiping, Fujian, 2017.

> The whole island of people from Gulangyu came to watch. I felt so crushed within. But in the midst of it, God reminded me of Matthew 5:10–11, "Blessed are those who have been persecuted for the sake of righteousness, for theirs is the kingdom of heaven. Blessed are you when people insult you and persecute you, and falsely say all kinds of evil against you because of Me. Rejoice and be glad for your reward in heaven is great; for in the same way, they persecuted the prophets who were before you." As these words came to my mind, I felt a surge of inspiration and energy. Then the sense of shame and humiliation left me, I was liberated! The Bible is indeed an ever-present help to me.

Mdm. Sun Yuying puts melody to Scriptures and sings them, Shandong, 2019.

The Bible to the Chinese Christians was indeed a memorized Scripture kept in their hearts, read from their memory.

Chen Caixian, an elderly believer, age 102, from Chongqing, lost both of her parents at a young age. She confessed that it was only when she met Jesus that she experienced and understood what it was like to be loved by a parent. She encouraged us to read and memorize the Bible and shared "the secret" to having a strong faith. This is wisdom from a centenarian:

Mdm. Chen Caixian reading the Bible with a church friend, Chongqing, 2020.

> I read and memorize the Bible every day. Now, as an old person, I can tell you that every word of the Lord is true. He is faithful and true to all his promises. Read his word till it goes into the depths of your heart, verse by verse memorize them all. You asked if I have a favorite verse. I don't think I have. I love all the books of the Bible, every chapter, every verse and

every word. It is only by reading his word that I am strengthened in my faith. I pray that the Lord will continue to enable me to share with others all the blessings and joy he has given me.

Chinese Christians so love the Bible that it is not uncommon that many have read the Bible many times over. It was reported in the 1990s that Christians from Wenzhou had read through the Bible from Genesis to Revelation more than one hundred times. And when the Reform and Open Door era began, many delighted in decorating their doorposts and walls at home with Scriptures and Scripture calendars so that their minds would be filled and saturated with it. A church in Wenzhou even constructed a big Bible and hymnal on top of their church building!

Copying the Word

Even when the Bible became more accessible and available after the establishment of the APC, some Chinese Christians continued to copy the Bible by hand. In a testimony collected in 2001, Wang, a Christian farmer in her thirties from Henan Province, shared that she hungered for God's Word after becoming a Christian. She discovered that reciting and hand-copying Scriptures left stronger impressions than merely reading it. She became so moved by the Lord's work in her life that she made a vow. She asked God to give her strength to copy the entire Bible so that more people would be motivated to read the Bible.

A church building with a Bible and hymnal constructed on the rooftop, Wenzhou, Zhejiang, 1998.

Painstakingly, she used small-size Chinese calligraphy, which she had learned from an old calligrapher whom she worked for, to copy the Bible. Even though she fell ill the following year and her family had even purchased a coffin for her, she persisted in hand-copying the Bible. In the process, Wang found much joy, comfort, hope, and healing. The mammoth task took her more than three years to complete, using 250 sheets of rice paper (measuring 364 by 196 mm) and more than forty calligraphy brushes. Even though she was poor, she refused to sell it when a printing press offered her RMB 3,000 for her handwritten Bible. Instead, she gave her handwritten Bible to the CCC as an expression of her love for the Lord and his word! The Bible was bound into four volumes: the Old Testament in three volumes totaling 1,520 pages and the New Testament in one volume of 481 pages.

Captivated by the Word

Through the Bible, many prodigal sons and daughters were captivated by the word, and returning to the

Christian Farmer Wang (left) who hand copied Scripture, 2001.

Father, they found their hope in Christ. Xiong Jing, an ex-gangster from Hubei Province was one of them. He was bringing home lots of money from his criminal activities, but his soul felt empty. Here's his story, collected in 2012:

> One day, I was given a gospel pamphlet on the streets that read "Jesus Christ is God." I was attracted to the name Jesus Christ. The name was familiar to me. I started asking my neighbors if any of them was a Christian who attended church. An elderly neighbor brought me to one. Soon, I bought a Bible from the church and started reading from the New Testament onwards. At first, I could not understand the first part of Matthew's Gospel, but I persevered and read on until I came to the "Sermon on the Mount"—then as if a bolt of lightning had struck my soul, I sat up straight and almost heard the voice of Jesus. I was so blown away by the Master's teaching that I kept on reading and reading till late at night.

Since his encounter with God through the pages of the Bible, Xiong's life was transformed. He left the gangs and the life of crime, and he even did housework and spent time with his young child.

The Bible is indeed no ordinary literature. Whether you're an ex-gangster or a student who failed your college entrance exams, the words contained in its pages can speak to you. Liu Jinzhi from Jiangsu Province was a high school student. When he failed his college entrance exams, he felt like it was the end of the world. Life ahead was bleak as he walked through the valley of utter hopelessness, and he wanted to end his life. He shared in an interview in 2010 that when a man reaches the end of the road, he finds God waiting for him:

> I cried out from the depths of my heart, "The God of my father, where are you? Can you save?" My eyes lightened up suddenly when I saw my father's Bible lying on the desk in a corner. It seemed to be glowing at me; beckoning me to pick it up. I began to read the Bible and immediately fell in love with it. It became the most precious book in my life. It gave me hope and guidance during this difficult time. It led me through the valley of the shadow of death to the green pasture and quiet waters; it helped me to understand that it was God who healed my deepest hurt. The void in a man's heart can only be filled by God alone. The more I read the Bible, the more I hunger for its daily bread. As the psalmist had written, "As a deer pants for flowing streams, so pants my soul for you, O God" (Ps 42:1). We have a thirst that can only be quenched when we read God's Word.

Obeying the Word and Being Transformed by It

Chinese Christians not only read, memorized, and copied the Bible, but they also made sure to obey the teachings in it. They examined their lives by the standard given in the Bible, choosing to be like the man who built his house on the rock (Matt 7:24). A simple everyday life testimony was told in 1991 of a rural Christian in Fujian Province who had borne a grudge against her brother-in-law. She felt troubled in her heart as they were not on friendly terms. One day, she read Romans 6:12, "Let not sin therefore reign in your mortal body, to make you obey its passions." She was so convicted in her heart that on her mother-in-law's birthday, she cooked an extra dish of delicacy for her brother-in-law. During those

Chinese Christians gathering to read the Word of God, Henan, 2010.

days, people did not have sufficient food, so preparing an additional dish required several days' supplies to be saved. From then on, friendly family relationships were restored. Praise the Lord!

Many Chinese have come to faith through reading the Bible, encountering the life-changing truths in it. God's Word has made them wise unto salvation and transformed them. Story after story of people abandoning their old way of life and embracing the new life in Christ was coming out of China. We see this in Liu Xinjuan, an examination invigilator. Here's her testimony shared in the mid-2000s:

Chinese Christians studying the Word of God, Nanjing, 2016.

> Like most Chinese people, I was told that we came to the world by accident, like everything else in this universe. If all things come to the world by accident, then there is no purpose in life and there is no ultimate meaning in this order-less and dark world. For this reason, I felt the hopelessness and meaninglessness of this world. I was also worried about many things in life. But after coming to faith, I found meaning in and through the Word of God. It makes my eyes and soul light up! To me, life's meaning comes from the biblical view of the origin of the universe and life. I have often been amazed by the beauty of things in the universe. For example, the blue sky, a leafy tree, a small flower, a fallen leaf, a chirping bird, a curious toddler … etc. They are so wonderful that I cannot help marveling at their beauty and wondering about their origin.
>
> The Word of God has really set my soul free! Verses from Philippians 4:6–7, Colossians 2:3, 1 Timothy 6:6–10 help me a lot. Indeed, I've got inner peace in my heart—which is really a great blessing from God. This precious inner peace makes me live a better and more joyful life. I've come to realize that the reason why I was so moody was that I used to focus on the world where there is no true hope at all; but now God has led me to focus on the Heavenly Kingdom where hope abounds, making me light-hearted and joyful.

Praise God for the transformative power of his word in the lives of the Chinese people! Indeed, as APC celebrated the 25-millionth copy of the Bible in 2000, Rev. Dr. Jen-Li Tsai, UBS Asia Pacific regional secretary and APC board chairman, reflected on how Scripture distribution has helped millions in China learn about Jesus and will continue to quietly sow the seed for future church growth in China. In his words, the Bible was acting like "water on dry ground in people's hearts," and Christians in China were "springing up like bamboo after the rain."

Passing On the Word

Chinese Christians were also teaching and passing on their faith to their children and their children's children. Here's a testimony from Yunnan Province:

> Madam Zhang Xiuyin came to the Christian faith in 1997 and has been reading the Bible to her grandchildren. When her eldest granddaughter was three years old, she brought her for a home visitation. The journey was fraught with difficulties due to poor road conditions. Madam Zhang recalled she was especially worried as she was traveling with a

young child at that time. Despite the somewhat perilous circumstances they were in, her granddaughter's response amazes her till this day, "Grandma, be strong and courageous. Do not be frightened, and do not be dismayed, for the Lord your God is with you." These were the words from Joshua 1:9 she had often read to her granddaughter!

We will see more testimonies of passing on the word in chapter 12, "Igniting Young Minds: Bible Ministry for the Family."

The Bible played a central and critical role not just in the individual lives of the believers but also in the corporate life of the Chinese Churches and meeting points. As church doors reopened in the 1980s and new ones were established, the Word of God was preached and taught at various platforms where people gathered around the Bible—Sunday services, baptism services, Bible study groups, prayer meetings, Bible reading groups, and seekers' classes.

Zhang Xiuyin and her grandchildren, 2020.

The Bible was also used at young people's fellowships, choir fellowships, blind fellowships, summer camps, winter camps, and revival meetings. The gospel was preached during Christmas, Good Friday, and Resurrection services. The Word of God brought blessings and comfort to people at church weddings, funerals, and memorials. The word was also brought into the homes of the elderly and sick, where family services and home baptisms were conducted and Holy Communion was served.

Gao Ying, a Christian from Beijing, shared how the preaching of God's Word in church and the faith of Christians led her to believe in Jesus:

> When the churches in Beijing were officially reopened in 1981, I attended my first church service at the age of twenty-five. The sermon that day was on Jesus and his dialogue with Nicodemus. That preaching left a deep impression on me. Another aspect that deeply affected me was the faith of the church members. In those days when the church had just reopened, there were no young people in the church and many Christians were still living in fear of persecution. Those who dared to declare that they were Christians openly were very strong in their faith. Encouraged by this and the powerful preaching that day, I found myself going to church week after week. I have never stopped attending church since.

Rev. Gao Ying, 1993.

> I cannot recall the exact moment I accepted Christ into my life, but I know that when the church held its first baptism membership class, I was among the first to register for it.

Gao Ying later studied theology and went on to serve as the vice president of the Nanjing Union Theological Seminary, China's national Protestant seminary.

Spreading the Word

As the word was read, memorized, and obeyed in the lives of Christians, it began to spread, and churches grew. There is something special about the act of gathering around an open Bible to hear it being read. As Romans 10:17 tells us, "So faith comes from hearing, and hearing through the word of Christ." When the history and origin of churches and meeting points in China were traced, many shared that they had, in fact, started as home-based Bible reading and prayer groups, an organic gathering of people from the same family or village, without the intention of starting a church. Yet, as the Word of God was read in these small groups, the Spirit moved people's hearts. Lives were changed, and these believers in turn led others into the kingdom. Church after church mushroomed and was birthed in the process. Many such stories could be told, but space only allows us to share three of them.

Anhui Province, early 1980s. Zhang was eighteen years old when his parents and sister accepted Christ after hearing the gospel. Although he was interested in Christianity, he felt that religion was for the old and sick. He was young and healthy and did not feel the need for a religion.

One day, an itinerant evangelist came to their home and shared the gospel with them. Zhang was excited when he saw the evangelist's Bible in simplified Chinese script. Because Zhang was a high school graduate and one of the rare few in his village who knew how to read at that time, the itinerant evangelist left the Bible with him, requesting that he read it to his family and other Christians in the village.

Man with his Bible at Jiang Pu Christian meeting point, 1987.

As Zhang read the Bible to them, he was moved by the Holy Spirit and became a believer not long after. He then began reading the Bible with greater diligence and eagerness on his own. He not only read the Bible to his family and other Christians, but he also shared the gospel with those who just joined them. And as he did this, something miraculous was happening—his faith began to grow, and people began to come.

Christians from neighboring villages heard about such a Bible reading group and flocked to Zhang's house to hear him read the Bible. Among them were unbelievers who were hearing about Jesus for the first time. Many repented of their sins and turned to Christ.

Mother and child at a Christian meeting point in Jiang Pu, 1987.

By 1987, over one hundred people were packed in Zhang's house and overflowing into the compound outside his house. It became a challenge for people when it rained or snowed. As they saw more people coming to the meeting, they began praying for a church building. They applied for a permit to buy a piece of land to build a church. When the permit came, the number of people gathering at his house had grown to two hundred.

By the time the church building was completed in the summer of 1993, the number of people attending the Christian meeting at Zhang's house had increased to three hundred. The purchase of the land and the construction of the church building were funded by the donations and resources of these three hundred believers.[2]

Although we may not know the name of the itinerant evangelist who visited Zhang and his family, we can be sure that his name is in the book of life. His simple act of visiting the family and leaving them with a copy of the Bible led to the conversion of Zhang and the birth of a church. What an amazing work the Lord can do with a man and his Bible!

Hengshan County, Hunan Province, 1990s. Meng Xiuying received Christ when she encountered the kindness and love of Christians in another valley who prayed for her when she was ill. Although she had a lot of work to do on the farm, whenever she could she started sharing her faith, walking from farm to farm, village to village. There was once she shared her faith with more than 70 people within a day. She and her husband began hosting Christian meetings in their small home. It grew and up to 200 people met there. From Meng's faith, there are now around 1,000 Christians in this area surrounding her village, and several churches have been built!

Meng Xiuying (right), age seventy-one, and her husband Li Yongfu, age seventy-two, Hunan, 2014.

Nanjing, Jiangsu Province, early 1990s. Tang, age sixty, was lying on her bed feeling hopeless. She had been in a serious car accident and suffered severe head injuries causing her to be almost totally paralyzed. One of her nephews who was a Christian encouraged her to read the Bible. Since she was unable to move her body and was confined to her bed, Tang took up her nephew's suggestion and began reading the Bible.

As Tang read the Bible, she was soon struck by the countless passages that revealed a God who had a profound love for all of creation, including her. "I learn through reading the Bible that there's a God and he loves and cares for all of us," said Tang. What happened next was equally amazing. As she continued to read and reflect on various Bible passages, she felt a change in her body; she soon realized that she was beginning to be healed!

Xin Qiao Church, Hunan Province, China. Twenty years ago, there were no Christians in this valley. Now there are around one thousand, thanks to the witness of Meng Xiuying, 2014.

---

2 Adapted from a story by Yick Bing, production supervisor, APC, June 1994.

Tang was so grateful for her recovery that she was determined to discover more about the God of the Bible. She then joined two other ladies for regular prayer and Bible study at one of their homes. By the end of the year, a healthy, mobile Tang was baptized! This group of three women started growing. More and more gathered to hear the Bible being read and to pray together. It grew so big that they had to buy an old house for their meetings. Eventually, this house also became too small, and they needed a new church. Gifts came from near and far, and believers helped with the construction of the church. And the church continued to grow.

Twelve years later, when Tang was interviewed, the church had eight hundred to one thousand people regularly attending the Sunday worship service. Between seventy and eighty of them gather every Friday for Bible study. At seventy-two years old, Tang was full of enthusiasm for Jesus Christ and for the church she had help found and develop.. When she talked, the words "Praise God" punctuated her speech. Her small and wrinkled fingers were surprisingly strong as she gripped the hand of every new Christian brother or sister she met. It is hard to imagine that Tang was almost totally paralyzed twelve years ago and how one suggestion by her nephew to read the Bible would lead to the birth of a church![3]

An eighteen-year-old youth starting a three-hundred-strong church? A sixty-year-old woman growing a church to a thousand members? What model or strategy did they follow? None except reading the Bible, obeying what is written in it, and praying. What can we say? Our God works in marvelous ways beyond our imagination. May we not be bound by our own expectations of how God might choose to work. First Corinthians 2:9 says, "What no eye has seen, nor ear heard, nor the heart of man imagined, what God has prepared for those who love him." Indeed, who could have imagined that the fires of revival would sweep across China so rapidly after the horrors of the Cultural Revolution; who could have expected the deep thirst and hunger for God's Word in the Chinese Christians, resulting in the wondrous work of God in and through them? These testimonies of Chinese Christians serve to spur us to love and obey the Word of God more and to know him afresh. The following stanza quoted by Rev. Luo Zhenfang, in his paper "The Role of the Bible in the Growth of the Church in China," sums up for us the passion for the Word of God in the lives of the Chinese Christians as we end this chapter:

> The Bible bears witness to Christ
> And only through the Bible
> Can we know the salvation of God
> The Bible is the Word of God
> That gives life
> God speaks to us through the Bible
> And the Church in China believes that
> Nothing in the Bible will be changed
> Until all is accomplished

---

[3] Adapted from *UBS World Report*, 2000.

7
True Vision

Braille Bibles for the Blind

And his disciples asked him, "Rabbi, who sinned, this man or his parents, that he was born blind?" Jesus answered, "It was not that this man sinned, or his parents, but that the works of God might be displayed in him."
—John 9:2–3

The only thing worse than being blind is having sight but no vision.
—Helen Keller, blind American author

When I was a senior in college, I was afflicted with an illness of the eyes that led to blindness. I was so grief-stricken that I wanted to die. After I embraced Christianity, I read the passage "forgetting what lies behind and straining forward to what lies ahead, I press on toward the goal for the prize of the heavenly call of God in Christ Jesus." I felt suddenly enlightened. Although I live in the darkness, my heart was illuminated by the Lord and my spiritual eyes were opened.
—A testimony from a young Christian in Shanghai

In the mid-1980s and 1990s, as Chinese Christians from the registered churches were gradually gaining access to the Bible, a group of people was still shut out from the Word of God. They were people with visual impairment. It was estimated that in the early 1990s, there were about 7.5 million visually impaired persons out of China's total population of 1.08 billion. Until 1995, there had been no printing press producing Chinese Braille Bibles for the blind in China. It was therefore an urgent task for the churches in China to look into meeting the scriptural needs of Christians with visual impairment. When and how did the Chinese Braille Bible develop? What was the level of braille literacy in China in the 1990s? How was the Braille Bible printing press set up in China? And finally, what was the impact of the Chinese Braille Bible on Christians with visual impairment?

The Braille System and the Development of the Chinese Braille Bible

Every January 4, the world remembers the birthday of Louis Braille, the man who invented the six-dot system based on the alphabet as a code for the blind in 1824. Braille lost his sight at the age of three in 1812. He injured one eye while playing with sharp tools in his father's leather workshop. Due to the spread of infection, he became totally blind.

At age fifteen, while studying at a blind school in Paris, he found out that the books in the school library were using actual words made in lead embossed on wax paper. Not only were those books heavy and bulky, but their prices were also prohibitive too. He then invented a system consisting of six raised dots that can be read by feeling with one's fingers, reducing the size and price of embossed books by nearly half.

When Braille was on his deathbed at age forty-three, he said, "God was pleased to hold before my eyes the dazzling splendors of eternal hope. After that, doesn't it seem that nothing more could keep me bound to the earth?" Braille understood that what mattered more was to have spiritual vision.

Two years after Braille died in 1854, the braille writing system was recognized and widely used. In 1878, the World Congress for the Blind voted to make braille the system of reading and writing for all blind people worldwide.

However, the braille system, based on the Latin alphabet, was unsuitable for the Chinese language. One of the earliest attempts to adapt it to the Chinese language was by a one-armed Scottish Christian, William Murray. In 1871, Murray, a Bible colporteur with the National Bible Society of Scotland (NBSS), arrived in China to distribute Scriptures. He learned Mandarin in Chefu and was based in Peking in 1873. During his time distributing Bibles, he came across the blind and poor who could not read. In 1874, he opened a private school for the blind with the support of NBSS.[1] Between 1877 and 1878, he tried to adapt the braille system to translate the Bible so that the blind and the poor could also read. A system based on numerals was revealed to him in a vision, a system that he successfully developed so that blind people could learn to read in a matter of weeks.[2]

Hence, the Murray Numeral-type system was created in 1878. Over time, the Bible, hymnals, and other books were published in Murray's numerical type. Schools for the blind were opened, a mission to the blind and illiterate was organized, and thousands learned to read, leading to a flood of Christian conversions among the blind and illiterate. The blind school founded by Murray became the Beijing School for the Blind,[3] one of the leading national centers for the blind in China today.[4]

Students at David Hill Blind School, Wuhan, ca. 1937. Used with permission from SOAS Library.

However, there were limitations to the Murray Numeral System as it was based on the Beijing language used in northern China. Missionaries working in the south found it unsuitable to adopt. Moreover, a limited number of characters could be represented in this numeral system. Hence, during the late eighteenth to the early twentieth century, other missionaries like David Hill, Amy Oxley, and William Campbell attempted to develop other reading systems for the blind and adapted the braille system for Chinese dialects such as Fuzhou and Cantonese.[5]

---

1 Wang, "Christian Missionaries, Blind Converts, and Braille Literacy in China (1874–1911)."
2 MacInnis, "William H. Murray."
3 https://www.chinadaily.com.cn/opinion/2007-04/21/content_856357.html.
4 Miles, "Blind and Sighted Pioneer Teachers in 19th Century China and India."
5 Argall, "The Woman Who Brought the Bible to Blind Chinese Children."

The need to promote and widely adopt the usage of the braille system in Christian missions in China first surfaced in the 1890 General Conference of the Protestant Missionaries of China. At the next conference in 1907, a resolution was made to look into developing a single language for the blind that could be used to serve all visually impaired persons throughout China. In 1913, the British and Foreign Bible Society and American Bible Society called for a meeting with other relevant mission organizations to discuss forming a standardized language system for the blind. The final agreement was to adopt the braille system and the language was to be based on Mandarin and not dialects. The result was the Union Braille System, the foundation for future revisions and for the current Chinese Braille Bible.

For the Chinese braille, sounds of the language (hanyu pinyin) rather than the characters are represented. It is written from left to right in horizontal lines running from top to bottom. Each syllable is made up of three braille letters: one for the consonant, one for the vowel, and one for the tone, though the tone marks are rarely used. Braille script for the consonants and basic vowels conform to international braille. Words are separated by spaces. Now the Chinese braille system was available, but were the blind in China learning Chinese braille?

A Blind Architect and A Little Girl's One Yuan– Beginning of Braille Literacy after the Cultural Revolution

The braille literacy rate in China in the 1990s would not have increased if not for the vision of a blind Christian, Xu Bailun.

Xu Bailun was a Christian architect living in Beijing. In 1971, when he was at the peak of his life, he became blind due to a medical accident. He was forty-two years old. Suddenly plunged into the abyss of darkness, Xu was devastated and even violent. Life was hell to him. He would rend his garments in the middle of the night, wishing that he could tear his chest apart and set his soul free.

After much loving care and encouragement from his wife, he finally decided to do something. He picked up the pen and started writing. He wrote stories for children—an area that he had observed was much lacking at that time. But it was not easy. It took him twelve years to publish his first novel. In that same year, his wife contracted cancer.

Xu suffered a second setback in his life when his wife died—she who had been his eyes and hands. That year, when everyone else was celebrating the Chinese Lunar New Year, he fell into deep despair and wanted to give it all up. Thankfully, he had a friend who financed his writing and encouraged him to use it to help people who are also blind. So, he plodded on, learned Chinese braille, and started a publication in 1985 called the *China Blind Children Literature*.

One day, he received a letter from a little girl. She told him about her younger brother who was eight years old and was blind. They lived in a rural village, and no school would take him. Whenever other children went to school with their bags, he would cry, saying he wanted to go to school too. Their mother had no choice but to sew him a school bag and let him go. He grabbed his school bag and went toward the place where he could hear children reciting aloud, which meant there was a school nearby. He would stand at the walls outside and try to follow the class inside. "But one day, my brother left and did not return. Later, we found his body in a pond outside the school, his hand still clinging on tightly to his school bag."

In the letter, the little girl pleaded with Xu to do something about the education of blind children in the rural villages. She even enclosed in her letter one Chinese yuan that she saved so that Xu could do something for blind children, and nobody would have to suffer the same fate as her brother.

Xu was deeply moved. Despite his physical limitations, he decided to do something. He began traveling from village to village, searching out blind children and trying to help them study alongside other children in mainstream schools. He trained school principals and teachers in Chinese braille and developed teaching materials and curriculum. In 1987, when official statistics showed that only 3.7 percent of blind children entered school, he launched the Golden Key Project to help them integrate into mainstream school. The project was so successful that in 1990 the Chinese government included the project in their policy for the education of the blind across China. Xu went on to found the Golden Key Center for Blind Children and became one of the pioneers championing education for blind children in China using braille. Amity Foundation, a Christian charity organization, was one of the sponsors of the Golden Key Project.

A Chinese magazine featuring Xu Bailun's story. Photo shows him in the village searching for blind children, 1996.

When he was interviewed in 1996 at age sixty-five, Xu said, "I would give all that I have to help more blind children enter the schools. This is my wish for the rest of my life." Xu was once trapped in the world of darkness. Yet, a vision within him gave him a purpose to live on. Because of this vision, more blind children grew up being able to read braille and had the world opened up to them, including the gospel message in the Bible.

How the Braille Bible Printing Was Set Up in China

Two sisters had this same vision within them as they traveled from Germany to Hong Kong in 1961. They were Lore Spilker and Maria Lange, German nuns from the Hildesheim Mission to the Blind (a German mission), which founded the Ebenezer School and Home for the Blind in 1897 in Hong Kong. The home took in blind girls who were abandoned and provided them with shelter and education. Sisters Lore and Maria also started the Christian Literature for the Blind (CLB) in 1978 to reach the blind with braille materials and tapes. They did so by setting up a small printing press.

Sister Lore, the chairperson of CLB and principal of the Ebenezer School had a special burden for the spiritual needs of the blind. Her heart yearned for them to know the gospel. In the early 1990s, when she discovered that there was no Cantonese braille available in

Diakonisse Lore. Source: h-bm.de.

Hong Kong, Sister Lore set out with a seventy-year-old blind woman to translate the Braille Bible from Mandarin to Cantonese. She also mobilized others to proofread, correct, collate, and print it. UBS provided USD$40,000 for the printing of four thousand Cantonese Braille Bible volumes.

It was the first time that the whole Bible was available in Cantonese for blind readers. Yet, the sisters soon saw a greater need arising as they began to extend their literature ministry to the blind in mainland China. It was estimated that there were about 8 million visually impaired people in China in the early 1980s. And they needed the Chinese Braille Bible.

In the fall of 1991, when the sisters heard about the establishment of APC, they got in touch with the leaders of UBS. "If sighted people have the right to have their Bibles, the blind people should have the same chance. So we started talking to people about the possibility of setting up a braille printing plant for Bibles in China [at APC]," said Sister Maria. Until that point, there were no printing presses or organizations in mainland China producing or providing Chinese Braille Bibles or Christian materials.

The need was tremendous. Visually impaired Chinese Christians are often the poorest of the poor—they are caught in a double bind of disability and poverty. Due to negative cultural perceptions and safety reasons, the blind are often kept at home by their family and thus are isolated from society. Without basic education, they are often unable to support themselves. But the situation was gradually changing in the 1990s with China opening up and with advocates like Xu Bailun championing education for blind children. The German sisters reckoned that braille literacy would increase as China opened more integrated schools and promoted education for the blind. As such, it would be critical to provide Braille Bibles for Chinese Christians with visual impairments. Hence, the sisters envisioned that a Braille Bible press with a larger capacity was needed.

Schwester Maria. Source: h-bm.de.

In April 1994, Sister Lore wrote a letter to Rev. Dr. Tsai Jen-Li, UBS regional leader. In it, she shared that CLB was in contact with 520 blind people in China who received Christian material from them. The number was rising but their printing press was too small and unable to cope with the demand in such a vast country. She also drew up a budget and proposal for setting up a Braille Bible press at APC, offering technical assistance from CLB, expertise, and the necessary software and text. The budget came to USD$260,000, which included labor costs for three years, to produce one thousand sets of Chinese Braille Bibles. The matter was shared with the leaders of the CCC, who also sensed the critical need for Chinese Braille Bibles to be made available. Without hesitation, they applied for permission from the authorities to set up a Braille Bible printing press.

The news of approval from the Chinese authorities came in June 1994. However, Sister Lore was at the hospital for advanced-stage cancer at the time. She heard the good news but passed away without having the pleasure of seeing the Braille Bible press. As I poured over the old records for this chapter, I found a memorial service program with a poem dedicated to Sister Lore about her obedience and the greater pleasure awaiting her. I was moved by it:

> My Lord spoke to me at dawn
> And I said: "Yes, Lord, I am here
> To do your will."
> The Lord told me he would be with me forever.
> The Lord walked with me all the way,
> And I gladly with him
> Through darkness and in light
> And in shadowed places.
> And my Lord said to me,
> "I am with you always."
> The Lord spoke to me in the evening
> And I said, "Yes Lord, I am here,
> I have done your will."
> And I put my hand in his
> And joyfully walked with him
> Into the bright dawn.

Binding a Chinese braille Gospel of Matthew at APC, Nanjing, 1995.

In due time, the Braille Bible press at Amity was set up with funding that poured in from the UBS fellowship as well as the Christian braille mission in Germany. Trial production began in June 1995, and the first Chinese braille portion of Matthew was completed in July. By September, most of the equipment had arrived and actual production could begin. The Gospels and the Book of Acts were the first to be produced.

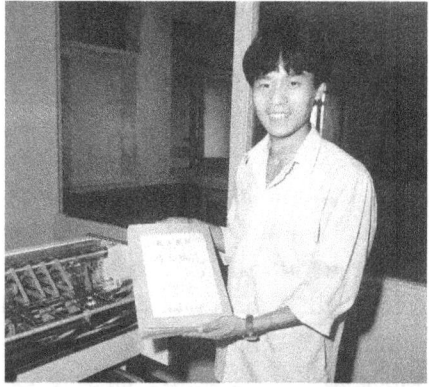

The first copy of the Chinese braille Gospel of Matthew, produced on the newly installed braille press at APC, Nanjing, 1995.

A set of the Braille Bible consists of 32 volumes.

In 1999, when APC celebrated the 20-millionth copy of the Bible, more than eighteen thousand Braille Bible portions had been produced. A strong demand was coming from the blind Christian community, but the braille production unit, which was not big, was not able to meet the demand. Hence, a second braille press was installed in 1999. A full set of the Braille Bible consists of thirty-two volumes and costs about US$270 to produce, compared to US$6 for a standard-sized Chinese Bible. Despite the much higher cost, we know that God's Word is priceless and its impact eternal.

As of 2020, thousands of Braille Bible sets, with thirty-two volumes in each set, have been printed and distributed with the support of UBS. What is the impact of Braille Bibles on Christians with visual impairment in China? The following testimonies remind us what true vision is: to set our sight heavenward, to put our hopes upon the Lord, and to see Jesus with our hearts.

Sister Maria Lange at APC, Nanjing, 1995.

A Blind Person Teaching Another Blind Person

In 1995, a Christian couple from Henan Province, Chen Zhongxin and his wife, found a blind baby boy abandoned on the street. They had compassion on him and brought him home despite being poor themselves. They named him Tianbao, meaning "heavenly treasure."

Unfortunately, their decision to adopt a blind baby was criticized by their family members. Finally, after three years, the couple decided to relocate to Beijing with Tianbao. Even though life was difficult for them, the couple was determined to send Tianbao to a school for the blind so that he could read the Braille Bible and understand the Word of God. So impoverished was the family that they had to pick up scraps and items thrown away by others. But they were comforted that Tianbao grew up to be a bright child, and at ten years of age, he was able to read the entire Old and New Testament in braille—something even sighted children may not be able to do.

Chen Tianbao, age ten, helped Liu Baojie, age thirty-six, to learn braille, Beijing, 2005.

At the same time, in another area in Beijing lived a blind Christian man in his thirties. His name was Liu Baojie. He lost his eyesight after a high fever during his high school days. Yet, amazingly, God used him to share the gospel with his family and relatives, and they came to know the Lord. But he was not able to read the Braille Bible and the school for the blind was not able to enroll him as he was overage. He felt sad and anxious as he longed to read the Word of God.

God answered the desires of Baojie's heart by bringing his "heavenly treasure" to him. Providentially, Baojie came to know Tianbao, who taught him how to read braille. As he learned braille from Tianbao, the heavenly treasures in God's Word were opened to him. At the time when this story was collected, Baojie was able to read the Gospel of Matthew. The two brothers in Christ formed a beautiful picture of finding true vision in life despite not being able to see.

So That the Works of God Might Be Displayed

Ma Wei, staff member of APC, working at the Braille Bible production unit, 2006.

Ma Wei is a staff member at the Braille Bible printing unit at APC. He joined APC in 1996 when the unit was set up, helping with the typesetting and proofreading of Braille Bibles. He was married and has a son. These accomplishments may seem rather ordinary to most people, but these are miracles to Ma Wei.

Ma Wei has been blind since his early childhood. As a child he found it difficult to accept his condition and to deal with day-to-day life. He constantly asked why he was different from other children and felt that nobody truly understood him. As he grew up, he also knew that his parents were grieved over his handicap, particularly how he could support himself and if he could start a family of his own.

Miraculously, God brought him to APC. "God guided me to the place where Scriptures for the blind are printed so that I could encounter him through his word. My heart was open to receive Christ Jesus as my Savior and I became a child of God."

One day, when Ma Wei heard a passage in John 9, his perspective toward his handicap changed. Verses 2–3 says, "And his disciples asked him, 'Rabbi, who sinned, this man or his parents, that he was born blind?' Jesus answered, 'It was not that this man sinned, or his parents, but that the works of God might be displayed in him.'" From this Bible passage, Ma Wei came to understand the reason for his blindness. He then felt that "God wants to perform a miraculous work in my life in order for his name to be glorified."

And so miraculously, Ma Wei met his wife, a sighted person, at APC. Both sides of the family were worried about their future and whether they could lead a normal family life. Despite the uncertainties and unanswered questions, they got married in 2006 with the blessings of their parents.

Again miraculously, they gave birth to a healthy son the following year. Ma Wei said, "This new addition brought my parents, my wife and me unspeakable joy. Whenever I am told that our son bears a great resemblance to me, I would respond with a smile and hope that our child will continue to grow healthily."

He added, "We continue to live simply day by day. We are not sure what our future holds for us; only God knows. However, we know that we are to cherish all that we have and not to worry over the things that we cannot see, touch or guess!"

I Teared Up When I Read God's Word

Zhang Mingli was born blind. He came to the Lord in his teens by listening to a gospel radio broadcast during the Cultural Revolution in the late 1960s. But because Bibles were scarce and Braille Bibles were even more so, Zhang never owned a copy of it until much later. It was in the year 2007, after being a Christian for nearly forty years, that he laid hands on his first Braille Bible.

"When I first received the Braille Bible, I read John 1:1. I kept tearing up as I felt God's Word. I was simply overcome with joy and excitement," recalled Zhang. "Braille Bibles were very rare during those years."

At sixty-seven years old, Zhang is serving actively in a church for the visually impaired in Shenyang City, Liaoning Province. "Praise God that over the years, the church has seen two hundred more blind people coming to Christ!"

Zhang Mingli, Liaoning, 2018.

Light Is When We Focus Our Sight on God, Darkness Is When We Do Not Do So

"Life as a blind person is hard," shared Honglin, age forty, a blind Christian from Liaoning Province. "From leaving the house, buying daily necessities, and visiting the doctors, to taking a bath. But I'll always go to God in prayers, and through prayers I've experienced the Lord's grace in my life."

Honglin had lost her sight gradually, and by age twenty, she was totally blind. When she first accepted the Lord as her personal Savior, she had hoped that God would miraculously restore her sight.

But that did not happen. As she grew to understand God's Word through reading the Braille Bible, her faith was strengthened. "I was convicted of this truth. Whether I can see or not, I will continue to believe in this God."

Over the years, Honglin has learned to put her hope in God. "Light is when we focus our sight on God. Darkness is when we do not do so."

Jesus Is My Bright Morning Star

When Li became blind, he wanted to commit suicide. He felt that he was such a burden to his family. But by the grace of God, he did not die. God brought him out of spiritual darkness to see his light when he heard the gospel over a radio broadcast. He heard that God loves him and wants to give him an abundant life.

In John 8:12, Jesus said: "I am the light of the world. Whoever follows me will never walk in darkness but will have the light of life." The good news of salvation immediately touched Li, and he invited God's light into his life.

Brother Li, 2020.

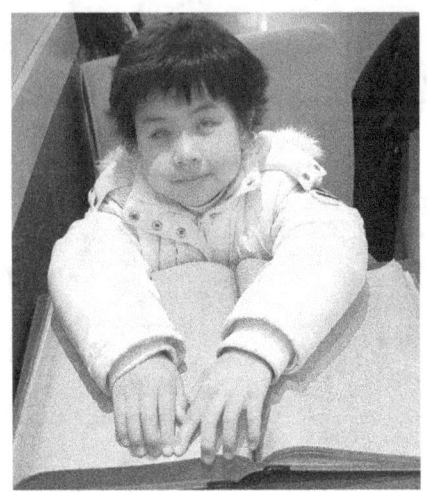

Eight-year-old Daifa reading her copy of the Gospel of Matthew in braille, given to her by UBS. Daifa was abandoned by her parents because she was blind, but she has found a loving home in Shanghai, where she learned about the Bible and was taught braille, 2010.

"God became the brightest morning star in my heart, and I became the first Christian in my family," said Li, age forty-nine. "Later, almost all my family members came to the faith, including my mother and brother."

"About six years ago, God answered my desire to be able to read his word when I received a complete set of the Braille Bible donated by the United Bible Societies through the church in China. The full Braille Bible, comprising thirty-two volumes, was the most precious thing I've ever received! I can lose any other belongings, but I can't afford to lose my Braille Bible! I read the Bible every day, and it's so worn out that I can hardly feel the dots clearly now."

Many blind Christians in China are poor and unable to pay for the full cost of a complete set of the Braille Bible. "I thank all UBS donors for loving and caring for the blind Christians in China. Through your selfless giving, you've helped to bring true light to us. Though we may live in physical darkness, you have helped bring hope to our lives."

Yi Yan Yan, age seventy-four, became a Christian when she attended a mission school for the blind as a child. Bible Societies helped fund Braille Bibles for her and the blind fellowship she attended, 2014.

Yunnan blind fellowship, 2011.

Through the invention of a blind boy in France, the compassion of a one-armed missionary from Scotland, the persistence of a blind architect from Beijing, the obedience of two nuns from Germany, and countless others who supported the setting up of the Braille Bible press, the visually impaired in China have had the Word of God opened to them in their language. We feel God's love for the blind in China and his desire to speak to them.

We thank God that over the last two decades, thousands of volumes of Chinese Braille Bibles have been produced and distributed to blind Christians in China. But there remain millions of blind people who have yet to gain true vision in Jesus. According to the China Association of the Blind in 2020, an estimated 17 million people in China suffer from visual impairment. Out of these 17 million, about 8 million are completely blind.[6] We end this chapter with a song written by Brother Li, whose testimony was shared above. Let us pray that many more visually impaired persons in China would see Jesus, the Bright Morning Star, and the Blue Sky in their hearts.

I have never seen an azure sky,
I never knew how clear the waters in the streams are,
I never knew the towering mountains,
I have never seen the faces of my loved ones.

You are the blue sky in my heart,
You are the living water nourishing my life,
You are more to be depended on than mountains,
You are the bright morning star in my heart.

Oh, my Savior Jesus, I love you,
I will praise your Holy Name in difficulties,
Your hand leads me through the rugged road,
I will see your gentle and kind face in heaven.

---

6   Gan, "China Has 8 Million Blind People, but Only 200 Guide Dogs."

8
Glows and Glitters in the Mountains I

Bible Translation for Ethnic Minority People in China

> After this I looked, and there before me was a great multitude that no one could count, from every nation, tribe, people and language, standing before the throne and before the Lamb. They were wearing white robes and were holding palm branches in their hands. And they cried out in a loud voice: "Salvation belongs to our God, who sits on the throne, and to the Lamb."
>
> —Revelation 7:9–10

> The greatest missionary is the Bible in the mother tongue, it needs no furlough and is never considered a foreigner.
>
> —William Cameron Townsend, founder of Wycliffe Bible Translators and Summer Institute of Linguistics

A Unique Group of People

"Have you heard about the Dulong people?" My colleagues and I were asked during a trip to Yunnan in 2017. "No," we replied. Our host from Yunnan Christian Council / TSPM proceeded to share about this people group. With a total population of five thousand, the Dulong (Derung) ethnic minority group in China is one of the smallest. Predominantly animists, they live in some of the most isolated terrain in all of China. Most are found in the village of Dulong River at the northwestern tip of Yunnan Province, bordering Myanmar and the Tibet Autonomous Region. The area is a little-known scenic place of forestry, mountains, and rivers. Prior to 2000, there were no roads to the village. Even now, roads are open only from June to November. Apart from this period, access to the village is closed because heavy snow from the mountains prohibits all forms of transportation.

Praise God that despite the inaccessibility, some of the Dulong people have been reached with the gospel, and a Dulong church has been established. There are about one thousand believers,[1] and they have their own preachers and fellowship meeting points. Dulong is one dialect of the larger Rawang group in Myanmar where the Bible has been translated into Rawang.[2] As there is still no written script for the Dulong dialect, some Dulong Christians have learned to read the Lisu Bible and preach in the Lisu language, which belongs to the same Tibeto-Burman language family as the Dulong. But will there be a day when the Dulong people can have their own script created and the Bible in their own language?

---
1 Li, UBS report.
2 https://www.asiaharvest.org/people-group-profiles#china-part-1.

The gospel is to be shared with all people and nations, all tongues and tribes. Surely this includes the 125 million ethnic minority people living in China. While there are officially fifty-five ethnic minority groups in China, there may be as many as five hundred people groups,[3] speaking 297[4] languages, and very few have a writing system. How will they be reached without the Word of God in their mother tongue? The following two chapters will look at the Bible translation and Scripture literacy work of pioneer missionaries in the nineteenth century and UBS in the twentieth century among the often-forgotten people in China.

For generations, ethnic minorities in China, like the Miao, Yi, and Hani people in Yunnan and Guizhou Provinces, have inhabited the cold and deep mountainous regions, some as high as 5,000 meters above sea level, where basic amenities are not easily accessible. They live in simple houses made from mud, sometimes bamboo, wooden poles, and planks, with straws or metal sheets as roofing. As for their livelihood, they are people who till the land, planting corn, potatoes, vegetables, and other crops. Like ethnic groups in other parts of the world, each of them has its own unique language, customs, traditions, and rituals. Many are particularly gifted in singing and dancing!

To the outside world, they are relatively unseen and unknown although a few groups like the Tibetan, Uyghur, and Miao have received more publicity in the mainstream media. Yet, to the Lord, none of them is forgotten, none unknown to him. He hears their cries, and over the centuries he has moved many missionaries to live and serve among them, to learn their ways of life, customs, and languages, and to translate the Bible so that they can hear him speak to them in their heart language.

---

3 Operation World—China.
4 Lewis, Simons, and Fennig, "Ethnologue."

An ethnic minority village in Yunnan, 1998.

A typical home in West Lisu mountain village, Yunnan, 2016.

A Black Yi mountain church in Yunnan, 2015.

Life of ethnic minority in the mountains, ca. 2000.

Late 1800s–Early 1900s:
How Bible Translation Contributed to Ethnic Minority Revival

I thank the Lord that through serving with the UBS Bible mission in China, I have learned more about the work of the early missionaries and the faith story of the ethnic minority people in China. When I visited the ethnic minority churches, some would share stories about the pioneer missionaries passed down through the generations, calling them affectionately by their Chinese names, like 党居仁 (James Adam), 柏格理 (Samuel Pollard), 富能仁 (J. O. Fraser).

Broomhall wrote that work among the ethnic minorities did not just "demand hardships and toil of no common order," but it was also "the most barren and unfruitful of soils."[5] One area of hardship and toil was language learning and Bible translation. To appreciate the importance of Bible translation for ethnic minorities, we will take a brief look at the pioneering work of the three missionaries mentioned above who ministered among the Miao and Lisu people in China during the late Qing Dynasty and the early period of the Republic of China. How did their Bible translation efforts impact the minority Christians, turning the "most barren and unfruitful soils" into the most fertile ground?

James Adam was a Scottish missionary who led the China Inland Mission (CIM) station in Anshun, Guizhou Province, in 1887. Notwithstanding discouragement and tragedies during his earlier years of ministry, he persevered and "visited 250 Miao villages and built relationships with many community leaders." Around 1900, he began translating the Bible with a romanized system for the Miao people and teaching them to read.[6] The Miao were amazed. Many of them believed that they once possessed a written language. But due to war, it was lost and destroyed. A pastor, Wang Mingji, said, "For thousands of years, we had been like the blind. It has been very bitter."

When copies of the first Miao Gospels supported by the British Bible Society arrived and were distributed, the Miao people felt as if the "once-upon-a-time lost books had been found ... and it told the incomparable story that Jesus loves the Miao. Only imagination can conceive what those meant to these hill men, some of whom traveled for days to view those books."[7] Soon, a revival broke out. Many came to the Lord. "We had over 300 in the house. Still they came from more and more distant places." Adam baptized hundreds of Miao as the spiritual awakening spread to other tribes in the region. One of which was Zhaotong, a town

James Adam, a Scottish missionary, arrived in China in 1887.

Gospel of John in Miao language printed by the British and Foreign Bible Society in 1908.

---

5 Broomhall, *Bible in China*, 106.
6 Hattaway, *Guizhou*, 128–29.
7 Quoted in Hattaway, 134.

in the neighboring province of Yunnan where Samuel Pollard, a Methodist British missionary, was stationed.

Pollard (1864–1915) arrived at Yunnan in 1886, a year before Adams. As Adams and his team were overwhelmed with the growing number of converts, they directed a group of them, the Big Flowery Miao, to Pollard after learning that they were living much nearer to him. This was the beginning of the Big Flowery Miao's mass conversions to the Christian faith. They did not come just by themselves nor just with their households but with their entire clans and villages, thronging and swarming every part of the mission station, from the courtyard to the living area to the kitchen.

Miao believers remembering Samuel Pollard at Shimenkan, Guizhou, 2014.

But there was not yet a Big Flowery Miao Bible for them. Pollard wrote, "We were caught napping. We had never imagined a revival coming in this way… No one among us knew the Miao language and at first all teachings had to be done in Chinese."[8] The Big Flowery Miao believers were undeterred—rising at five in the morning to learn to read in Chinese their newfound faith till the wee hours of the next morning. However, it was not ideal, and translation of the Bible into their language remained imperative and urgent.

Pollard's tombstone in Shimenkan, Guizhou, 2014.

As there was no written Big Flowery Miao language, Pollard lost no time in creating a writing system for them in 1904, taking inspiration from another Methodist missionary who served among the natives in North America. With the help of local assistants, Pollard produced a translation of the New Testament in 1917 and many hymns. The Big Flowery Miao Bibles arrived on the backs of twenty-nine horses, and all of the copies were sold within two hours![9] Amazingly, the Pollard script caused a ripple effect on the other ethnic groups. The written scripts of two other ethnic minority languages in China, the East Lisu and Black Yi, are, in fact, borrowed from the Pollard script! According to Yunnan Christian Council / TSPM, today more than half of the Big Flowery Miao population in Yunnan has recognized Jesus as their Lord and Savior, and the Pollard script is still being used.

The Gospel of Mark in East Lisu printed by the British and Foreign Bible Society in 1912.

---

8 Broomhall, *Bible in China*, 107.

9 Nida, *Book of a Thousand Tongues*, 295.

Arriving in 1908, about twenty years later than Adam and Pollard, J. O. Fraser was a British missionary of the CIM stationed in Yunnan Province. Having a consuming passion for the salvation of the tribal people, Fraser began to live among the West Lisu people, ate their food, and learned the difficult Lisu language. Like the Miao people, the Lisu did not have their own writing system. But they had a legend that said one day a White man would come from far away and bring the Lisu their own books and their own king that they had once lost. This legend made the Lisu people open and receptive to the gospel.

James O. Fraser with Lisu converts.
Used with permission from OMF.

In 1938, Fraser, along with other workers, developed a writing system for the Lisu and translated the New Testament into their language.[10] With the Lisu New Testament, not only were the spiritual lives of the Lisu believers nurtured and edified, but Lisu Bible teachers and evangelists could also be raised up and trained. Today, about 30 percent of the Lisu in Yunnan Province are Christians, and they continue to use the Fraser script!

Battles in the Spiritual Realm

What is so special about holding and seeing God's Word printed across the paper in one's own language? C. S. Lewis said this about reading, "We seek an enlargement of our being. We want to be more than ourselves … we want to see with other eyes, to imagine with other imaginations, to feel other hearts, as well as with our own."[11] If this can be said about secular literature, what more the Bible! The act of reading the Bible is a sacred one, and for many ethnic minorities, it involves battles in the spiritual realm.

From interviews with ethnic minority believers, I was told that for countless generations, many ethnic minorities have been trapped in the stronghold of animism and superstition, alcoholism, and gambling addiction. A Ganyi Bible translator said that because of the lavish funeral rites and animal sacrifice, many Yi people felt that they "couldn't even afford to die." On top of that, they were also despised and oppressed by others. Darkness and misery were all they knew. Dare they believe and imagine another kind of life for themselves—another kind of existence that Christ promises to all who trust in him?

Praise God that many did. Through reading the Bible in their mother tongue and the labor of the missionaries, they have felt God's heart, imagined other possibilities, saw with the eyes of faith, and became more than themselves. Through the Bible, they heard God telling them that they matter to him, he has not forgotten them. As they read how he came to them, they entered his story and found their unique place in it. As a result, revival broke out, and thousands upon thousands of them have come out of spiritual darkness into his marvelous light. This was the undeniable impact of Bible translation among the ethnic minorities in China.

---

10 McConnell, "God's Mission to the Lisu," 24–34.
11 Lewis, *An Experiment in Criticism*, 137.

Observing this phenomenal movement, Wang Aiguo, deputy director general of Yunnan Province Administration for Religious Affairs, said, "Missionaries labored for more than ten years but saw very little effect, with just a handful of converts. Then, suddenly in the late 1800s, a large number of Miao people came to faith as a result of the ministry of Samuel Pollard. Why did they embrace Christianity in large numbers? I think the answer lies very much in the Christian message itself. It has given the ethnic minorities a sense of identity, purpose and dignity."

The 1980s to 2020:
Ethnic Minority Bibles Printed with the Support of UBS and Its Impact

During the Cultural Revolution (1966–1976), ethnic minority believers suffered for their faith, and some were executed. Many of their Bibles were destroyed. As churches reopened in the early 1980s, they were in dire need of Bibles. As early as 1983, CCC/TSPM had started to print ethnic minority language Scriptures, namely the Lisu Bible (fifteen thousand copies at Wuxi, Jiangsu Province), the Black Miao New Testament (ten thousand copies at Kunming, Yunnan Province),[12] and the Wa New Testament.

The focus during this period was to print Bibles that had been translated by the early missionaries and their local assistants before 1949, using old copies preserved by the churches through the decades. But without a dedicated Bible printing press and support and given the growing needs of the ethnic minority churches, the church leaders knew that what they could print was only a drop of water in the ocean.

With the establishment of APC, more ethnic minority language Bibles were printed with the support of UBS. The first print run at the press began in 1989. Bibles in Korean, Lahu, Jingpo, and Lisu as well as New Testaments of the Miao (Black) and the Black Yi language were printed, totaling 110,000 copies of Scripture. Subsequently, other languages like Dai and Wa were also printed.[13] Based on the APC production reports from 1989 to 2013, CCC/TSPM printed nearly 300,000 copies of ethnic minority Bibles and 60,000 ethnic minority New Testaments with the support of UBS.

As Bibles were made available and the Word of God spread in China, more ethnic minority people were coming to faith. The transformative power of the gospel was so evident that it caught the attention of a religious affairs government official, Ms. Zhang from Yunnan Province, who gave this account in 2002 of the Lahu ethnic minority people:

Lahu Bible distribution in Yunnan, 2001.

> I know of a thirty-four-year-old man, Zhang Zasuo, who took drugs and had sold off all his family belongings to feed his

---

12 Loh I-Jin, document on APC chronology, 1989.

13 About two thousand copies of the New Testaments in the Dai language were printed in 1993, and about ten thousand New Testaments in the Wa language were printed in 2004.

drug addiction. After becoming a Christian, he managed to kick his addiction within five days! He has bought a Lahu Bible and is reading it every night before going to bed.

In another Lahu tribe, there were many who took drugs. In 1964, the government had sent officials to control the situation, but the problem remained. Later, someone preached the gospel to them, and they believed in the Lord. Following that, they gave up their drug habit one by one. In 1990, a church was built in this village. These are the amazing works of God. In yet another village, people were steeped in superstition, they used to take their livestock and slaughter them as sacrifices to the idols. After becoming Christians, they were no longer involved in idol worship. That is why I say that Christianity is the best.

Praise the Lord for using the testimony of our Lahu brothers and sisters in Christ to speak to a government official! William Cameron Townsend said, "The greatest missionary is the Bible in the mother tongue. It needs no furlough and is never considered a foreigner." This has proven true for the Chinese Bible and now for the ethnic minority language as well.

My first ethnic minority Bible distribution was in Yingjiang County, Yunnan Province, in 2013. We were giving out the Jingpo Bible to hundreds of Jingpo Christians who had gathered for the event. At that time, without knowing the history of the Bible in China, I was surprised to hear that many of them were receiving the Bible in their heart language for the first time. This was the second print of the Jingpo Bible. The first print was twenty-four years ago, in 1989, which explained why it would be the first Bible for many of them.

Shang Yuehan, age twenty-two, who was at a Bible distribution told me about the need for the Bible in his mother tongue: "This is my first Jingpo Bible! I've been reading the Bible in Chinese. Now I can read it in my own language! I am so grateful to God and United Bible Societies for bringing the Bible to us. It is very hard to find a Jingpo Bible here. But believers need it so much for our spiritual growth, especially for believers who cannot read the Bible in Chinese. Without the Word of God, we won't have the right knowledge, and we do not really know for ourselves what we are believing in."

At the Bible distribution, I met some leaders of Jingpo Church who were knowledgeable about the history of the Jingpo Bible. I was moved by how serious and eager they were to share with me about it. According to them, the Bible was first translated from its original languages of Hebrew and Greek into the Jingpo language in 1926 in Burma. It was done by a Swedish Baptist missionary, Ola Hanson, after thirty-five years of laboring among the Kachin (another name for the Jingpo tribe). Both the first and second prints of the Jingpo Bible by APC were based on his translation.

Shang Yeuhan with his Jingpo Bible, Yunnan, 2013.

A Jingpo Christian in her traditional costume and headdress at the Bible distribution, Yunnan, 2013.

Many expressed their immense gratitude for having the Bible in their own language. "We are very thankful towards United Bible Societies for sponsoring the Jingpo Bibles," Pai Zharen, a Jingpo church staff member told me. "The Jingpo Bible is a symbol of God's love for our tribe by rescuing us from the darkness and giving us his word in our own language. It is his grace among us."

"The Jingpo language is something close to our hearts. Reading the Bible in our own language brings us closer to God as it is the spoken language among family members and friends," shared Jin Juhua, a Jingpo church leader.

Ethnic Minority Christians' Thirst for the Word of God and the Need for the Bible in Their Languages

By the twenty-first century, only a handful of ethnic minority groups in China have the Bible translated into their language. The vast majority of the ethnic minority people still do not have God's Word in their mother language. Driven by their desire to read God's Word, some ethnic minority Christians have tried to pick up the Chinese language and were grateful to have Chinese Bibles. In 2000, an ethnic minority (Big Flowery Miao) church in Guizhou Province with nearly four thousand believers shared their experience receiving free Chinese Bibles from CCC/TSPM with the support of UBS:

> We live in a poor region, and it is hard for us to be able to own a Bible. In several meeting places, there is only one Bible and one hymnal for the whole congregation. In slightly better places, an average of ten families would share a Bible and a hymnal. Therefore, when we received the free Bibles from you, some brothers and sisters in Christ wrote a song in the Miao language,
>
> > Heaven is great and earth is great, but greater is the gracious favor of God
> >
> > Father is dear, mother is dear, but dearer is the love of brothers and sisters in Christ
> >
> > Around us are many good things, but better is the goodness of Christ's truth.
>
> More than two thousand brothers and sisters in Christ gathered in festive costumes for a thanksgiving and distribution service. They sang Hymn 201 Gift of Bible while they were in the queue. We did three things after that: (1) began evening Bible classes, (2) set up a church choir in each meeting place, and (3) repaired the church to get ready to share our faith with others.

When I came across this testimony in the archives, I thought to myself: What a wonderful response; can you imagine the exponential impact on this ethnic minority group if the Bible were available in their own language?

Over the years, even as more ethnic minorities are learning Chinese, we have been told not all of them are proficient in the language. Said one East Lisu Bible translator, Elder Yang, in 2003, "About 70–80 percent of us do not read Chinese. Not having the Bible in our mother tongue will greatly affect the development of our faith and spiritual growth." In some cases, as noted above, only the New Testament has been translated. And these New Testament translations were done in the late 1800s and early 1900s and probably need revisions.

Miao Rev. Wang Zhiwen, grandnephew of Rev. Wang Zhiming who was executed during the Cultural Revolution in China, said, "For many years, Miao believers could only read from the NT. They have very little knowledge of the OT. They could only hear about it from extracts of Rev. Wang Zhiming's sermon. Hence, translation of the Bible is essential to the Miao people."

Li Jiaxing, a Ganyi Bible translator, hopes that with the translated Ganyi Bible more from his tribe will come to know God: "In my village, people have been bound to animistic belief for a long time. I believe God's Word has the power to shape and influence the entire Yi tribe people, and for generations and generations to come."

In a nutshell, the ethnic minority Christians were facing three predicaments—many cannot read the Chinese Bible, some do not fully understand the old version of the New Testament, and the majority have not read the Old Testament. This implies that their spiritual growth and development will be stunted, and they will have difficulty sharing their faith with others. Therefore, the ethnic minority churches in China saw the pressing need to translate the Bible into their mother tongue. In the 1980s and 1990s, some of the elders and preachers among them took the initiative and courage to form Bible translation teams. Some of these include the Big Flowery Miao, East Lisu, and Black Yi minority groups.

However, the demanding task of Bible translation requires scholarship and expertise spanning a few areas like biblical studies, linguistics, and translation theory. Most ethnic minority Bible translators, being rural people, have limited education and theological training. It is also rare to find anyone who is proficient in the English language in which most biblical resources are written or the biblical languages of Hebrew and Greek.

Moreover, ethnic minorities are spread over the mountainous regions in China. Even people from the same group inevitably have some differences in their dialects that contribute to the difficulty of Bible translation. The task seemed insurmountable. How was the gap going to be closed? How would God use UBS, whose mission is to make the Bible available for everyone, to come alongside the ethnic minority churches in China?

Black Yi Bible translation team, Yunnan, 2000.

Black Yi Bible translation team, 2016.

UBS's Support of Bible Translation in China

As Chinese Churches reopened in the early 1980s, the first initial Bible translation support given by UBS took place as early as 1983, even before the establishment of APC. A workshop was held in Kunming, Yunnan Province, to train translators for several minority language projects in the province. For various reasons, this was not able to be followed up, but some of the translators continued their work. Contact was reestablished in 1992 when another training was conducted. Following that, East Lisu, Big Flowery Miao, and Black Yi translation teams received help from UBS via the Yunnan Christian Council / TSPM.

In 1998, a milestone meeting was held at Kunming, Yunnan Province. It was attended by the leaders of CCC/TSPM, Yunnan Christian Council / TSPM, the Religious Affairs Bureau, UBS, and fourteen representatives and Bible translators from eight ethnic minority groups. This meeting marked the beginning of the partnership between CCC/TSPM and UBS in Bible translation with the blessings and approval of the Religious Affairs Bureau. It both kick-started and resumed Bible translation work among seven ethnic minority groups: Big Flowery Miao, West Lisu, East Lisu, Wa, Black Yi, Ganyi, and White Yi.

During this period, Wang Aiguo, deputy director general of Yunnan Religious Affairs, played an instrumental role in supporting ethnic minority Bible translation. Possessing a good knowledge of the ethnic minority groups in China and recognizing the positive social and cultural impact of the Christian faith on them, he helped facilitate the partnership between the churches in China and UBS. As a result, Bible ministry flourished among the ethnic minorities. When there was a question of the choice of script for the Lisu Bible translation, he listened to the sentiments of the Lisu church and allowed the old Lisu script to be used in the Bible translation instead of the new one. In an interview in 2015, Wang said, "It is of fundamental importance that the Word of God be translated accurately since it is the basis of the Christian faith. I think UBS was the most reliable organization to work with for this matter."

Kua Wee Seng, Bishop John Chew and Wang Aiguo at Yunnan Theological Seminary, where the students come from different ethnic minority groups, 2013.

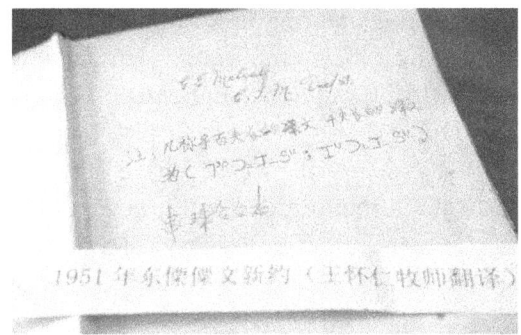

The 1951 edition of the East Lisu New Testament translated by George Metcalf, is on display at the Bible translation center.

Yang Hai'en and Yang Xianguo at the Bible translation center. They are a father and son who were involved in the East Lisu Bible translation. One is holding the 1951 East Lisu New Testament translated by George Edgar Metcalf and the other the East Lisu Bible completed in 2016.

Over the years, UBS, whose mission is to make the Bible available for everyone, has come alongside the ethnic minority churches in China in this endeavor. Overseas Christians, through the Bible societies, have given support toward Bible translation, helping ethnic minorities in China to hear God speak in their heart language. With the support, Bible translation training and workshops have been conducted, and UBS translation consultants and officers have been deployed to the various Bible translation teams to check and review translation drafts, ensuring faithfulness to the original text.

In addition, equipment like computers and furniture have also been provided, and Bible software like Paratext shared. Living allowances were also given to the Bible translators, who were usually pastors and preachers serving in the local church, supporting themselves and their families through subsistence farming. With the living allowances, they could then devote most of their time to translation work. In some cases, motorbikes were also gifted to Bible translators who lived far away from the Bible translation workspace.

UBS also supported the construction and set up of a Bible translation center in 2003 on the fifth floor of the Trinity (Sanyi) International Church in Kunming, Yunnan Province.

Visitors from UBS at the Bible Translation center with ethnic minority Bible translators, Yunnan, 2014.

The translation center enabled the Bible translators to meet at a central location in the city with the visiting UBS Bible translation consultants and officers for training, discussion, and checking of their drafts. Beautifully decorated with colorful handicrafts, costumes and old tools of the ethnic minorities, the center is like a mini museum with display cabinets showcasing old Bibles and newly translated ones. The center was where I have beautiful memories of spending time with the Bible translators, listening to their journey and the heartbeat behind their work, some of which are recorded in the next chapter. Besides the center, the fifth floor also has guest rooms where the translators could stay for a couple of weeks before returning home.

Praise God for the example set by past missionaries who labored among the ethnic minority people in China, carrying the light to their souls. It is inspiring to see how the ethnic minority Christians in China kept their faith during the Cultural Revolution. It is humbling to see how, despite all their limitations, ethnic minority Christians took the initiative to translate the Bible into their own language. And it is amazing how the Lord granted favor with the Chinese authorities to expand the Bible work among the ethnic minorities. We shall continue the story of the ethnic minority church in China by looking at the labor of the people involved in Bible translation, the impact of the Bible translation on Christians, and Scripture literacy in the next chapter.

9
Glows and Glitters in the Mountains II

Bible Ministry to the Ethnic Minority People in China

> Is not my word like fire, declares the LORD, and like a hammer that breaks the rock in pieces?
> —Jeremiah 23:29

> It is in prayerful dependence upon the One who inspired the prophets and the apostles of old that someone today can make this same message "a living fire" in the hearts of men and women.
> —Eugene Nida, executive secretary for translations, American Bible Society, on the work of Bible translation

Dr. Yu Suee Yan at the Big Flowery Miao Bible launch, 2009.

Every Bible translation is a long-term investment of one's time and energy, a lengthy process involving drafting, checking, reviewing, correcting, typesetting, and proofreading. Who would give ten to twenty years of his or her time to a laborious task without expecting any material reward? Probably very few. Yet the ethnic minority Bible translators in China have courageously taken up the monumental task and trusted God to carry them through. Despite lacking theological and translation scholarship, they have persevered and inspired many with their commitment and humility. They also understood that this is not just the responsibility of the Bible translators; it is a shared endeavor involving the local church community and the support of overseas Christians. Bible translators often double up as literacy teachers in churches. Scripture literacy goes in tandem with Bible translation to help ethnic minorities engage with God's Word in their own language. In this chapter, we catch a glimpse of the labor that goes into Bible translation, the impact of God's Word, and the continued engagement with the word through literacy classes.

Labor of Love

One of the first completed translations under the partnership between the registered Churches in China and UBS was the Big Flowery Miao Bible. Completed in 2008, the Big Flowery Miao Bible took no less than twenty years to see the light of day. Dr. Yu Suee Yan,

UBS global translation advisor, who worked closely with the Big Flowery Miao team for more than a decade said, "The Miao translators are very dedicated to their work. They left behind their families in their respective villages, stayed together in the translation center in Wuding, and labored for years. It has been a blessing to work with these dedicated Miao Christians."

Big Flowery Miao Bible translation team with UBS staff, 2000.

East Lisu Church, Yunnan, 2009.

Believers overflowed outside the church at the East Lisu New Testament launch, Yunnan, 2009.

Launch of the East Lisu Bible, Yunnan, 2016.

Speaking of the labor of the East Lisu Bible translators, Dr. Yu, who also worked with them, gave a beautiful description, "As farmers they sow their seeds every spring with a sense of anticipation. And then they will wait with great expectation for the harvest. When they think of the harvest in summer, they will forget their hard labor. A bright smile breaks through their weather-beaten, wrinkled faces. When God called them, they put down their plow shears and picked up the other plow that Jesus gave them. Eyes fixed on the cross, they followed their Savior." The East Lisu New Testament was launched in 2009 while the complete Bible was done in 2016, with consultation given by Dr. Simon Wong, UBS global translation advisor.

The Bible translators knew that it was an undertaking that would have been impossible without the support of their family and the Christian community. Li Shaoxing, a Ganyi Bible translator who served for sixteen years and thought of quitting several times, said,

> My wife and parents told me, "Don't give up. We are people of faith; we face difficulties together as a family. We will back you up." Their unwavering support for me is very precious. My fellow Bible translators are always cheering me on, helping me to deepen my understanding of the Bible. Our church also gave us a lot of moral support and prayed for us all these years for wisdom and understanding from the Lord. I know they are all longing to see the Word of God in their own language. Practical support and encouragement from UBS also helped me and the team to persevere. I am grateful to them. Without all their support, I would have quit many times over.

Bible translators also expressed their gratitude to UBS Bible translation consultants with whom they worked closely. "We appreciate Dr. Simon Wong who reminded us to handle the Word of God carefully and to hold ourselves responsible to the believers who will be reading the translated Bible. Support and investment of resources from UBS has given us the confidence to finish the task," shared Rev. Bao Guangqiang, Wa Bible translator, Yunnan Province. The Wa Bible translation team was formed in 2002. In their long journey of Bible translation, they moved from using handwritten manuscripts to manual typewriters to computers. The translation was finally completed in 2015.

Wa Bible launch, Yunnan, 2016.

How did it feel to see the fruit of one's labor? A heart bursting with thankfulness was what Elder Bi Hongzheng, age fifty-six, one of the earliest members of the East Lisu Bible translation team, experienced. He was one of the few who stayed from 1992, when the team was formed, to 2013, when the translation was completed. After more than two decades, he was able to witness its launch in 2016. He said,

Wa Bible launch, Yunnan, 2016.

> Praise God, I am blessed to witness the work from start to finish. I've seen with my own eye the Bible translated and printed in our ethnic language! The value of the East Lisu Bible is immeasurable. If it were not for the support of UBS, we don't know when we could have the whole Bible in our own ethnic language. We can't thank UBS and all its supporters and donors enough. I have often shared with fellow East Lisu believers that it is like we are going to heaven by holding the hands of brothers and sisters in Christ from UBS.

Most of all, they knew that they could not do it without God holding their hands. There was a clear recognition that God was their helper and provider. Throughout the last twelve years of translating the Bible into the Black Yi language, Elder Zhang Quanwei has seen God provide for him and his family. There was no lack, and with God's provision, he was able to send his children for university education. He said, "Also, I didn't know how to use the computer software at first, but God provided help by allowing me to attend a two-week computer course supported by UBS. His divine provision was what enabled me to stay on the translation work till its final phase in 2013."

A Century of Waiting: Milestones in Bible Translation

From the stories of the Bible translators and believers, I learned that the completion of a Bible or New Testament translation can be a bittersweet experience for many of these ethnic minority groups, an occasion where one can be overwhelmed with mixed emotions. The reason is that many of these groups have waited at least a century to see the Bible in their own language since the gospel first reached them. Also, due to the long process of Bible translation, some translators and ethnic minority Christians, especially the elderly ones, did not live to witness the completion of the translation work.

At the launch of the East Lisu New Testament in 2009, Rev. Yong Haiwen, age forty-one, an East Lisu pastor who is a fourth-generation Christian, said, "I am now holding the East Lisu New Testament which for generations my ancestors had hoped to see." The gospel first reached the East Lisu people in 1903. Even though the New Testament was translated in 1947 by British missionary Rev. George Edgar Metcalf

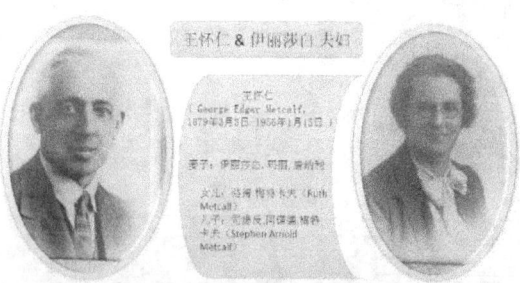

George Edgar and Elizabeth Metcalf served among the East Lisu in the early 1900s.

Believers in their traditional costume at the White Yi New Testament launch, Yunnan, 2015.

Black Yi believer with her Bible, 2018.

White Yi New Testament launch, Yunnan, 2015.

Black Yi believers, 2018.

and his team and was published by the Hong Kong Bible Society (China Bible House, Hong Kong Street) in 1951, it did not reach the East Lisu Christians in Yunnan Province.

White Yi Elder Li Wangsan said at the launch of the White Yi New Testament in 2015, "Christianity came to the White Yi people about a century ago. Today, a century later, I am so thankful that we finally have the New Testament in our own language. A part of our culture was lost for many decades, now we have our language in written form."

Imagine what a jubilant moment it must have been for the ethnic minority churches during a celebration held in 2016 in Kunming for the long-standing partnership between UBS, CCC/TSPM, and Yunnan Christian Council / TSPM. The special occasion marked the first publication of the East Lisu Bible, Black Yi Bible, and Wa Bible and the reprints of the West Lisu Annotated Bible, Big Flowery Miao Bible, and White Yi New Testament, totaling 120,000 copies of Scripture.

After the celebration in Kunming, some UBS guests and I traveled to Lincang County, Yunnan Province, where we were privileged to join in the launch of the Wa Bible at a church. Upon arriving, we were welcomed by the Wa believers with exuberant singing and clapping. Decked in their striking red-black costumes and beaded headdresses (for the ladies), they formed a line under the scorching hot sun to receive us.

What touched me also was to see Lahu believers at the celebration of the Wa Bible launch. They even performed a song in Lahu to share their joy with the Wa believers! It was like a heavenly scene to me. As the Wa Bibles were distributed, tears and heartfelt joy were seen on the faces of the Wa believers, who could hardly believe that they were holding the Bible in their very own heart language, having waited almost a century for it.

"Praise God that the Wa Bible has been translated! An ethnic group without its own literature is like one without a soul. This is a historical moment for the Wa ethnic group. Our culture is much more enriched now by having the Wa Bible. The Wa churches used to only have the New Testament (translated in 1938 by American missionary William Young and his team), which felt like having only one arm, now we have both arms!" shared Rev. Bao Guangqiang, Wa Bible translator, Yunnan Province.

The Wa Bible was completed in 2015 and launched in 2016. Rev. Bao continued, "Over the years, because of my experience in translating the Wa Bible, I have been recognized outside the church community to be an expert in the Wa language and culture. From time to time, I've been interviewed by people involved in policymaking and academia. The Wa Bible was also used as a reference in the compilation of the Wa-Han (Chinese) dictionary. But what touched me the most was the excitement of fellow believers when they read the opening line of the Bible in Wa: 'In the beginning, God created the heavens and earth.'"

There are currently a few other ongoing Bible translations for the ethnic minorities in China. Let's pray that it does not take another century to see God's Word being translated into more languages of the ethnic minorities! Let us also pray that more ethnic minority language Bibles be printed in China!

"A Living Fire": The Impact of Bible Translation on Ethnic Minority Christians

Welcome by an elderly believer at a Ganyi Bible distribution.

What is the goal of Bible translation? Eugene Nida said this about Bible translators and their work—they are "deeply conscious that the message which they were rendering was in a special sense God's Word, not man's. It is in prayerful dependence upon the One who inspired the prophets and the apostles of old that someone today can make this same message 'a living fire' in the hearts of men and women."[1]

I find this imagery not unlike what is expressed in the Chinese idiom 薪火相传, which means passing on the torch of knowledge and skills through the generations, except that we are talking about passing on the torch of the Heavenly Message of God.

How then was this "living fire" felt in the hearts of the ethnic minority Christians? What difference did it make to them to be able to read God's Word in their own language?

An East Lisu preacher said about receiving the New Testament in her own language in 2009, "When I read the Bible in Chinese, I felt as if my schoolteacher was speaking. But

---

1 Nida, *Book of a Thousand Tongues*, xiv.

East Lisu Bible translation team, Chinese Church, and UBS leaders.

when I read the Bible in the East Lisu language, it was like my papa and mama talking to me. God becomes closer and more intimate."

Even draft copies had a tremendous impact on the believers. As part of the process of Bible translation, drafts were shared with the local church community for the purpose of obtaining feedback. A Black Yi Christian, Li Benchong, shared about a draft of the Book of Genesis he was given in 2009:

> A few years ago, I heard that a team of brothers in Luquan County had begun translating the Old Testament into our Black Yi language. It has always been our dream to catch a glimpse of this translation. When the day finally came, we could not contain our excitement and joy when we could read from this little book that is a draft copy of Genesis. We can now have a better understanding of what our pastor has taught us. It is like God has finally spoken. He is really speaking to us now. We have found out for ourselves more details from the Book of Genesis. For example, how God called Abraham, how Abraham obeyed and loved God. His beloved son was born to him only when he was one hundred years old. When God asked Abraham to sacrifice his son, he did not hesitate to offer his son as a living sacrifice. Comparing Abraham's faith and love for God with ours, we are ashamed that we have so little faith. There are so many beautiful things to behold.

For Bao Bai Ai, a Wa believer from Yunnan Province, it meant breakthroughs in several areas:

> Before having the Wa Bible, my faith was not strong. During my wife's illness, I had been involved in idol worship and animal sacrifice even as a Christian. I regretted it as I saw that it was all futile. Now with the Wa Bible, I've come to know God and his will better. In the church, there is much more emphasis on preaching,

Bao Bao Ai with his Wa Bible.

Mongolian Bible translators holding the trial edition of both the Four Gospels and the New Testament. According to the Inner Mongolian Christian Council / TSPM, the Mongolian Bible will be ready in 2024.

Ethnic minority language Bibles. Left, top-down: White Yi New Testament, East Lisu Bible, Lahu Bible, Wa Bible, Jingpo Bible. Right, top-down: Inner Mongolian New Testament Trial Edition, West Lisu Bible, Big Flowery Miao Bible, West Lisu Annotated Bible, Black Yi Bible.

reading, and studying God's Word in the Wa language. My son, who was a drug addict and whose marriage was badly affected, experienced a breakthrough when I brought him to a Wa Bible reading group. Now my son, daughter-in-law and I have been immersing ourselves in the pages of the Bible till it became quite worn out! I repented of my previous actions and the Lord has transformed my life and my family through his word. Praise God!

To date, about 650,000 copies of Bibles and New Testaments in ten different ethnic minority languages have been printed at APC and distributed for free by the churches in China.

Translation of Bible Resources for Ethnic Minorities

Steps have also been taken to provide the ethnic minorities with Bible resources to help them deepen their understanding of God's Word as well as to equip pastors and preachers for their preaching ministry. One example is the Lisu Annotated Bible. In 2015, the Lisu Annotated Bible, which was based on the annotations in the Chinese Annotated Bible, was translated by a team of Lisu Bible translators and published by CCC/TSPM with the support of UBS. Together with other guests from UBS, I was privileged to attend its launch.

West Lisu Annotated Bible launch, Yunnan, 2015.

Lisu Rev. Yu Wenliang, who served as the leader of the translation team shared with us that since 1990, 135,000 Lisu Bibles have been printed and distributed. At the same time, they also see the need for annotated Bibles, study Bibles, and other spiritual resources to aid the spiritual growth of the Lisu believers and strengthen their biblical foundation as a defense against cult groups. "Hence, in 2009, with the support of UBS, we started the work of translating the notes in the Chinese Annotated Bible into Lisu."

Rev. Yexi, a member of the translation team, added,

In the process of translating the Annotated Bible, we also made some corrections to the Lisu Bible and hence revised it. This helps the believers to have a more accurate translation of the Bible on top of having some explanatory notes.

On the need for such a resource, Lisu Rev. Li Chunxing, age thirty, said, "Lisu people are coming to know God, but the church is lacking in good pulpit ministry. Preachers usually rely on limited Chinese resources, which are not in their mother tongue. So the translated Annotated Bible is a very valuable resource for pastors and preachers. It will improve the quality of our sermons!"

West Lisu believers with their annotated Bibles, 2015.

Thank God for the Lisu Annotated Bible and let's pray for ongoing translations for other Bible resources for ethnic minorities Christians so that more will be able to have a deeper understanding of God's Word.

Scripture Literacy for Ethnic Minorities

Bible translation for ethnic minorities often goes hand in hand with Scripture literacy—teaching and helping them to read their own written script. There are two main reasons for this. First, most of the ethnic minorities communicate through oral tradition, transmitting cultural values and beliefs via word of mouth in the form of storytelling, songs, etc. Language learning is hence passed down orally, and their writing systems were usually created by the missionaries. Besides the Bible, most of them have almost no other existing written literature.

Wang Chumin (second from right) with her family, 2016.

This is evident in the comments by an East Lisu Bible translator, "The East Lisu Bible translation has great implications and significance on our culture and history. The East Lisu Bible is the most important religious and cultural literature of our tribe. Hence, for a long time, learning the East Lisu language and reading the Bible is inseparable."

Second, the Chinese language is being taught in schools and is the medium of instruction. Even for ethnic minority groups like the Lisu, which has a written script (created by Fraser) and a small mass media industry, the Lisu language is not taught in schools. They either learn it at home or church.

Therefore, ethnic minority Bible translators are keenly aware of the need to teach Scripture literacy to their fellow believers, and this is usually

Lahu Scripture literacy class, 2023.

done concurrently with Bible translation, where trial editions are printed and circulated to the local Christian community. This helps ensure that when the Bible is fully translated, some believers will already be able to read it for their spiritual nourishment and growth. To this end, numerous Scripture literacy classes for ethnic minority churches have been organized by the CCC/TSPM with the support of UBS.

In 2016, my colleagues and I visited a White Yi Scripture literacy class in a village in Yunnan, attended by about one hundred people. We were moved by the hunger of the White Yi believers to learn to read the Scripture and the fact that some of them had taken leave from work, returning from the counties and cities, to participate in the class held in the village.

West Lisu Scripture literacy class, Yunnan.

Wang Chunmin, age thirteen, one of the youngest students at a White Yi literacy class said, "I may be able to read Chinese, but I don't fully understand what I read. However, when I read the White Yi Bible, I can understand it much better and feel more satisfaction."

Elder Yang Sousou, age thirty-eight, the overseer of a two-hundred-strong White Yi church and a student in the literacy class, told us, "We are truly able to gain more understanding reading the White Yi Bible compared to the Chinese Bible, which not many are able to read, especially older believers who did not go to school. So I look forward to helping my church learn to read the White Yi script."

Churches continue to conduct Scripture literacy classes even for Bible translations that had been done before 1949. One of them is the Lahu ethnic minority church. Zhang Nasi, a Lahu farmer serving in the church choir, said, "Through the literacy class and communal reading of the Bible in our ethnic Lahu language, I have discovered an inner strength. The collective experience of studying Lahu and engaging with the Scriptures has empowered me in ways I couldn't achieve alone. This class has not only deepened my understanding of the Bible but also fostered a stronger connection to my heart language. Now, I can read and comprehend the Lahu Bible, no longer relying solely on sermons. I am truly grateful for this transformative experience."

Ethnic minority preachers have also experienced breakthroughs in their teaching and preaching ministry through Scripture literacy. Li Nawa, a Lahu lay preacher, shared, "When I was studying at the Bible School, I relied on Chinese translations as I couldn't read Lahu, my native language. Joining the Lahu literacy class transformed my ministry. Now, empowered by reading and preaching directly in Lahu, my heart language, I have deepened my understanding of the Scriptures. This shift has brought

White Yi Scripture literacy class participant, 2016.

remarkable convenience and profound impact to my ministry, allowing me to convey the message with greater accuracy and resonance."

Besides Christians, Scripture literacy classes have also caught the interest of unbelievers. White Yi Bible translator Elder Huang shared, "We have unbelievers, for example, White Yi school teachers who teach Chinese in the schools, wanting to learn the White Yi script from us. We foresee that this will be a great opportunity to share our faith with them."

Participants of West Lisu Scripture literacy class, 2016.

Another example came from the Lisu church. During a visit in 2016, I was amazed to hear that unbelievers in the Lisu news media sector have been using the Lisu Bible as their dictionary as it is the only written script offering a wide range of vocabulary and phrases! Rev. Li Moxi, Nujiang Christian Council / TSPM chairman said, "Since seven or eight years ago, Lisu news reporters and radio broadcasters have sought the help of Christians and consulted the Lisu Bible in their writing and reporting. We are grateful to Fraser for creating the script and very glad that the script could help in the development of our community today."

Yu Yong Guang, a member of the West Lisu Annotated Bible translation team summarized the importance of Scripture literacy in these words, "In order to continue the work of spreading the gospel, building and strengthening the spiritual life of believers and passing down the Lisu language and cultural heritage, Scripture literacy is necessary."

Over the years, besides Bible translation and Scripture literacy, UBS Bible ministry among the ethnic minority churches in China has expanded to include equipping and supporting needy lay preachers, gifting Bible motorbikes to lay leaders, and providing training and resources for young adult ministry, which will be covered in the subsequent chapters.

It is inspiring to know that since the days of the pioneering missionaries, God's Word, like a "living fire," is still burning bright among ethnic minority churches in China. Through Bible translation and Scripture literacy classes, the Word of God is continuing to spread among the ethnic minority Christians who hunger for it in their heart language. Praise God that in the 2000s, ethnic minority churches in China entered a new dawn when some Bible translations were completed! It was no ordinary achievement in the history of the ethnic minority churches in China. They are now finally able to experience what it is like to hear God speak to them in their heart language. Not only were they being drawn closer to God and sharing their faith more effectively, but they were also proud to contribute to the cultural preservation of their tribe. There are however still many ethnic minority groups in China without the Scriptures in their mother tongue. This prayer from IllumiNations, a Bible translation alliance of which UBS is a part, reminds us to look to God in the unfinished task:

> God, Your Word is more precious than all that I possess.
> Your Scripture gives light to my path and directs my steps.
> Through Your will alone, lives are transformed and minds made new.
> So I now pray for all people that do not yet know You.
> For You've promised that Your voice by every tribe and nation will be heard.
> So equip us by your breath to provide every heart language with your Word.
> Amen.

10
A Light for Every Season

Scripture Portions, Selections, and Gospel Booklets

> To make an apt answer is a joy to a man, and a word in season, how good it is!
> —Proverbs 15:23

> I began to understand a certain truth: when God created us, he left a void that only he could fill. When we attempt to fill this void with things like success in career, wealth, and relationships, we realize we can't.
> —Li Mengyu, age twenty-two, came to faith after a Christian friend handed him a Gospel booklet *No Longer Lonely*

Grand Meetings in Humble Booklets

Small and light, it can be held comfortably with one hand. You can bring it anywhere and read it whenever you want. Some may find the Bible too intimidating and the New Testament too long, but nobody would reject reading a Scripture portion or a Gospel booklet. You can even read it in one sitting. It is always within your reach, and it can reach you in ways beyond your imagination. Finally, you can multiply its benefits by giving it to someone else.

Scripture portions and Gospel booklets distributed in China.

Since the beginning of the Bible society's work in China in the 1800s, Scripture portions, selections, and Gospel booklets have always been at the heart of the ministry. As the names suggest, these booklets contain a part of Scripture or one of the Gospels. Because of their shorter length and smaller size, a higher volume was usually reported to have been handed out by Bible society agents, missionaries, and colporteurs. Canvassing and distributing these Scripture portions often gave them a valid reason for entering either a busy city or a quiet local village that might otherwise be a harder enterprise.

Through the pages of these small and humble-looking booklets, Chinese people were given the opportunity to meet the Lord of the universe and hear him speak to them about some of life's deepest issues. One is reminded of the accounts in the Gospels where Jesus met individuals. He addressed them personally and specifically on issues that concerned them. These unique individuals encountered the Lord Jesus and knew that he had spoken to them. Often through questions and words of truth, he spoke into their lives, in each of their unique circumstances. We recall Peter fishing and catching nothing, the Samaritan woman drawing water at the well, Nicodemus coming to Jesus in the night, the rich young ruler seeking eternal life, the robber crucified beside Jesus asking to be remembered.

Likewise, God has been meeting the Chinese through his word in these handy, portable booklets. Since the early 2000s, UBS has supported several provincial Christian Councils / TSPM to produce, print, and distribute these booklets. Over the past two decades, an amazing variety of Scripture portions and Gospel booklets have been developed based on different themes, special occasions and seasons, social concerns, and major national events. Many Chinese Christians said that the booklets were not only beneficial to themselves, but they were also like a window, opening up opportunities for them to share about Jesus with their family and friends. Below are selected stories about the unique circumstances under which some of these booklets were developed and their impact on the lives of individuals.

The AIDS Prevention Scripture Portion

Even as China has emerged from the COVID-19 pandemic, it was only in recent decades that it was battling another virus—the human immunodeficiency virus (HIV) and the disease it causes, AIDS. Having first appeared in Africa in the 1960s, the virus spread to China in 1985, when the first case was reported, and then later in 1989, when an initial outbreak and cases of people infected were recognized.

Wang Zhiwei's parents were among those infected with the deadly disease. Five-year-old Zhiwei lived with his parents and grandmother in a village in Zhumadian Prefecture, Henan Province. His parents, who were farmers, had recently heard that selling their blood could fetch RMB 90 (equivalent to USD$13 now) each time, equivalent to more than a month's income. Being poor and faced with a bad harvest, Zhiwei's father went. But, sometime after selling his blood, Zhiwei's father became ill and died. His mother followed suit a year later; both husband and wife were just thirty-two when they passed on. It was later found out that his father had contracted HIV/AIDS while donating blood and passed the disease to his wife. The deadly disease was also passed to little Zhiwei, who was born with it.

Wang Zhiwei, Henan, 2005.

Of all the provinces, Henan Province in central China, where Zhiwei and his family came from, was among the top five hardest hit by the virus in the late 1990s. One of the major causes was illegal blood trading. This most populous agricultural province in China was struggling with extreme poverty. Bad weather conditions and challenging terrain in certain parts of the landlocked province had resulted in a dismal harvest and poor income. So when they were told that 800 cc of blood could fetch over a month's worth of income, many poor farmers and village people donated blood. Unfortunately, it was later discovered that these underground traders flouted safety precautions and used recycled needles and syringes.

UBS CP coordinator Kua Wee-Seng (center) with a group of Christians with HIV/AIDS at Shang Quan Village Church in Zhumadian Prefecture, Henan, 2005.

The rosy promise of some income to survive a bad harvest turned into a nightmarish prospect of a deadly disease as mortality increased at an alarming rate. By the 2000s, many of these blood donors had died, leaving behind their children and aged parents. It was believed that in some villages, almost a whole generation of people had been wiped out. More tragically, the incurable disease was spread to some of their young children, whose lives were cut short. Little Zhiwei succumbed to the disease and died at eight years old.

In Shaanxi Province, cases of people infected with AIDS were also beginning to surface in the 1990s.[1] In response to the health crisis, a Christian meeting point under the Shaanxi Christian Council / TSPM started an AIDS awareness and care ministry. Volunteers from the meeting point went around in the community and their neighborhood in a borrowed pushcart for recycled items carrying handwritten leaflets about AIDS and AIDS prevention, tirelessly handing them out to passersby.

Soon, these materials developed into an HIV/AIDS Scripture booklet. It addressed the Chinese Ministry of Health's concern about inadequate AIDS education by providing some basic information about the disease, including its harmful effects and channel of transmission as well as prevention and control measures. The other part of the booklet contained selected verses of encouragement highlighting what the Bible says about God, human beings, and his love for people. Written by Rev. Wang Jun, a leader of Shaanxi Christian Council / TSPM, readers were reminded of God's presence with them, his acceptance of them, and that his love is greater than death.

When approached by the Shaanxi Christian Council / TSPM to partner with them, UBS responded readily, raised the necessary funds, and supported the printing and free distribution of hundreds of thousands of HIV/AIDS Scripture booklets in the 2000s to Yunnan, Henan, and Shaanxi Provinces. Guo Hui Qin, a believer from a church in Shaanxi Province, said after receiving the HIV/AIDS Prevention booklet,

---

1 Xiang, Hua, Li-fang, Bai-suo, Wen-hui, Qiang, Lu, Meng, and Ai-hua, "Reported HIV/AIDS Cases in Shaanxi Province, 1992–2010."

We were extremely grateful to be given free copies of a booklet that educates us about the prevention of AIDS. This booklet helps us to understand the social responsibility of a Christian. It explicitly teaches about showing the love of Christ to people infected with AIDS, who need love, care, and concern. At the same time, the teachings of the Bible are also included adequately to better equip us to become the light of the world!

We trusted God that with each booklet that was given out, AIDS patients and their families would be reached with the good news of Jesus Christ and that Christians would be equipped with another resource to bring the love of God. As in the case of Wang Zhiwei, it was heartening to know that before he passed on, Christians from a church in his village cared for him and his grandmother. Most of all, they shared the gospel with Zhiwei and gave him a copy of the *Pictorial Bible Stories*, and Zhiwei came to know the Lord Jesus. On his deathbed, they could hear Zhiwei crying out, "Jesus, please save me!"

In 2021, the churches in Shaanxi were once again sensing the need for a reprint of the AIDS Scripture booklet and approached UBS for support. UBS readily supported the reprint of 100,000 copies of the booklet.

Gospel Booklets for the FIFA Women's World Cup and 2008 Olympics

Scripture portions were also designed for special events to open more opportunities and avenues for the Word of God to be read and heard in China. The FIFA Women's World Cup and XXIX Olympiad, both hosted by China in 2007 and 2008, respectively, were such events that offered great opportunities.

In September 2007, the fifth edition of the FIFA Women's World Cup was held across five cities in China. The event captured the imagination of many Chinese and a football fever was raging among them, particularly the young. While the team from Germany grabbed international headlines by winning the World Cup, two Christian footballers from the Chinese team would go on to make headway in the hearts of the local Chinese, paving the way for the gospel to be heard and strengthening the faith of many believers.

Gospel booklet featuring Han Duan's testimony, 2008.

How did that happen? Right after the Women's World Cup, the churches in China wanted to take advantage of the football fever that was still running high. By God's providence, friends of UBS CP approached two Christian players in the national team—Han Duan and Liu Yali—to publish their testimonies in Gospel portions. Both readily agreed.

Han Duan, named by FIFA as one of the players to be reckoned with, confessed that in her journey as a national player, there were more downs than ups, more failures than successes. As the striker who scored ten goals for China in the 2007 Four Nations Women's Tournament, she attributed her abiding sense of joy and peace to her Christian faith. This faithful reader of the word went everywhere with her Bible and believed that God has his beautiful purposes behind both the sweet and bitter moments of life.

Han Duan's faith was, in fact, so contagious that a fellow player, Liu Yali, was inspired to consider the gospel for herself. In her testimony, she shared how the concern and prayers of Han Duan drew her to faith. It was not common in those days for people to be open about their faith, especially when they were famous, up-and-coming celebrities. Praise God that these two ladies were willing to make a stand for Jesus.

Before long, the two Chinese-English Gospel portions—*To Be Great* (featuring the Gospel of Mark) and *Power of Love* (featuring the Gospel of Luke) with testimonies of Han Duan and Liu Yali, respectively—went into printing at APC. With the support of UBS, more than 200,000 copies of *To Be Great* and *Power of Love* were printed and distributed in churches, young adult groups, seminaries, Bible schools, and shops owned by Christians.

The testimonies of Chinese Christian sports personalities like Han Duan and Liu Yali were timely for both seekers and believers in China. Since the beginning of the reopening of the churches in China in the 1980s, most conversions had taken place in the villages among the poor, the elderly, and women. Due to poverty and limited medical services in the rural areas, many of them had come to faith because of physical healing. As such, many people have associated Christianity in China with the old, rural, sick, and handicapped. Thanks to the testimonies of Han Duan and Liu Yali, people's perceptions are changing. This can be seen in the feedback the churches received.

Li Hong, age thirty-four, a seeker who attended a church in Nanjing, wrote, "All along I thought that those who turn to Christianity are people who have illnesses. After reading the booklet, I now know that Christians are good people. I wish to find out more about the faith."

Huang Qin, age forty, also a seeker, shared, "My husband is a Christian, but I'm not. I often think that he is superstitious and backward in his thinking. I have an aversion to religion instinctively. But when he brought the booklet *Power of Love* for me to read, I realized that Christianity is not a superstitious religion, rather it is a good religion. Jesus Christ is a compassionate and loving person."

Believers, especially the younger ones, were also inspired by the testimonies and spurred on in their faith. Here are some testimonies we collected.

"Han Duan is a public figure, and she is able to talk freely about her faith, glorifying God. But I have never admitted that I am a Christian in public, among friends. Han Duan's dependence on God and her faithful prayers are what I want to learn from," shared Liu Jianmin, a senior high student who hailed from Henan Province.

"Among the youngsters, they tend to have the idea that believing in Jesus is likened to having an emotional crutch. But the English language is one of the most important skills they are pursuing. Moreover, they are also attracted to famous and important people. *Power of Love* is a booklet about China's famous football star, and it is also bilingual—so it is a wonderful combination that reaches them!" said Su Zhen Zi, age twenty-one, a believer who attends a church in Henan Province.

After the FIFA Women's World Cup, China was again in the limelight for another sporting event, this time on an even bigger scale—the XXIX Olympiad held in Beijing in 2008. To China, it was a momentous event to showcase its new self to the world, a coming of age of sorts. To the Churches in China, it was a golden opportunity to sow the Word of God broadly, a chance not to be missed.

"It is not only a sporting event," said Elder Fu Xianwei, chairman of the national TSPM. "It is also to promote mutual understanding, sharing the message of peace and friendship with all the people around the world." The international event drew nearly 2 million visitors from other parts of China and abroad, on top of the sixteen thousand athletes and officials participating in the Summer Olympics and seven thousand in the Paralympics. As with other Scripture distributions, permission from the authorities needed to be obtained. This was even more necessary for a highly regarded, major international event. Would consent be given?

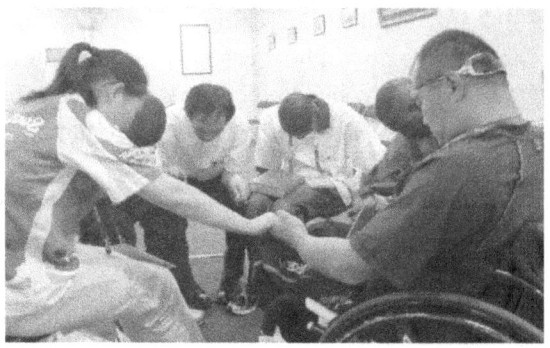

A pastor praying with athletes at the Beijing Olympic Village, 2008.

In December 2007, eight months ahead of the Olympics, good news came. The occasion was the 50-millionth Bible celebration at APC. Minister Ye Xiaowen of the State Administration for Religious Affairs, an invited guest at the celebration, announced in his congratulatory speech that Scriptures printed at APC would be made available at the Beijing Olympics! It was a significant development in UBS Bible ministry's support of the Churches in China—the first time that UBS was partnering with the Churches in China for an international event on a massive scale.

Another breakthrough came just three months before the event. The Beijing Organizing Committee granted CCC/TSPM permission to use their official emblem free of charge on the cover of the bilingual Four Gospel Portions—the first time the committee has done so without charge! This good news was announced by Elder Fu, with applause from the audience, at the opening ceremony of APC's new and larger site on May 18, 2008. It was a double joy! Without further delay, APC printed fifty thousand copies of the Chinese-English Four Gospel Portions with the emblem, supported by UBS, to be made available for athletes, coaches, and officials participating in the Olympic Games. Another fifty thousand copies were later printed.

The special edition of the Chinese-English Four Gospel Portions in the Today's Chinese Version and the Good News Translation, used with permission from UBS and American Bible Society respectively, 2008.

Three months later, at the Olympic Village chapel and churches in Beijing Olympics and other venue cities—Qingdao (venue for sailing); Shanghai, Shenyang, Tianjin, Qinhuangdao (venues for football preliminaries)—the Word of God in the Four Gospel Portions was within reach of anyone who wanted to read it.

In addition, another ten thousand copies of the Chinese-English Bible (CUV/ESV) and thirty thousand copies of the Chinese-English Catholic New Testament (NRSV/SBV) printed by APC were made available during the Olympics. Places of worship within the Olympic Village were also set up by the Beijing Olympics Organizing Committee to provide religious services for participants. The churches in Beijing was asked to provide the religious personnel to man the chapel and to conduct worship services and prayers.

The Chinese-English Bible (CUV/ESV) was published with the help of UBS and the British and Foreign Bible Society (BFBS). BFBS holds the international publishing rights to the ESV from its publisher, Crossway, and this was the first time that ESV was published and distributed in Mainland China! Praise God that Bible and Scripture portions were also available at the churches in Beijing for sale and distribution to Chinese visitors to Beijing.

The churches in Beijing also opened their doors to welcome visitors to their worship services. Many Christians volunteered during the Olympics. The Beijing Olympics was, as Elder Fu Xianwei said, "not only a sporting event." While the winning athletes received their precious and hard-won medals at the Olympics, we know that many others received the everlasting Word of God and "an inheritance that is imperishable, undefiled, and unfading, kept in heaven" (1 Pet 1:4) for them.

Scripture Portions during the COVID-19 Pandemic

The idea of a Scripture portion for the COVID-19 pandemic came before the global health crisis took place. On a visit to the Brazil Bible Society bookstore in the summer of 2017, my colleague saw a series of bookmarks that caught her eye. The series was entitled "Come to Me," printed with Bible verses inviting people to come to Jesus with their pain and sorrows.

She immediately thought of the Chinese believers and how they would benefit from these bookmarks with selected verses from the Bible, especially the Psalms, addressing different human emotions—fear, anxiety, anger, distrust, hopelessness, grief.

Copies of the Scripture portion, "Come to Me," were distributed amid the COVID-19 pandemic.

Upon returning to Singapore, she shared the idea with church partners in Jiangsu Christian Council / TSPM, who readily took up the idea. As China has urbanized and developed at a breakneck speed, its people have experienced emotional and psychological distress. It is estimated that 173 million people in China have a mental disorder,[2] and many of them do not seek treatment due to the stigma related to mental illnesses. The churches in China saw the value of such a booklet.

After some discussions, it was agreed that instead of separate bookmarks, a booklet of the same title and similar content would be produced. However, for various reasons there was a delay in the design and production of the booklet. "We spent more time on this than on other Scripture portions. There were many rounds of reviews and editing!" she recalled.

---

2 *The Lancet*, "Mental Health in China."

It was only in the fall of 2019 at the beginning of the COVID-19 pandemic and worldwide lockdown that the copies of booklets were ready to be distributed. The timing was perfect. The *Come to Me* booklets, filled with carefully selected Bible verses and photos inviting people to come to Jesus with their fears and anxieties, were distributed just as the pandemic hit China. Praise God for the positive feedback from recipients as their spirits were uplifted by the Word of God.

Mdm. Li* from Jiangsu Province was one recipient. What could be worse than having to live under the fear of the relatively unknown virus that was spreading around the world? For Li, it was battling tuberculosis at the same time. As the Chinese saying goes, it was "adding frost to snow." Confronted with her own mortality, Li was gripped by a deep sense of helplessness. Yet nobody is beyond the reach of our loving Savior. Li's Christian friend, Zhang, passed her a copy of the *Come to Me* booklet after knowing that her friend was in distress. As Li read the booklet, she found her anxiety and sorrow gradually lifted and replaced with a sense of peace. God was speaking to her through the Bible verses. She came to Jesus in her helplessness, and she discovered a truth: God is greater than any disease. By faith, she received Jesus as her Lord and Savior and is attending church with Zhang!

Mdm. Liu Maohua, recipient of the *Beyond Disaster* booklet, Shandong, 2020.

At the beginning of the COVID-19 pandemic, another Scripture portion introduced to the churches in China was *Beyond Disaster*. It is a spiritual first aid developed by American Bible Society that helps people understand and process their emotions, struggles, and questions arising from the aftermath of trauma by taking their pain to the cross of Jesus.

The resource was introduced to the Nanjing Union Theological Seminary. Prof. Yan Xiyu and his team in the publication department of the seminary looked at the material, which was already translated into Chinese, and saw the value of making it available to people. They believed that it was important to help people deal with trauma, especially with the onslaught of the pandemic. After making some adaptations to the material, it was sent for printing with the support of UBS. Thus far, 100,000 copies have been printed and distributed to the churches in China.

For Liu Maohua of Shandong Province, *Beyond Disaster* came at the right time. She was experiencing multiple stressors in life. Like many others, she was worried that her family would be infected by COVID-19, especially her husband who was working. In addition, her grown son's marriage was on the rocks, and her thirteen-year-old grandson was not managing his emotions well. She said, "Thank God for the booklet, which has relevant verses to deal with specific emotional distress. It has been a great help to me in managing stress with the Word of God and by going to him." Liu found the booklet so helpful that she shared the contents of the booklet with her family and friends on social media. "Praise God that I could share with my son and grandson from the booklet. My grandson has opened up to me now with his struggles. The booklet also provided me with opportunities to share about Jesus at my workplace!"

In Season and Out of Season

Li Mengyu came to faith after reading the Gospel booklet *No Longer Lonely*, Henan.

Over the years, a wide array of Scripture portions and Gospel booklets have been produced, and millions of copies have been distributed. These booklets feature themes like loneliness, God's love for the world, finding hope and direction in life, the wonders of creation, as well as testimonies of Chinese Christians and famous personalities.

It would take another chapter to give an account of how each Scripture portion and Gospel booklet was developed and produced and its impact, but here is some selected feedback on these booklets based on various themes, which we hope will bless your heart and inspire you.

Yang Weiping, age thirty, from Henan Province, came to faith through reading the *GPS of Life*, a Gospel booklet on finding hope and direction in life, which contains the Gospel of John and quotes by Christian personalities. She said,

> I received the *GPS of Life* from some Christian friends who visited me when I was hospitalized. Having nothing else to do, I read the booklet cover to cover. When I finished, I was filled with remorse at not having recognized God's grace before. Now, I understand God's love for sinners, including myself. I have struggled with living a morally upright life and have done wrong in many ways. God's Word is powerful. Now, I want to walk closely with him and live a holy life as his child. I have recommended this booklet to my friends. I hope God's Word will bring new life to them as well.

Xiao Ye, a migrant worker from Jiangsu Province, received *The Lord Protects You*, a booklet consisting of selected Bible verses primarily from Psalms, Luke, Mark, 2 Corinthians, and Jeremiah. He also came to faith. He said, "I have seen lots of suffering around me and concluded that human comfort will never be enough. Then I read this booklet and got to know that there is a Higher Being protecting us. In the past, I used to think that there must be some kind of 'superpower' in the universe, but I did not know who this God was. Now I know that he is Jesus. I believe in Jesus now!"

Li Qiang, from Henan Province, was a wifebeater with a skeptical mind. He was given *My Cup Overflows*, a booklet featuring the Gospel of Matthew and the conversion testimony of a Chinese lady. When he read the booklet, he wondered to himself, "Can God really be so good?" When he came to the Gospel of Matthew, he felt the weight of his sin and knew he was wrong to beat his wife. He broke down and repented. The next morning, Li Qiang went to church and asked Jesus to be his Lord and Savior. Li's home life, once filled with violence, was now a haven.

Pu Meili, a shop owner, found that leaving the booklet *A Gift* at her shop was an excellent way to reach unbelievers. First produced and published by the Bible Society of Singapore, *A Gift* presents the gospel message in a comic form and addresses the core issues of life that are relevant to society today. She said, "*A Gift* is a good book. Customers who enter my shop would pick up a copy and read it; hence, the seed of the gospel is planted!"

Some high school students were given *A Gift* by their family members. Xu Gang, an eighteen-year-old high school graduate said, "This booklet says that many scientists are Christian. It surprises me! I didn't know this before as I had this deep impression that science and God cannot co-exist!" Another eighteen-year-old student who was given *A Gift* observed, "This is the first time I read that some scientists named in this booklet are Christians. The life stories of these scientists are available in my school textbooks, but no one has ever told me that they believed in God!"

Christian businesswomen and staff who distribute Scripture portions to customers. The portions are published by the Jiangsu Christian Council / TSPM with help from UBS, Nanjing, 2010.

In 2012, the Gospel booklet *A Living Hope*, featuring the Gospel of John and the testimony of the American Chinese NBA player Jeremy Lin, was given out to churches. Good TV Broadcasting Corp had kindly given permission for the use of Jeremy Lin's testimony and photograph. Many Chinese Christians said Lin's testimony was a good conversation starter for them to reach out to their family and friends. Twenty-five-year-old Chen Xiaowei said, "People may not have the patience to read through the whole Gospel.

Pu Meili, age forty-one, displays Scripture portions in all three of her shops in Nanjing. The booklets are published by the Jiangsu Christian Council / TSPM with help from UBS, Jiangsu, 2010.

Scripture portions are offered to customers in this clothes shop. The booklets are published by the Jiangsu Christian Council / TSPM with help from UBS, Jiangsu, 2010.

A Light for Every Season

Gospel booklet featuring Li Yan's testimony, *Run toward the Goal*.

Zheng Yu Man, Chen Xiao Wei, Run Li Fan with Gospel booklet featuring testimony of Jeremy Lin.

Scripture portion *Words of Encouragement* was distributed to people affected by the earthquake, Sichuan, 2008.

Jeremy Lin, a Taiwanese American basketball player, being interviewed by Good TV.

With Jeremy Lin's testimony as an opening, sharing how God's Word has guided his life, people are attracted to read on." According to Chen, she and her two other friends gave out about one hundred copies of *A Living Hope* to their unbelieving friends and family members. We pray that many among them will come to faith in Jesus.

Over the past few decades, millions of Scripture portions, selections, and Gospel booklets have been printed and distributed for free to churches across China and at special international events. This is astounding considering how China used to be a Bible desert just forty years ago. With these booklets, gospel seeds were scattered and sown. Some have landed on good soil and grown. While we do not have all the names of the Chinese people who read these booklets and received Jesus into their lives, we know that their names are all written in the book of life. They are known by the Lord, who spoke to them in each of their unique circumstances and met them where they were. Praise God!

11
Fan into Flames

Scripture Literacy Classes and Discipleship Resources for Believers

This Book of the Law shall not depart from your mouth, but you shall meditate on it day and night, so that you may be careful to do according to all that is written in it.
—Joshua 1:8

Scripture literacy classes not only teach us how to read and write, but more importantly, they also teach us about God's truth. And God's truth protects us from the lies of the evil one.
—Sun Yingli, age fifty-five, Shandong Province

A Second Chance

Mdm. Chen Lianzhen (first row, left) with her fellow Scripture literacy class students, Chongqing, 2014.

Chen Lianzhen, age seventy, a retired rice farmer, woke up early one morning to head to church, even though it was not a Sunday. It was because of a special event at church that day—Chen and sixty others were attending their first Scripture literacy class! A sense of anticipation saturated the air as the booklets and Bibles for the class were distributed. Zhang Jianhua, the class teacher, who is also a preacher at the church, began teaching the class the first lesson on God's love. The sanctuary was then filled with resounding echoes as the whole class recited after her: "God loves me; God loves you; God loves him; God loves us."

The Scripture literacy class was held at Mengen Church in Baiyang, a quiet county town in Wanzhou District, northeast of Chongqing. Mengen Church is situated at the upper reaches of the famed Three Gorges of the Yangtze River. "Baiyang," a term which literally means "white sheep" in Chinese, is a town with about fifty thousand people, many of whom are either very old or very young because most adults have moved to the cities to find work.

According to Zhang Jianhua, age forty-four, the only preacher in Baiyang, the church served about four hundred believers. Seventy percent of the church members were illiterate. They had never dreamed that they would be given a second chance to learn to read and write. Like many others of her generation, Madam Chen did not have any formal education. "I was the eldest child in my family, and being a female meant that the chance of me going to school was zero!" remarked Madam Chen. "I am extremely happy to be given a chance to learn how to read and write at this age!"

Gaining Literacy through Reading the Bible

Madam Chen's story was collected during a trip to Chongqing in 2015. This was one of my best trips because I met with elderly Chinese believers who were so joyous to learn to read and write through Scripture literacy classes. Many of them were brimming with gratitude to God and to overseas Christians who helped support the classes.

Madam Chen was one of the 65 million people, age fifteen and above, who were illiterate in China according to a 2010 World Bank statistic. The number was probably higher if the semiliterate were included. The Chinese word for illiterate is "文盲," which can be loosely translated as "word blind." In the Teochew language (spoken in southern China), the colloquial term for illiterate is "blind cow." Perhaps to the Chinese, not being able to read and write is akin to the plight of being blind.

The illiterate are shut out from the world of the written word—road signs, menus, signs at public places, letters, and documents, not to mention books, newspapers, etc. They see the written words but are blind to their meanings. This makes them dependent on others and opens them up to possible harm and danger. Worse still, in many cultures including the Chinese, the knowledgeable and learned are highly esteemed, while the illiterates are usually looked down upon. Undeniably, many illiterates suffer from inferiority and low self-esteem.

Rev. Yin Jianhui came to know the Lord through reading the Bible for a group of elderly believers in the 1980s.

For Chinese Christians who are illiterate, there is one more struggle and a far-reaching one—not being able to read the Bible for themselves. As the churches in China grew exponentially between the 1980s and 2000s, it was observed that the majority of the Christians were from the rural regions of China. Among them were many women who did not have a chance to go to school due to poverty or being born during the war-torn period of the 1930s to 1940s. As one elderly Chinese Christian woman said, "There wasn't enough to fill our stomachs in those days, let alone go to school!"

However, as more Bibles were made available, some illiterate Chinese Christians were sharing amazing testimonies. They started as illiterate or semiliterate and could only recognize a few Chinese characters, like their own names. But after joining a Bible reading group at a church, listening to and following the Bible text, they gradually gained some level of literacy. Some illiterate Christians were able to recognize more and more characters after a few rounds of reading through the Bible. As one Christian lady who was a part of a Bible reading group in her village in Hunan Province said, "Before, I was illiterate, so at first I turned the Bible upside down. But now I've got more confidence, and I manage to read."

In some cases, non-Christian neighbors who were literate were asked to help read the Bible for the Christians. Since reading materials and Bibles were not in abundance, especially in the 1980s, literate people were willing to help so that they could use the opportunity to practice their reading. In the process, some were themselves converted by helping to read the Bible!

This was the testimony of Rev. Yin Jianhui, age fifty-one, from Hunan Province. In 1983, Yin was asked by a group of seven or eight elderly people in her neighborhood to read the Bible to them because they were illiterate. She was in her late teens and had just finished high school. Thinking that it was good to help people, she agreed. "I would read a passage of the Bible to them, and then they would discuss and explain it. One elderly lady, who owned the Bible and had been a Christian for many years before the Cultural Revolution, would explain what we had just heard. I would sit and listen to the explanations, then read them another passage, and so on. Six months later, I became a Christian!"

Yin Jianhui went on to be an ordained pastor and was appointed the president of the Yiyang Municipal Christian Council in Hunan Province, overseeing the work of 265 churches and continuing to read and teach the Bible to believers in China.

Praise God for using illiterate Christians to lead literate people to him!

UBS's Involvement

As the Christian population in rural China grew, the number of adults needing help to read the Bible increased. Many who could not read the Bible were feeling helpless. So churches tried conducting Scripture literacy classes to help illiterate adult believers. Many churches were amazed by the turnout as even some younger believers came for classes. People in their forties and fifties wanted to learn to read too. However, due to a lack of resources and manpower, not much

A Scripture literacy class in Shaanxi, 2013.

could be done, and most churches could not sustain the classes in the long run. Part of the reason was that churches in China were growing so fast that some churches did not even have a permanent pastor or preacher, let alone a Scripture literacy teacher or facilitator. What could be the solution?

Literacy class teacher with students, Shaanxi, 2013.

The request came after a UBS delegation's visit to Anhui Christian Council / TSPM in the early 2000s. There, the church leaders shared another problem that was common in most churches in China—many preachers and seminary students were not adequately supported. They either depended on meager family savings or financial support from their spouses or parents. Some preachers also took up part-time jobs to supplement their income, which took away time from church ministry and their families. The UBS delegates present asked themselves what they could do to help the church.

An idea came to Kua Wee Seng, UBS CP director (1999–2021) and the leader of the delegation. Why not ask the preachers and seminary students to be Scripture literacy class teachers while UBS funded the Bibles, class materials, and teacher allowances? The proposal was readily accepted, and Anhui became the pilot province. A similar model was adopted in the registered churches in Henan, Jiangsu, and Shandong during the next couple of years. Later, partnerships also started with other provinces to conduct Scripture literacy classes.

The Top Five Impacts of the Scripture Literacy Classes for Adults

As classes were run, stories from the churches poured in, testifying to the power of learning to read God's Word. Here are the top five impacts of the Scripture literacy classes gleaned from interviews done by UBS staff and me.

1. Bringing about Spiritual Growth and Development

The writer of Hebrews said, "Anyone who lives on milk, being still an infant, is not acquainted with the teaching about righteousness" (5:13). And in 1 Corinthians 3:8–9, Paul said that the Christians at Corinth were not ready for solid food as they were still infants in Christ. As churches in China grow in number, they need to also grow spiritually from infants to mature adults. They need to learn to feed on the word themselves. Praise God that through the Scripture literacy classes, many illiterate Christians were beginning to read the Word of God themselves for their spiritual growth and development.

Yang Qinggu (right) with a fellow Scripture literacy student, Chongqing, 2014.

Just being able to turn to the right Bible passage was an accomplishment. Yang Qinggu, age sixty-six, a corn and potato farmer from Chongqing shared, "Before attending the Scripture literacy classes, I used to feel anxious during the service, not knowing how to turn to the Bible passages. And I also cannot follow the sermon well. I lagged behind the others who could read. Now I am very happy that I can read and turn to the right Bible passage!"

Elder Lei Gengtang, age fifty, from Shaanxi Province, shared about the challenges faced by illiterate Christians he was shepherding. "It's a challenge to learn about their faith. Because they can't read or write, they are not able to remember what they have heard since they can't write it down. It's hard to see spiritual growth without literacy." The village church was seeing change as Scripture literacy classes were launched. Wu Liuxuan, a fifty-one-year-old fruit farmer, came to know the Lord three years ago. She never went to school and had found it hard to remember what was preached every week. On the reasons for coming to the Scripture literacy class, she shared, "I want to learn to read and write so that I can make sermon notes and spread the gospel. Now, not only am I learning to make notes, I also want to attend Bible school one day! People laugh at me, but I will do it step by step."

Many illiterate believers desire to draw close to God by reading his word, but they are often discouraged by the many words they do not know. With Scripture literacy, many were

Liu Guanxian, Chongqing, 2015.

motivated to read the Bible. Liu Guanxian, age fifty-eight, a crab farmer from Jiangsu Province, relished the opportunity to learn how to read and write God's Word. Coming from a big family, Liu did not have a chance to go to school. After knowing the Lord a few years ago, Liu began learning to pray and sing hymns at a Christian meeting where he and other believers gathered, but they stopped short of reading the Bible because they were all illiterate.

"It used to be impossible for us to read the Bible on our own. With the class, thanks to the donation of UBS, we are able to read and understand the Bible better! Bible reading is important as it will enable believers to resist the assaults of the evil one. Because we have a better knowledge of the Word of God, we experience more peace and joy. Now, I am so glad to be able to make simple notes during sermons and review them at home after the service!"

One of the Scripture literacy teachers, Duan Linhong from Shaanxi Province, shared in her reflections: "During class time, we prayed together and sang praises to God. In addition to writing and reciting Bible text, I require students to read the Psalms and Proverbs. The Word of God is the bread of life. Not only do students learn to read the Bible, but they are also fed spiritually by the Spirit of God through the reading of his word."

2. Defending against Cults

In 1999, the September issue of *Tian Feng*, a CCC/TSPM publication, ran a feature article on the threat and influence of cults in China. As the new millennium, 2000, was approaching, false teachers and heretical groups were on the rise, spreading their doomsday message and bringing chaos and confusion to church congregations in China. One example was the *Dongfang Shandian* (Eastern Lightning), which teaches that Jesus Christ has already come to earth a second time in the bodily form of a Chinese woman. Another was *Mentuhui* (The Disciples), a cult started in the early 1990s by Ji Sanbao, a farmer from Shaanxi who claimed to be the second Christ. Cults prey on illiterate or semiliterate rural believers who are not able to read the Bible and have difficulty finding out the truth for themselves. They are not able to fact-check to ascertain if certain claims are true or false.

Zhou Yinian, a literacy participant said, "It is important to read the Bible because it is the Word of God and I want to put his word in my heart," Chongqing, 2014.

The article's writers said, "Many believers in these [rural areas and city suburbs] areas either don't own a Bible, have never read a Bible, or do not fully understand what they read in the Bible. Alongside this, many rural believers have a low educational level and a poor understanding of the faith." Like learning to tell a counterfeit dollar note from a genuine one, the writers concluded that the best defense against cults was for every believer to arm themselves with biblical truths.

Scripture literacy classes would be the first important step toward that defense. Hu Jiangrong, forty-one, a pastor from Shaanxi Province, shared, "When they can read, then we can show them how to differentiate between the truth and false teachings of the cult groups."

The urgency for rural believers to gain Scripture literacy continues after 2000. In fact, in 2016, the Chinese government reported that there were fourteen officially named cults, twelve of which were related to Christianity. Today, CCC/TSPM continues to alert believers via its official website about the false teachings of the cults and their infiltration strategies.

In truth, it has been observed that the suspension of church services at the height of the COVID-19 pandemic has created a vacuum allowing cults to take advantage of vulnerable believers. Coupled with a lower level of digital literacy, elderly believers who access their church's official WeChat account (an all-in-one messaging app) for audio sermons have become more susceptible to the pull of false teachings when they are misled to cult websites.

As one Scripture literacy student from Chongqing, Chen Guangju, age seventy-three, said, "God's Word is the lamp unto my feet and the light unto my path. If I did not learn to read God's Word, I would not know right from wrong. I would be lost. Scripture literacy is important for those of us who have never been to school before."

3. Gaining Self-Confidence and Dignity

It has been well researched and attested that attaining literacy can improve one's self-esteem and confidence. Being able to read and write opens a person up to more social interaction with others, leading to a healthier life. Attending Scripture literacy classes is a practical way for illiterate Christians to step out of their shyness and comfort zone and break free from psychological and spiritual barriers to learning. This is perhaps especially so for younger illiterate believers.

A Scripture literacy teacher from Henan Province, Wei, recounted her experience teaching a young lady who had never attended a single day of school. Her mother died prematurely, so she had to support her family and look after her younger siblings. Wei shared: "When I bent down close to her to look at her writing, she covered them up with her hands because she felt she wrote badly and was too shy to show me. Tears were swelling up her eyes, and she wanted to give up learning to read and write. I paused to counsel, comfort, and gently teach her, hand-over-hand, going over some of the more difficult words. Gradually, she became more at ease and was even able to write "以马内利" (Immanuel).

For older believers too, gaining literacy is an important personal milestone. Li Fenglian, age sixty-nine, recounted her experience with holding a pen in her Scripture literacy class: "In this class, I held a pen for the very first time in my life. I trembled initially, but now I hold the pen with greater confidence. I am overjoyed that I am able to read and write now after attending the class since 2009. My class teacher is very caring and approachable; she patiently explains the difficult characters to us. Thank God for this Scripture literacy class!"

Other Scripture literacy students shared the simple joy of being able to get around when traveling, recognize public toilet signs, read information boards at bus stops, and study with their grandchildren.

4. Drawing People into the Kingdom

These Scripture literacy classes were free for all, and among the people who came were seekers of the faith. Church leaders from Shaanxi Province shared the following insights in 2014. "As a result of starting these classes three years ago, the illiteracy rate has been halved from 40 percent to 20 percent," reported Elder Lei. "I think literacy classes are going to double up the speed of (church) growth." He shared that not only did the classes benefit the Christians but they had also attracted non-Christians. The church at Meng Zhuang village had seen thirteen come to faith. Rev. Hu Jiangrong from the same province had also seen growth in his congregation as a result of the literacy classes in Zhu Lin village: "Ten percent of the class students have come to faith. I am so happy to see these people whom I have known my whole life coming into the kingdom of God!"

Women take part in a literacy class at Meng Zhuang (Dream Village) church, Shaanxi, 2013.

In another rural part of China, Scripture literacy classes are attracting family members to know the Word of God. In a testimony collected in 2020, Zhao Ying, a young lady who attended Scripture literacy class with her grandma, said, "I think the class is particularly meaningful. Besides supporting my grandma to learn, I can also listen to the teacher sharing Bible stories. I know more about the Bible now than ever before. I enjoy coming to these classes more and more because I can feel the love, care, and peace here."

A lady with her grandma at a Scripture literacy class, Gansu, 2020.

5. Energizing and Edifying the Whole Body of Christ

A Scripture literacy teacher from Henan Province, Zhang, was impressed and encouraged by her students' hunger to learn. "The response for these classes was overwhelming." She added, "The majority of these students were women and older folks who have had little or no formal education at all. As we progressed, their attentiveness in class, diligence, and hunger for learning touched my heart so much that they spurred me on towards giving my best in teaching."

A particular quote from an elderly Scripture literacy student continues to motivate UBS staff and donors to treasure the Word of God. When asked why she bothered to learn to read the Bible in her old age, she replied, "Precisely because I know I am going to meet my Lord soon, I do not want to be guilty of not having known and read his word!"

Large print Bibles with thumb indexes are given free to Scripture literacy students.

Notebook of a Scripture literacy class student.

As believers have a renewed hunger for God's Word, they are energized to step up and serve in church. A report from Shaanxi Province shared that spiritual growth has also led to church revival—literacy teachers testified that students who had graduated from literacy classes were filled with gratitude in their hearts. Not only did they come more regularly for church meetings, but they also participated more actively in church ministries.

Praise God that, as of 2020, with the support of UBS, hundreds of thousands of illiterate Chinese Christians have been taught to recognize at least one thousand Chinese characters, enabling them to read the Bible with relative ease for their spiritual growth and development.

Moving from Scripture Literacy to Spiritual Maturity and Discipleship

There continues to be a great need for Chinese Christians to engage with God's Word for spiritual growth and maturity. While it is heartening to hear of many illiterate Christians in China learning how to recognize the words in the Bible and getting into the word themselves, it is the beginning of a spiritual discipleship journey toward maturity and Christlikeness. And this journey has been a challenging one for the churches in China.

In my interactions with Chinese church leaders, this is often what I heard: Due to the severe lack of pastors and Christian resources in China, many rural Christians are not able to be properly discipled. Coupled with the fact that pastors and preachers are usually not paid adequately, it has not been easy for the churches in China to raise up full-time workers. Consequently, with the lack of proper shepherding and guidance, some Chinese Christians either remain baby Christians or become nominal and apathetic believers.

The situation was well delineated by Rev. Chen Yiping,[1] a veteran pastor from Fujian Province, who wrote, "The churches in China are growing, but there is a potential crisis. As the number of believers keeps climbing, the quality is compromised. Look around in the churches, there are many sheep without shepherds. Whenever I visit rural churches, I come across many believers who are not clear about their beliefs. Some are just blindly following. As a result, they are also susceptible to the lure of cult groups."[2]

To support the churches in China in their urgent need to build up believers, in 2019 UBS started to come alongside some Provincial Christian Council / TSPM by providing

---

1 His testimony is featured in chapter 6.
2 From the preface of *The Abundant Life*.

a series of discipleship materials, *The Abundant Life* and *The Abundant Grace*, published by the CCC/TSPM. The first covers the basics of Christian faith and teachings; the second covers the basics of understanding the Bible and how to read it for personal growth. The series, which is designed for small group settings, comes with a leader's guide.

Praise God that with the provision of the discipleship materials, some of the churches have reported encouraging testimonies. One of them was a church in Feicheng County, west of Shandong Province.

Elder Wang, Shandong, 2022.

Like in other churches, Elder Wang shared that they have members who only come on special occasions like Easter and Christmas, members who are not concerned about the church and not serving in any ministry. Some have backslidden and stopped coming altogether. With the COVID-19 pandemic leading to the suspension of church services, she saw that the spiritual life of the believers was adversely affected.

It was at this same time when the discipleship materials had arrived at their church. "To our surprise, we realized that the materials we received from UBS were just what we needed!" Elder Wang and Preacher Zhen Shasha, her co-worker, then began using the materials in small groups held in the church whenever possible, pouring into the lives of the believers. And the Spirit of the Lord began to work among them.

A participant of *Abundant Life* and *Abundant Grace* small group study, Shandong, 2021.

Elder Wang shared, "God surprises us! From one small group, we have grown to more than twenty groups now representing about 240 people. And from our church, we have gone to

Discipleship training at a church, Gansu, 2021.

share this small group format using the discipleship materials with fourteen other churches in Feicheng! More and more people are interested in joining a small group." In fact, at one time, the church ran out of materials and had to reuse them while some group members hand copied the book.

What is the draw of this small group format combined with the usage of the discipleship material? According to Elder Wang, a small group setting helps the church in two areas—it encourages relationship building and drives pastoral care.

"In small groups, people find it easier to ask questions, open up, and share. When relationships are built, there is mutual support, love, and a sense of belonging. Secondly, as we go through the discipleship materials, it helps us to know where people are in their spiritual life and how we can come in to shepherd them more effectively."

A small group using *The Abundant Life* discipleship materials, Gansu, 2021.

Elder Wang and Preacher Zhen were especially encouraged to see members who were previously diffident opening up to share and actively participating in the discussion. "Regardless of a person's educational level, he is able to build his spiritual life in the Lord and benefit from the spiritual disciplines taught in the materials. I believe that when our spiritual lives are being built, we will bear fruit," shared Preacher Zhen.

Praise God that Elder Wang's church has seen personal spiritual growth in its members. "They now understand the importance of spending time with the Lord, and even those who had little education have started journaling," shared Preacher Zhen. "One of the key benefits from the small Bible learning group is accountability to have their personal time with the Lord regularly."

Elder Wang added, "More have also stepped up to serve in church. People are on fire for the Lord now. They are bringing the gospel to their family and friends. Backslidden believers are also coming back to the Lord. We truly see God at work among us. Praise the Lord!"

Besides helping to provide existing discipleship materials, UBS is also supporting Churches in China in their attempt to develop a more systematic approach to biblical discipleship training. Plans are also underway to adapt and develop contextualized discipleship materials that would resonate more with Chinese believers. The hope is that when Chinese Christians are discipled and grounded in the Word of God, they will grow in maturity, live out biblical values, and become the salt and light to the world in which they live.

It is exciting to see that, through Scripture literacy for adults and biblical discipleship programs, Chinese believers are getting help to be more engaged and anchored in God's Word. Many are growing deeper in their faith and walk with the Lord and some have embraced biblical discipleship as their lifelong journey. In the next two chapters, we shall see how families and those who are hurting emotionally have turned to the Word of God to find guidance, strength, and light.

12
Igniting Young Minds

Bible Ministry for the Family

But Jesus said, "Let the little children come to me and do not hinder them, for to such belongs the kingdom of heaven."
—Matthew 19:14

The *Pictorial Bible Stories* explains the origins of the world and human beings, and the spiritual lives of Bible characters. It helps the young to understand God, his wonderful creation, and his truths.
—Ren Hui, young people's ministry leader from Shaanxi Province, early 2000s

Passing on the Baton of Faith

Jiangsu Province: A Rural Village in the Early 1970s
The Cultural Revolution had been happening for a few years. Tonight, the sky was jet black and the stars shone brightly. Junior Zhang wondered if people would still come. It was almost ten o'clock. Being the only Christian family in the village, his mother would host meetings at their house every week. This week was no exception, even though more people had recently been rounded up by the Red Guards. Slowly, his house was filled. One, three, five, ten, fifteen, twenty. The meeting started with prayer, and then they would sing softly. His mother, being schooled, read the Bible—the only Bible around, handwritten beautifully by his granduncle. She exhorted the group to cling to their faith. Junior Zhang was impressed that they were all leaning forward and taking in every word being read and preached. He too listened. And they did this week after week.

Early in the morning, while the air was still chilly and Junior Zhang was still asleep, he could sense his mother's presence by his bedside. He opened his eyes and saw that his mother's eyes were closed. She was praying for him, just as she did every morning.

The situation for the Christians got tougher. There was an eighty-year-old woman in their village, Preacher Wang, who was put under house arrest. To support her financially, Christians in the village collected donations and tasked Junior Zhang with the job of delivering the money to her. Eventually, Preacher Wang was called up for public interrogation. The Red Guards dashed this frail old lady against the ground for refusing to deny Christ. The scene haunted the young boy. That night, Zhang prayed to God that he would one day serve him as a faithful preacher like brave Granny Wang.

Years later, Zhang trained to be a preacher and became an ordained pastor. Since China's opening in the 1980s, the Christian population in Jiangsu Province has mushroomed to more than 2.4 million. Serving as the chairman of Jiangsu Provincial TSPM, which has the oversight of more than 4,600 churches and meeting points, as well as being the president of Jiangsu Seminary, Rev. Zhang Keyun is recognized today as the leader of the Jiangsu Protestant churches. His vision is to raise up China's next generation of pastors and preachers, and to this end, he has partnered with UBS on several Bible ministry projects for the seminary and churches in Jiangsu.

Rev. Zhang Keyun in his office, Jiangsu, 2015.

Shandong Province, 1990s

China experienced an economic boom after Deng Xiaoping took the country on the path of reform and opening up. Little Yuekai was under the care of his grandparents as both his dad and mom were out working. Night had just fallen, and all was quiet. Yuekai was looking forward to a bedtime ritual with his grandmother—reading Bible stories. His granddad was a preacher who suffered during the Cultural Revolution, and his grandma was an excellent Bible storyteller. Tonight, as they read the story of David and Goliath, Yuekai wondered how tall David was. As tall as him? His granny's soft and gentle voice fell into his ears and ignited his

Bible lecturer Liu Yuekai, Shandong, 2019.

imagination as he brought the story into his dreamland. He fell asleep on his granny's lap with the Bible beside them. This was how he was raised—cradled by Bible stories and the faith of his grandparents. Day by day, his love for the Bible grew.

Today, Yuekai, age thirty-four, is a seminary lecturer on Old Testament survey, Christian education, and applied theology. He teaches both seminary students and lay preachers from Shandong Province. But there are three others to whom he is especially anxious to pass on his love for the word—his three little children. Following the tradition of his granny, he and his wife read Bible stories to their children and gather them twice a week for family worship. He desires to raise them up just as his granny did—in the word and the faith.

Hebei Province, 2014

By now, the economic miracle in China was well known. Life has improved vastly for many Chinese. Most families have only one child, and these children have been given the title "little emperors." Many of them have a sense of entitlement, but it seemed that Jianan was different.

She was the youngest volunteer at her local church. Her responsibility was to lead four- and five-year-olds in singing, tell them stories from the Bible, serve them drinks and biscuits, comfort them when they cry, and last but not least, bring them to the toilet. "Two years ago, I saw that there is a great need in my local church, so I decided to serve here," shared Jianan earnestly. "Even though there are challenging days like when the kids throw tantrums, I see those times as opportunities for me to learn to be patient and to depend on God through prayer. God helps me to see each child as his unique creation." How did a young person grow up to have such a positive and selfless attitude? "Since I was five years old, my grandma would read the Bible to me and sing hymns with me. She would do that without fail every day. She is the person who has influenced my life the most," recalled Jianan, who now reads through the Bible once every year. "My parents would also have family devotional time together, especially on days when my father is home and not away on business trips. They would teach me from the Bible and pray with me."

Jianan with her mother, Hebei, 2016.

Jianan especially enjoys reading the Psalms and Proverbs. She said, "Even though what schools teach is also important as it will be useful for making a living, what the Bible teaches is more valuable because the Word of God lasts forever, it teaches us wisdom and truths that the world can't."

From One Generation to the Next

These three interviews were conducted on different occasions for different purposes, but I was amazed as I saw the common thread in them. Through the generations, many Chinese Christian families have been passing on the baton of faith to their young. They are sharing their love for God and his word with their children. We see in the lives of Rev. Zhang, Yuekai, and Jianan the influence and impact of the family and community of faith on their own faith. While each generation has to know God for themselves and personalize their faith, the journey often starts at home or in the church.

Chinese Catholics too talked about how the faith was passed down to them from their forefathers through the Bible. Sister Ren, who served in a parish, was one of them. In a testimony in 2010, she shared how the Catholic faith was passed on to her by her grandfather and father through Bible stories:

> The Bible has already started its work in me since I was a child. My forefathers were all Catholics, so my family has a strong Catholic background. As far as I can remember, when I was a child, my parents had been extremely concerned about my spiritual growth. My maternal grandfather and my father would often tell me stories from the Old Testament. As these stories were told in a creative manner, I was very captivated by them. Even today, I have vivid memories of these stories being told to me—the calling of Abraham and the testing of his faith, stories of Joseph in Egypt, etc.

However, the spiritual needs of Chinese Christian families remain huge and diverse. Not all are able to pass the baton of faith well. Moreover, the past few decades of rapid urbanization and economic transformation in China have strained families and churches. Families are more dispersed and breaking down as traditional values are not as closely observed. Living standards have gone up, causing more to focus on accumulating material possessions. Social media competes for the attention and time of both young and old, which has affected relationships across the board. The work of raising the next generation in the faith and rooted in the word has become more challenging. Of much concern to both Chinese authorities and churches is the tens of millions of children left behind in the villages as working-age adults poured into urban areas for employment.

He Cuiyang (middle), a believer from Henan, takes care of two of her grandchildren, 2016.

In light of these complex challenges, the Chinese Churches since the early 2000s have been supporting Christian families in a variety of ways—through providing Bible resources and Christian reading materials for the young, training young people's ministry leaders, supporting summer programs, and conducting biblical parenting workshops. The heart of these programs is building families centered on the Word of God, anchored in biblical truths and wisdom.

Bible Resources for the Young and Training for Adults

Coming from a non-Christian family, Kua Wee Seng, UBS CP director (1999–2021), shared that being invited by friends to attend church as a child was a precious and important part of his spiritual journey. When he visited some Chinese Churches in the early 1990s, he observed something that was concerning—parents brought their children to church for adult Sunday worship, but the children were not meaningfully engaged. He then discussed it with the pastors, and the local church soon started a childcare ministry. They began to tell Bible stories to the children, but they did not have any Bible materials for the young and requested help from UBS.

Children's Bible storybooks published by CCC/TSPM with free distribution supported by UBS, 2005.

At that time, Wee Seng and his wife were using *Pictorial Bible Stories*, published by Cook Communications Ministries in 1996, to tell Bible stories to their two young daughters. When the book was introduced to the Chinese church leaders, they saw that it would benefit the churches and Christian families with children. Work began to make it into a reality. Praise God that translation into Chinese was soon done by Christian Communications Limited, and the authorities approved printing *Pictorial Bible Stories* in a bilingual format!

In 2003, twenty thousand copies were printed and distributed to Protestant churches in China over four years with the support of UBS. Featuring one hundred Bible stories selected from the Old Testament and New Testament in Chinese and English, with colorful illustrations, this was the first major Scripture publication for the young by CCC. It especially catered to the young—those who want to read Bible stories and learn English at the same time. Copies of *Pictorial Bible Stories* were distributed to many churches, including those in Yunnan, Hebei, Hunan, Jiangsu, Chongqing, Shaanxi, and Henan.

Bible resources for young people.

Many young people who received the *Pictorial Bible Stories* gave positive feedback. One of them, eleven-year-old David from a church in Henan, said: "There used to be many things in the Bible that I did not understand, but since our church started a class for young people like me, the teachers taught us stories in the book and that has helped me to better understand the Bible." David continued, "Now I know that Jesus came to this world to save sinners like me. He wants us to love and care for one another. I want to be a good witness for Jesus."

Stories of Jesus in manga style, a young adult resource produced by CCC/TSPM.

Another recipient, Qin said, "Reading the Bible is no longer a difficult task for me. This book has simplified the Bible words, so I can now understand God's Word better. It helps me to grow as a Christian."

Song, who had read many books, said, "When I opened *Pictorial Bible Stories*,

Children holding copies of the *Pictorial Bible Stories* they use in class, Henan, 2011.

something more powerful attracted me. I am touched by God's holiness, greatness, and love for his people. I want to obey God's Word and be an obedient child of his."

At the end of each story, application questions encourage readers to bring the biblical truths they learn into their daily lives. Testimonies were shared about how lives young and old were changed as a result of churches using the *Pictorial Bible Stories* in their young people's ministries.

One such testimony came from a village church in Yunnan Province. The young people's ministry was set up in 2012 by a Christian couple, Pu Hongyan and her husband, right in the church kitchen due to a lack of space. It grew from ten to nearly one hundred young people within a few years. The couple, graduates of Nanjing Union Theological Seminary, was

Ethnic minority teacher Li Zhiqiang with children at church, Yunnan, 2018.

Children in a church looking at Scripture materials, Hunan, 2014.

Children and adults gather for an activity at a church, Henan, 2013.

grateful to receive the *Pictorial Bible Stories* as teaching material for their young people. "This is an extremely appropriate material for our ministry here. It is very readable and encourages the young to form the habit of Bible reading and to apply God's truths in our lives, myself included!" shared Mrs. Pu.

Dongqin was one of the young people in the ministry who tried to apply God's truths gleaned from the *Pictorial Bible Stories*. She used to hate her father. Like many men in the village, her father was an alcoholic. When in a drunken state, he would go into a rage, physically abusing Dongqin and her mother. Dongqin shared that she would shout back at her father and then hide and lock herself in the room. Many times, she had contemplated running away from home. She felt miserable and helpless. But after joining the young people's ministry in her church, her perspective about people changed.

"I learned that my father was enslaved to sin. I have also sinned by shouting at him. My church teacher taught me how I should respond to my father." Gradually, whenever her father was drunk, she learned to help him sober up and tried to console him. Praise God that over time, her father was so moved that he quit drinking and started attending church. Dongqin said, "I had always thought that the fault lies in other people. After attending church, I learned that we are all sinners; we will fail. But Jesus still loves us and accepts us. Slowly, I learned to also accept others, be grateful, and love others."

Praise God for the young people's ministry that came alongside the parents to nurture the faith of young people. Mrs. Pu shared, "Many parents, concerned about basic survival issues, are busy working. They need support to bring up their young ones in the Lord, to love them with the Lord's love. My heart goes out to these young ones; some are left behind with their grandparents. As the church, this is the least we can do for the young people who are the future of the church and the country."

Here is another testimony of life change that came from a church in Shaanxi Province, shared by a young people's ministry teacher, Wan Sha. She had taught a class of twenty students using *Pictorial Bible Stories*, and one of the application questions was about reaching out to and loving others who are poor and in need.

Young people's class in Hebei, 2014.

We had just finished lunch and I was doing the dishes in the kitchen. Two kids came in and asked me softly, "Teacher, can we give the leftover rice and eggs to Jing? Her parents are divorced, and her granny died of illness. The house is just left with Jing and her grandfather. They are very poor and have been collecting scraps for a living." At that moment, I felt both guilt and joy. Guilty for not knowing the needs of this girl called Jing and joy knowing that the love of God is in the hearts of these little ones. That afternoon, the kids brought me to Jing's house—it was a single small room where they did their cooking, washing, and sleeping. We also met Jing's grandfather and talked with him. When we shared with him about God, he willingly accepted Jesus into his heart and said he would go to church with Jing. I am amazed at how God has changed these kids. They used to be very rowdy and disinterested. But by God's grace, he has molded them into caring individuals, loving and looking out for one another.

Besides the *Pictorial Bible Stories*, the Chinese Churches were attempting to create relevant teaching materials to engage the young ones. Amid a lack of teaching curriculum, a significant moment came when the authorities approved a set of materials known as the *Good Fruit Series* developed by the Zhejiang Christian Council / TSPM and published by CCC/TSPM. It was one of the first contextualized teaching materials for the young by the Churches in China. In addition, reading rooms with Christian books were set up in churches to inspire and encourage young people to form good reading habits and discover biblical truths found in stories and comics.

Teachers browsing Scripture materials for the young (*Good Fruit Series*), 2014.

Besides Bible resources, Chinese churches were also training more teachers to lead the young. In 2015, a church in Hunan Province held summer training for leaders of young people's ministry. Forty leaders from thirteen districts across the province gathered at You County Christian Church for a time of equipping and fellowship. Some of the topics covered were pedagogy of young people's ministry, the process of teaching and learning, understanding young people's needs, creative ways of Scripture memory and Bible storytelling, and classroom management. Time was also allocated for lesson demonstrations where teachers could evaluate one another.

Sixty-eight-year-old Mdm. Tang Songbo from Hengyang County, the oldest participant in the group, shared, "Young people's ministry concerns the growth and revival of the church in China. If we do not do anything now, the church may not have a future."

"We know that children are going to be leaders of society. They are people who will shape the future. It is so important for us as teachers to be led by God, to continuously learn and be equipped so that we can teach the children well," shared Ms. Lei Xiaoyu, age fifty-one, from Changde City in northern Hunan.

It was a training that the teachers looked forward to, with a few of them traveling for about ten hours to reach You County. "I'm very thankful for this opportunity to be in the body of Christ, to meet fellow teachers who share the same burden!" said Ting Fei, age forty-five.

Zeng Zhenhua, age twenty-eight, said, "I'm learning what it means to love the kids. To bring them up in the way of the Lord is the most important task. We have been given the mission and responsibility to help our young ones know God's love, to pass on the faith to the next generation." About the *Good Fruits Series*, Lei Xiaoyu said, "It is useful in helping teachers use creative methods to tell Bible stories, and through memory verses and art and crafts to help children learn."

Summer Programs for Young People

Sensing the urgency to impart biblical truths and pass on the baton of faith, some churches started organizing summer programs for their young people. An example is Jinhong Church in Yunnan Province. The summer of 2017 was to be an extraordinary one for more than sixty young people from the ethnic groups of Yi, Hani, Dai, Lahu, and Han. They came together for three days of Bible teaching and fun activities to learn about God, their identity in Christ, and sexual purity. The programs left a deep impression on the young people. Let's hear from them.

Sunny: "In the past, I had come across Christianity and the history of ancient Israel in books. All of that was head knowledge. After listening to the teacher's explanation of the Bible, I learned that it isn't just a collection of historical facts but also a source of emotional support in hard times for many people—including me. Through this summer program, I have come to a new understanding of God. In the past, he was just my father's God. Now, I know him as my God too."

Joy: "I've been feeling inferior to others since my father passed away three years ago. This camp has taught me that I am unique. In the past, I only knew that I was a created being, but now I realize that I am fearfully and wonderfully made. Now, I am learning to pray for myself to overcome my feelings of inferiority. Thank you! Without this summer program, we would not be able to learn so much. I feel that I have a new life now."

Leonard: "In the past, my primary experience of God was through the testimonies of my elders. I began to doubt God when my classmates in school ridiculed me for my faith. Faced with this pressure, I started to distance myself from church and the Bible. Through this summer program, however, I have come to recognize the importance of God's Word, and I want to get to know God through his word. I want to walk more closely with him and draw strength from his word daily. I am thankful for this opportunity to learn so much."

A church elder: "When we spoke to the parents about this summer program, many of them were moved to tears when they heard their children's reflections on their relationship with their parents. I wish we had done this much earlier."

A young people's ministry leader: "This is the first time we have conducted a young people's summer program of this scale. The outcome has surpassed our expectations! All of them participated actively in the programs, and many shared their experiences candidly. Feedback from the participants has been very positive."

Biblical Parenting Workshops

In Chinese society, the family is recognized as a basic component. In the Christian tradition, the home is the natural environment for the incubation of faith as implied in what Paul wrote to Timothy: "For I am mindful of the sincere faith within you, which first dwelt in your grandmother Lois and your mother Eunice, and I am sure that it is in you as well" (2 Tim 1:5 NASB). And it is done in the simple day-to-day interactions, telling of God-stories as the psalmist says in Psalm 145:4, "One generation commends your works to another; they tell of your mighty acts" (NIV).

Parenting workshop, 2021.

Every prayer uttered, every Bible story told, every hymn sung, and every testimony shared is an encounter with the living God. Through these acts of worship at home and in the faith community, the young are being brought to the presence of Jesus. And in his presence, they are being touched and transformed.

Christian parents play a key role not just in their children's physical and mental development but also in their moral development and spiritual growth. While it is true that it takes a village to raise a child, the spiritual role of parents is not to be delegated to the church. However, many parents need help in this daunting journey. Not all have developed the habit of reading the Bible to their children. Nor do they all spend enough time with their children. Recognizing the

Parenting workshop, 2021.

need to help Christian parents in their parenting journey, registered churches in China since 2019 have begun to conduct biblical parenting workshops. The vision is to help build families that are centered around the Word of God, where stories like those of Rev. Zhang, Yuekai, and Jianan can continue. We captured some of the feedback given by parents who attended the workshops in Jilin and Yunnan Provinces.

Young adult leaders' training, 2021.

Tang Hongtao: "Children are often deemed as 'little troublemakers' or 'debt collectors' of their parents, but the Bible says that children are 'the inheritance from the Lord' and that they are a reward. According to the Bible, as parents, we can also learn from our children. In the process of raising children, it is important to correct our own mistakes in a timely manner and make up for our lack of biblical truths. I learned that we should see parenting as an opportunity to renew ourselves spiritually. This course is very practical and has improved our ability to be parents."

Li Hui: "One key thing I learned is to be intentional in accompanying my children. I've quit my bad habit of browsing videos on my phone, and I now intentionally carve out time to be with them. I've also promised to celebrate their birthdays. I said, 'Papa will make time for you.' No matter how tired I am after a day's work, I try to spend time with them. I want to work hard at expressing unconditional love and acceptance to my children instead of merely scolding them."

Lou Juan: "I realized that I had been spending a lot of time on my mobile phone, and I did not listen attentively to my children when they talked to me. I've also learned to rely more on God in my parenting. I now try to read the Bible with my children, teach them God's Word, and pray together with them more often. I need to learn to live by faith more, trust in God, and look to Him."

Yun: "This course helped me to reflect and repent. I realized that I have never accepted my children for who they are, much less anything about them that is inconsistent with my expectations. At the same time, I began to reflect on my relationship with God. My wife and I confessed and repented of our sins before God, received acceptance and forgiveness from him. We asked for wisdom and empowerment from God to build our family."

It is heartening that, as the Chinese Churches grow in maturity, many Christian leaders and parents are recognizing how critical it is to raise the next generation of Christians rooted in God's unchanging word. From Christian materials and summer programs for young adults to workshops for Christian parents, Christian leaders and parents are playing a key role in shaping the future of the church. With the recent decades of rapid urbanization and economic transformation in China, the work has already become more challenging. Praise God that many have caught the sense of mission and urgency to lay a strong spiritual foundation for the young ones, seizing the time they have and working while it is still day. Let us continue to stand in the gap together with the Churches in China for the next generation of Christians!

13
In the Shadow of the Cross

Bible and Mental Well-Being

My God, my God, why have you forsaken me?
>Why are you so far from saving me, from the words of my groaning?
>
>—Psalm 22:1

To give light to those who sit in darkness and in the shadow of death,
>to guide our feet into the way of peace.
>
>—Luke 1:79

Some experiences in life are so painful that they cause deep and lasting sufferings. That "suffering" is what we call trauma.
—Trauma Healing Institute, an initiative by the American Bible Society

Shufen has been an ordained pastor since 2019. For a period of time, her spirit was low, and she had the thought of giving up on herself. It was so bad she couldn't even eat or sleep well. It started when she felt that she had been misunderstood at work. Badly affected, she cried during the work meeting, which made her feel weak and vulnerable. Things got worse when nobody seemed willing to listen to her. People around her, including her husband, assumed that the issue was unforgiveness.

Finally, she couldn't go on and decided to seek counseling help. She said to her Christian counselor, "The Scripture said, 'The old has gone, the new is here!' I know it theoretically, but I can't put it into practice. What happened to me? Today, I mustered the courage to come to you for counseling; otherwise, I'm afraid that the depression will continue. I could be mentally ill or do something silly." Thank God that through six sessions of counseling, Shufen was able to receive help, learn to manage her emotions and pressures in life, and bounce back from her depression.[1]

The Long Shadow of Ill Mental Health

Globally, about 280 million people suffer from depression.[2] In China, the number is 95 million, according to data released by the 2022 China Mental Health Survey, published in the national newspaper, *People's Daily*. The main causes are emotional stress, parent-child relationships, and unexpected emergencies like accidents and serious health issues.

---
1 Adapted from Feng Shuxian, "To Strengthen Mental Resilience: Stay Mentally Healthy."
2 WHO website figure, 2023.

In the Asian context of honor-shame culture, ill mental health carries with it a cultural stigma. It remains a taboo for people to talk about it openly, making it an aspect of life that is generally neglected. As the Chinese value personal and social harmony, to bring such issues into the open will mean disrupting the stability. The fear of damaging one's reputation and being socially isolated further deter people from seeking help. The result is many feel they have no choice but to put on a facade and hide their problems.

The COVID-19 pandemic undoubtedly exacerbated the problem. According to the first national survey on psychological distress in China done in 2020, 35 percent of respondents experienced distress, including anxiety and depression.[3] The pandemic brought stresses to the fore, triggering latent mental and emotional problems that might be dormant in some people. It has been observed that the trauma of lockdowns and wider collateral effects of the pandemic like food insecurity may have been worse than the virus infection itself. Even amid the lifting of restrictions, concerns about resuming routines and transmission of new strains of the virus lingers. As such, the impact of the pandemic on mental well-being is far reaching and will be long term.

Toward Mental Resilience for the Body of Christ

In the context of the Chinese Churches, the issue can be even more delicate. Generally, the importance of Christian soul care and developing mental resilience has yet to be fully embraced among Chinese Christians. As the Chinese value diligence and putting community above self, the idea of setting aside time to care for oneself sounds doubly self-centered to the Chinese Christian. Meeting the needs of the congregation is often the priority. Moreover, there may be some misconceptions about mental health. Not only does it take courage to admit that one's soul is hurting as seen in Rev. Shufen's case, but Chinese Christian workers may also have self-imposed expectations, blaming themselves for not being spiritually stronger when they feel low. Chinese Christians may even wrongly perceive depression as a lack of faith or a result of one's sin. Thus, very few will seek counseling help.

Thankfully, in recent years, some Churches in China have started to recognize how important mental and emotional well-being is to the overall health of the church and its full-time workers. Seminars and workshops on pastoral counseling and mental well-being have gradually been held in a few provinces for pastors and lay leaders. More Chinese Christians are now familiar with the idea of self-care and the importance of rest. Some are beginning to pay attention to the condition of their inner life and emotional well-being. However, this is only the beginning, and with the pandemic, caring for the mental well-being of the body of Christ has become more urgent. Hence, UBS offered to partner with the Churches in China to support them in this critical area.

Thus far, UBS Bible ministry in China has been focusing primarily on Bible printing and distribution, publication, providing Bible resources, and equipping. What would it look like, and what would it take to support the Chinese Churches in this relatively new area of Bible engagement to help people develop emotional and mental well-being?

---

3 *The Lancet*, "Mental Health after China's Prolonged Lockdowns."

Healing Wounds of the Heart

By God's providence, the American Bible Society has developed a Bible-based trauma healing (TH) program based on the book *Healing the Wounds of Trauma* written in 2001, which could be adapted and contextualized for use in the Chinese Churches. Believing that healing heart wounds happens best in the heart language, the book has been translated into more than 150 languages, including Chinese.

Trauma healing materials adapted into Chinese.

Originally developed to help victims of armed conflict in central Africa, the TH program combines wisdom from the Bible and best practices in mental health. It deals with pertinent questions like, If God loves us, why do we suffer? How can the wounds of our hearts be healed? Trauma is defined as painful life experiences that cause deep and lasting suffering. The heart of the program is to help people encounter Jesus, our Wounded Healer, to experience his love and healing from trauma.

Using a participatory learning approach, people who come are encouraged to learn and share in small healing groups. With the help of a trained facilitator, participants process their feelings as well as listen to the stories of others. They tell their stories of grief and pain, bring their heartaches to the cross of Jesus, and allow God to carry them on a journey of healing, forgiveness, and restoration. To empower and equip more people to help others, the TH program also caters to those who want to be trained as healing group facilitators as well as to become trainers of facilitators.

Trauma healing workshop at Yunnan, 2020.

In 2019, the TH program was introduced to two provincial Christian Councils / TSPM. However, the pandemic broke out, and things came to a halt. Like in other countries, borders to China were closed, and COVID-19 preventive measures and restrictions were put in place. Would it still be possible to carry out any trauma healing program?

Thank God that, in July 2020, he opened the way for a more in-depth explanation of the program to Yunnan Christian Council / TSPM via a virtual meeting. Church partners in Yunnan Christian Council / TSPM saw the timeliness of such a program for believers to receive help as well as for more lay leaders to be trained. Twelve months later in July 2021, when it became possible to conduct onsite programs, Yunnan Christian Council / TSPM held its first trauma healing workshop with the support of UBS. Fifty participants attended the two-day workshop and gave positive feedback.

Trauma healing workshop at Yunnan, 2020.

Individual time with the instructor at a trauma healing training, Hubei, 2023.

In 2022, the more advanced materials of the TH program were also translated into Chinese and contextualized for the Chinese Churches using stories and examples with which Chinese participants could better relate. "Thank God for the TH program. My hope is that in time to come, the Chinese Churches will design and develop their own material so that it will be a program that is by and for the Chinese Christians, in their context and culture," said Kua Wee Seng, UBS CP director (1999–2021).

Praise God that thus far about 350 have received basic training to become healing group facilitators. Rev. Luo of Yunnan Christian Council / TSPM said, "Trauma healing program is a new initiative. It is very applicable to what we are facing now. We have selected our core team of lay leaders to attend the training so that they can in turn help those who are emotionally wounded and hurting. We are heartened by the positive feedback given, and we look forward to partnering with UBS in expanding this program to more cities and counties."

Participants who attended the TH training to become healing group facilitators gave their feedback. One lay leader shared, "We really need this training because, in our churches and meeting points, there are those who have just lost their loved ones, those whose marriages are in crisis, and those who are having trouble making ends meet. The training is indeed much needed and timely."

Another lay leader who serves at a Christian drug rehabilitation center in Yunnan Province said, "This is something new to me. It's easy to see physical wounds but not wounds of the heart. I've gained a better understanding of trauma healing. Through the sharing sessions, I saw the greatness and power of God in each participant's life, which gave me a new understanding of God. I am eager to use what I've learned in my ministry."

"What touched me most during the training was the patient help given, explanation, and personal participation of the instructor, and the enthusiastic learning attitude of fellow trainees," said

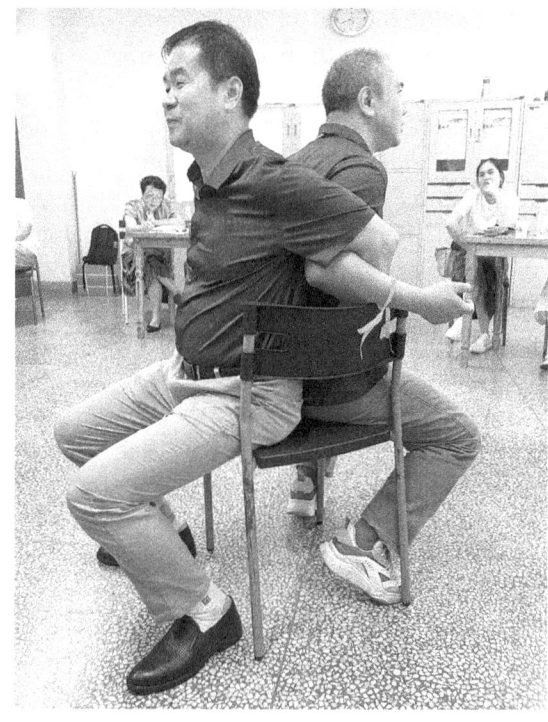

Activity during a trauma healing training, Hubei, 2023.

another lay leader from Yunnan Province. "During the practice session, I realized that if we do not try something new, we will remain stagnant. Only when we try, then can we know our own shortcomings and know how to improve. I've gained more motivation and confidence to help others now."

A lesson on "Caring for the Caregiver" resonated with many lay preachers. A participant wrote that the facilitator encouraged them to learn to say "no" and acknowledge their vulnerability and limitations, suggesting that preachers need to set healthy boundaries and spend time having personal spiritual devotion and rest. Many participants felt that this was what they needed to hear most.

The TH training has recently expanded to other provinces like Hubei and was met with positive feedback. For Rev. Lei Yingjian, age forty-five, who has been involved in end-of-life care and bereavement ministry at his church, the TH training has proven to be both timely and useful. "Too often, we offer simple platitudes without paying attention to the emotions of the person who is going through the pain," he shared. "Now, through the workshop, I've learned the importance of addressing the deeper layers of emotions that people grapple with. When we do not help others to face their grief and loss, we are truncating the process and misleading them on a 'false bridge,' which is a shortcut and does not lead to true healing and restoration."

In the Shadow of the Cross

Are more of such TH training and workshops needed? We turn to a testimony of Yang, a lay preacher serving in Yunnan Province, to get a better picture of the day-to-day struggles of full-time workers. This is her journey toward healing and restoration, shared in 2022.

Overwhelmed

Ten years ago, my husband and I moved to this remote county to serve. It was just after we got married. At first, the desolation of this place made me want to run away. There were only a handful of elderly believers at our first Sunday service. We used to serve in a vibrant and growing young adult ministry, so this was a huge change. In recent years, I found myself being overwhelmed by the sufferings of our congregation. A believer lost his son to cancer not long ago. Subsequently, he discovered that he himself also has the same disease. We prayed fervently as a church for him, but his condition continued to deteriorate. Another sister-in-Christ was asking me to pray that she could divorce her husband. He has been in multiple adulterous relationships, and their son has often gotten into fights with his father to the point of using kitchen knives.

During times like these, I felt as if heaven's gates were made of iron bars, blocking all my prayers. I asked God, "Why are these things happening?" I couldn't sleep well and became negative. I didn't know how to deal with these heavy emotions and burdens I was carrying. It was unbearable. I couldn't help the people who came to me. I felt so helpless that I sometimes even wondered if I was fit to be God's worker. Why is it that other churches are always talking about all the positive news, while ours is always in trouble? Then someone said, "It's because you didn't pray enough, you didn't have enough faith, you didn't have the spiritual power." This frustrated me as if an ungodly pastor like me caused all the problems!

Lamentations and Letting Go

It was during this time that the TH workshop was held. As I entered the conference room, my eyes immediately landed on the phrase "Take Your Pain to the Cross." I thought to myself, "This is exactly what I need." During one of the sessions, the trainer encouraged us to write our own laments and sorrow to God just like Jeremiah the prophet. It was a new experiment for me. It was as if I experienced another dimension when I expressed in written words the thoughts in my mind and the prayers in my mouth. Behind every word I penned was a real experience. In my lament, I cried out to God. I was honest with him about my feelings, giving him the pain of my helplessness and bitterness.

Then I realized that I had many misconceptions about ministry. I learned that there are times when we must accept that there is nothing we can do and that we are limited in our power. And we must also accept other people and allow them to have their moments of weakness. I can be there for those who are going through hard times and support them. Yet, I know that these burdens are not for me to bear alone. How things may turn out is beyond my control. But I know I can commit and surrender them into the loving hands of the Lord and put down the heavy load.

A participant practicing taking her pain to the cross, 2023.

Preacher Yang visiting an elderly believer who was unwell, Yunnan, 2021.

Preacher Yang with some elderly believers, Yunnan, 2021.

Coming to Terms

The truth is church workers themselves can be traumatized, and many feel that they cannot share with believers and have no one to confide in. They rely on themselves for a long time, which causes them to suppress their negative emotions. All of us need help. I thank the Lord for his perfect timing in bringing me to this TH workshop. Although we only have a glimpse of this topic and have not yet explored it deeply, the workshop has raised our awareness and provided us with a new tool for our ministry—so that we don't have to serve with too many tears, don't have to give up due to our weaknesses and don't have to be ashamed of our vulnerabilities. Listening is love and there is power in sympathizing with one another.

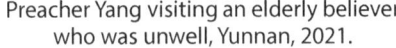

The Bible speaks to all aspects of our lives including our mental and emotional health. Notably, the largest group of psalms in the Psalter is the Psalms of Lament. To grow in maturity requires Christians to grapple with the issue of human suffering and pain. Whether it is suffering during the Cultural Revolution or mental and psychological distress in today's fast-paced society, it is encouraging to see that Chinese Christians are continuing to experience Immanuel, the reality of God with us through his word, by taking refuge in the shadow of the cross. Some of them are learning to go beyond the surface of things to care for their inner lives. As the Churches in China grow in numerical strength, let us also pray that they will grow in mental resilience and emotional strength in the Lord through his word!

14
Fuel for the Fireplace

Bible Ministry to Seminary Teachers and Students

And He gave some as apostles, and some as prophets, and some as evangelists, and some as pastors and teachers, for the equipping of the saints for the work of service, to the building up of the body of Christ.
—Ephesians 4:11–12 NASB

UBS has not only put the Bible into the hands of the people but also placed it in their hearts through such Bible teaching courses!
—Mr. Gu Chuanyong, Jiangsu Religious Affairs deputy director general, on the Bible seminars for pastors and preachers, 2014

"A Hundred Years to Nurture a Person"

A Chinese proverb says, "It takes ten years to grow a tree, but a hundred years to nurture a person" (十年树木, 百年树人). The Chinese understood that much time, effort, and resources are needed to develop and grow a person. The same goes for developing and training an important group of people who are instrumental in determining the health of the church—the pastors, preachers, priests, and nuns.

In the 1980s, as the Churches in China reopened and the number of believers grew, one of the critical and urgent needs, along with providing Bibles, was to train people to serve full-time church ministry. They were needed to explain and teach the Word of God, to nurture the faith of millions of new believers, as well as to run the church administration. However, theological seminaries and Bible schools were closed, just like churches, during the Cultural Revolution from 1966 to 1976. Some were taken over by the authorities and repurposed. Theological education could not be carried out, and for many years, no pastors and preachers were trained. At the same time, the previous generation of clergy was growing old, retiring, or had passed on. Hence, when the churches reopened in 1979, the older generation of clergy was thinning out and a new generation was missing.

At a church in Sichuan. Chinese Churches face a severe shortage of pastors.

It was not until the early 1980s and 1990s when seminaries and Bible schools gradually reopened that the Churches in China began to train and develop pastors and preachers. But the phenomenal growth of the church was outpacing the rate at which seminaries could produce pastors. Over the past two decades, even though the national average ratio of ordained pastors to believers in the registered Protestant churches in China has decreased from 1:8,700 to 1:6,700, the gap is still wide.[1] The severe shortage of pastors resulted in many churches and meeting points, especially those in the rural regions of China, having no designated pastor or elder. They relied on either visiting pastors or lay preachers for their spiritual nurturing and growth.

Beginning in the 1990s, leaders of the Churches in China saw the pressing need to train more pastoral staff to nurture the faith of the believers and for the healthy development of the church. Bishop Shen Yifan, general secretary of CCC, identified the training of leaders to be a key factor in running the church for the future of Christianity in China. He said in 1993:

> If we cannot give better Christian nurture to the people who join the church so that they can grow better in their understanding of the Christian faith, if we cannot train more young leadership and promote young leaders to key positions in the church, or if we cannot provide enough Christian literature, then I think there is less chance for Christianity to grow in a healthy way in China.[2]

Since then, the national church leaders of China have identified developing leaders and training full-time church workers and lay preachers as the top priority for the church. In fact, even in the recent five-year plans of the CCC/TSPM on the Sinicization of Christianity in China (2018–2022 and 2023-2027), a major task for the church was to "continuously standardize theological education and accelerate the pace of personnel development."

Bible Resource Support from UBS in the Early Years

Even before the establishment of the APC in 1987, UBS's support for the Churches in China had already begun—donating scholarly Bibles and Bible resources. The purpose was to help rebuild seminary libraries, which were largely destroyed during the Cultural Revolution.

Scholarly edition Bibles and resources for Churches in China.

According to records, in 1979 after Chinese Christian leaders initially established contact with UBS, they requested scholarly publications, including biblical texts in Greek and Hebrew plus a set of the Helps for Translators series for Nanjing University to rebuild their library. In 1982, copies of the Translator's Handbook series, the Greek New Testament, and other books published by UBS were sent to Nanjing Theological Seminary from New York. In 1984, five hundred copies of RSV annotated Bibles were also sent.

---

1 The ratio 1:8,700 was based on 3,000 pastors and 26 million Christians in 2016; 1:6,700 was based on 6,000 ordained pastors and 40 million Christians in 2021. Figures are based on official reports by the CCC/TSPM.

2 Philip Wickeri, "Interview with Bishop Shen Yifan," *Amity News Service*, April 15, 1993.

By the 1990s, as more seminaries were opened, UBS continued to provide scholarly books including *A Concise Greek-Chinese Dictionary of the New Testament* and the newly published Today's English Version / Today's Chinese Version (TEV/TCV) diglot Bible. A complete set of Translator's Handbooks was also sent to Yunnan Seminary for a UBS-sponsored Bible translation workshop. A major item for the Sheshan Catholic Seminary was the *Novum Testamentum Latine* (Latin New Testament). Catholic church leaders also requested a hundred copies of the TEV for students to use as a study text.

Deeper and Wider Partnership

In 1999, at the plenary meeting of the CCC/TSPM, Rev. Su Deci, vice president and general secretary of the CCC, explained the condition of the Chinese church's theological reflection and training this way:

> After the Chinese Church reopened in the 1980s, it put all its efforts into reopening and rebuilding work, leaving little time or energy for serious theological reflection. Similarly, theological seminaries have tended to concentrate more on practical theology and basic Bible knowledge, to churn out enough pastoral workers as quickly as possible to serve the church's growing population. Pressures of demand, lack of trained teachers and limited resources have precluded the serious study of history, philosophy or theology in seminaries. There is thus a need to strengthen the clergy's ability for theological reflection and provide more in-depth training than are currently available for lay leaders.[3]

Building on the good working relationship between UBS and the registered Churches in China in the early years, new projects were embarked upon to further resource the seminaries in a more concerted manner and to help them raise the academic standards of theological education in China. Support was also given to churches and Bible schools to strengthen the Bible preaching and teaching of pastors and lay preachers and to encourage ongoing theological reflection and learning. These initiatives were like fuel to keep the fire of revival burning in China.

Kua Wee Seng (UBS CP director, 1999–2021) explained the strategic importance of supporting Bible preaching and teaching in churches and seminaries, "Besides having the Bible, we need good Bible teaching, research, and scholarship. So we help to equip the pastors and lay preachers. But we also need to go upstream—impact the students at the seminaries, who have a longer duration of ministry and impact on the congregations. If we enhance their biblical resources, which will be used by the students and lecturers, they will be able to better understand the Word of God, and they will be better ministers of God's Word in the churches."

To this end, several Bible programs and initiatives have been implemented in a multi-pronged approach to support the seminaries as they train a new generation of clergy and equip existing pastors and preachers. We shall look at multiple ways in which this was done. In this chapter, we will look at partnerships focused on developing seminary teachers and students. In the following chapter, we will look at Bible programs that seek to empower pastors and lay preachers through supporting churches and Bible schools.

---

3 "The Time Is Ripe for Building Chinese Theology," *Amity News Service*.

Scholarships, Attachment Programs, and Bible Symposiums

Scholarships are granted to seminary teachers interested in furthering their studies in biblical studies. The earliest recipients were two Chinese seminary teachers—Hu Huiping and Shi Wenhua. They were sponsored by UBS to do a two-year degree in biblical exegesis and translation at Trinity Theological College (TTC) in Singapore, and they graduated in 2003 with a Master of Theology.

"My desire is to become a well-qualified Old Testament lecturer. The two painstaking years of study have built up my faith and confidence. I wish to express my heartfelt thanks to UBS for your support, encouragement, and prayers," said Huiping upon graduation at TTC. Shi Wenhua, who came from Anhui Province, said, "Millions of Chinese are still in darkness, and they need the salvation of God. The Holy Spirit has given me a strong burden and mission for these people in my heart. I thank God for guiding me to complete my Master of Theology at TTC and for the support of UBS. I hope to be able to better serve the churches in China."

Both women went on to pursue PhDs—one in Old Testament studies and the other in New Testament studies—in the UK with UBS's support. The achievement was a key step in the development of Bible work in China.

Another recipient of the scholarship to do a two-year degree in biblical exegesis and translation at TTC was Geng Weizong. Upon completion of his studies, Geng returned to China to teach biblical studies at Huadong Theological Seminary, a regional seminary. In addition to teaching at Huadong, he has also contributed significantly to theological education and biblical studies for the churches in China. Today, Rev. Geng serves as the vice president of the CCC.

Seminary students from China who are doing biblical studies at TTC in Singapore as well as those pursuing a PhD in biblical studies at Nanjing Jinling Union Theological Seminary (NJUTS) in China are also considered for scholarships. These scholarships are a great encouragement to the recipients and support the Chinese Churches to develop talents in biblical studies to ensure greater competencies in Bible teaching, research, and translation.

Mr. Cao Zhenlei, a scholarship recipient from NJUTS in 2021, said that it is important for him to understand God's Word better so that he can be more equipped to teach at churches or seminaries in the future. "I am determined to devote my life to the study of God's Word. I want to expound biblical truths so that all (myself included) can be edified. I am very grateful to the United Bible Societies for this generous support. You have freed me from worries about my financial limitations and have blessed me spiritually."

Another area of support was through attachment programs. In 2013, two Bible teachers from China were at TTC for a four-week attachment program sponsored by UBS. It was their first visit to TTC and to Singapore. They were Rev. Tu Zhijin of Shandong Theological Seminary and Rev. Xu Changxiu of Sichuan Theological Seminary. Both have the mission of helping the churches in China to produce competent Bible teachers and preachers in their respective provinces. And they needed some fresh input themselves. Hence, when the opportunity arose to learn from an academic mentor to consult on teaching and research matters, they were grateful and delighted. In addition, they had full access to the TTC library facilities for independent research purposes.

On his attachment experience, Rev. Tu said, "I am very touched by their great commitment and willingness to help the churches in China. TTC is such an excellent center for higher learning. Continued support from UBS in sponsorship of Bible teachers will certainly help the Chinese church in the long run."

Bible symposiums and seminars on Old Testament and New Testament studies were also organized for Bible teachers from seminaries and Bible schools across China to update their understanding of biblical studies and the latest research advancements.

The first Bible seminar on the Old Testament, jointly organized by NJUTS, CCC/TSPM, and UBS, was inaugurated in 2012 by the Rt. Rev. Dr. John Chew, UBS Global Council Member and former primate of South East Asia. The four-day seminar was attended by twenty-one Old Testament lecturers from seventeen regional and provincial seminaries and Bible schools all over China.

Dang Gaiqin, a lecturer from Shaanxi Bible School with more than twenty years of teaching experience, remarked: "This Old Testament Bible seminar has widened my perspective and stirred me to be more inquisitive to delve deeper into the Bible text. I am more motivated to work harder and to find answers for myself."

Zhang Shuilian, a teacher at Zhongnan Regional Seminary for twenty-four years, said the seminar enlightened her. "It has also given me a renewed impetus to Old Testament teaching!"

Riding on the success of the Old Testament seminar, the first New Testament seminar was launched in 2015, and twenty-four New Testament lecturers from twenty-two seminaries in various parts of China attended. Cui Jinghuan, age thirty-four, a New Testament teacher from Heilongjiang Theological Seminary shared, "Now I have a deeper and clearer understanding of New Testament themes. This knowledge will enhance my teaching method and choice of teaching topics and form the basis for professional reflection."

Besides professional development, financial support to help seminary teachers stay on the job was another important area. Many seminaries that lack funds and resources often struggle to pay their teachers and retain them. Thus, UBS was called upon to support the seminaries in paying Bible teachers, especially those from more difficult and needy backgrounds. Helping one Bible teacher stay on the job means more pastors and preachers can be trained in China.

In 2019, I met Liu Tingting, age twenty-nine, a Bible teacher from Shandong Theological Seminary and a recipient of financial support. The soft-spoken, long-haired woman has a younger sister who suffers from congenital cerebral palsy. A few years ago, her father had to stop work due to a severe lung infection. She said, "Even though that means I'm the sole breadwinner in the family, I believe that God's grace will carry us through step by step, day by day. So support from UBS is a tremendous help to my family and me! God has never failed me. His grace is greater than any crisis my family and I have faced." I was impressed by the faith and tenacity found in such a young-looking and petite lady. May the Lord's grace and wisdom be upon her as she serves in the theological seminary and cares for the needs of her family.

Liu Tingting, a Bible teacher from Shandong Theological Seminary.

Bible Resources for Seminaries and Bible Schools

Another important area is helping seminaries build up their libraries. Although most of the seminary students will not study overseas and most Bible teachers will not obtain a scholarship or have an overseas attachment, the works of theologians and scholars can be brought to them. In fact, it has been said the library is the heart of the seminary. It is an intimate and integral part of the school—the center where seminary students and teachers have dialogues with theologians, writers, and thinkers through the centuries. The place where they absorb, adapt, or wrestle with what they read and make sense of what they are studying. Simply put, books are the lifeblood of seminaries and Bible schools. They fuel the theological and spiritual development of seminary students as they grow to become ministers of God's Word and charge forward to advance his kingdom.

Opening of the BRC at NJUTS, 2012.

To this end, a major initiative was to set up Bible resource centers* (BRCs) at China's national theological seminary of the Protestant churches, NJUTS, and at the National Seminary of Catholic Church in China. With the support of the British and Foreign Bible Society and UBS, a BRC at NJUTS was set up in 2012 after two years of preparation. The BRC has an area of 84.5 square meters and houses 4,800 titles and four computers with English and Chinese biblical studies software. According to Liu Meichun, NJUTS library director, the seminary has the largest collection of biblical resources in Mainland China! In 2014, the BRC at the National Seminary of Catholic Church in China was opened. It housed nearly three thousand titles as well as computers with biblical studies software.

Lord Stephen Green and Lady Jay Green, with Rev. Dr. Chen Yilu (executive vice president of Nanjing Seminary), in front of the seminary's BRC, which was funded by UBS with the support of Bishop Radford Trust established by Lord Stephen Green and Lady Jay Green, 2014.

To help these national seminaries keep abreast with the developments of scholarly research in biblical studies, new titles have been added over the years to enlarge their collection. In 2020, the BRC in NJUTS expanded its walls, moving from the second floor to the ground floor. It now houses eight thousand titles and has a larger study area for the students. A long-term goal of this initiative is to produce Bible researchers who can offer a higher level of theological training and to develop Bible scholars with strong biblical foundations, attaining a level of scholarship that is comparable with international standards.

What did the students and Bible teachers say about the BRCs?

Du Nana, studying at NJUTS in 2013, said that the books at the BRC had helped her to take her calling as a minister of God's Word more seriously. She shared, "God used the books to make the Bible and preaching come alive for me, spurring me on." Praise God that Du, who hails from Shandong Province, has since gone on to further her theological education in biblical studies after graduating from NJUTS.

Du Nana, a student at the Nanjing Union Theological Seminary.

The BRC also attracted Bible teachers from other provinces. Ma Xiaoqin, a Bible teacher from Shanxi Bible School who first visited the BRC of NJUTS in 2012, was moved to see the books. He said, "It's amazing to see the wide collection of books here. I could feel how these authors must love the Bible so much. They had spent so much time writing to share with us their precious thoughts and insights!"

Some biblical resources arriving at the library of the National Catholic Seminary, Beijing, 2012.

Li Wei, a priest in training at the National Catholic Seminary in 2015, said, "There are very few resources in biblical studies in China. The books in the BRC have not only increased our understanding of the Scriptures but also our interest in biblical studies."

Soon the regional seminaries in China were also requesting biblical studies resources from UBS. Hence, besides BRCs, Bible resource rooms (BRRs) were also set up at five regional

Cardinal John Onaiyekan visiting the BRC at the National Catholic Seminary in Beijing, 2018.

theological seminaries from 2013–2016, namely, Huadong Seminary, Yanjing Seminary, Sichuan Seminary, Zhongnan Seminary, and Dongbei Seminary. Reference books related to biblical studies, furniture, and computers with Bible software were donated to these seminaries to supplement their libraries.

He Yongbao, a student from Sichuan Seminary, commenting on the Chinese Almega software, said, "Thank you for providing the Bible software. I can conveniently read up on a lot of resources and hermeneutic books when doing assignments. This software is extremely helpful for students and teachers in their research."

Students at Guizhou Bible School with Bible tools on their desks, 2016.

"The setting up of the BRR at Dongbei Seminary has brought about big changes. Being a teacher, we need to have access to new books, both from China and overseas in our respective academic fields. In particular, as a New Testament teacher using the resources in BRR has greatly improved my teaching content and broadened my view," said Gao Meilian, a Bible teacher from Dalian, Liaoning Province.

"Thank God for the BRR at Dongbei Seminary, especially when I was completing my thesis. It affords a wide range of reading materials that stimulate my thinking and increase my interest in learning. The resources here have broadened my view and helped me to understand the Scriptures more deeply. Some of the newly published books challenged my past understanding of Scripture. It caused me to realize my poverty of knowledge and made me hunger more for the truth," said Shen Lifeng, a student from Jilin Province.

Next, BRRs were set up at fifteen provincial-level seminaries and Bible schools. Praise God that over the years twenty-two seminaries and Bible schools across China have been equipped with Bible resources, and the BRCs and BRRs are continuing to be updated with new titles and publications.

Furthermore, UBS has also received requests to support Bible Training Centers (BTC) with Bible resources. These BTCs are a level below the seminaries and Bible schools, training

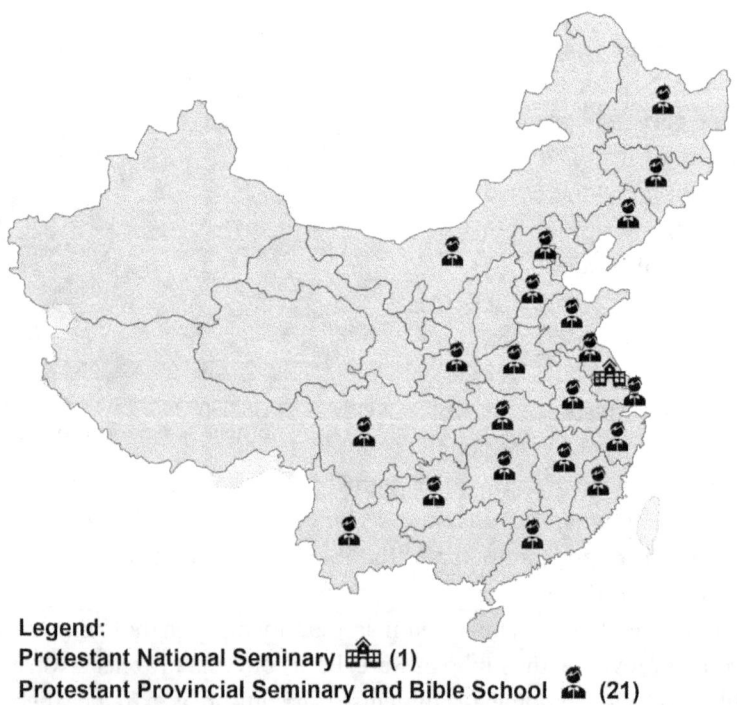

Guizhou Bible School plus 21 Seminaries and Bible schools in China.

lay preachers and lay leaders. There are more than a hundred such centers in China. With the acute shortage of ordained pastors, lay preachers and lay leaders who are trained at the BTC provide vital pastoral support to the Chinese Churches. Equipping BTCs with basic Bible resources provides students with a strong biblical foundation as they serve their home churches. So far, UBS has supported seven BTCs since 2019 and hopes to extend the project to more BTCs.

Bible resources not only feed the minds of the students and teachers, but the sight of them also warms their hearts and energizes their spirit. Zhou Yaqin, an alumnus and current staff member of Baotou BTC, Inner Mongolia, said, "I would like to thank the United Bible Societies' donors for their generosity and burden for the Lord's ministry. When we see these books, we feel their love for God, and it is an inspiration to us all. They serve as a reminder for both teachers and students that we are not alone in dedicating our lives to God's ministry. Praise the Lord!"

Zhou Yaqin, an alumnus and staff member of Baotou BTC, 2022.

BRCs and BRRs provide reference materials meant for common use at the library. However, to be a diligent student and teacher of God's Word, one also needs some essential Bible resources by one's side. For needy Bible students and teachers who are not able to afford basic Bible resources for their studies and teaching, a set—consisting of a Bible commentary, study Bible, concordance, and Bible dictionary—is given to them free.

Bible resources for students of Henan Bible School, 2009.

Bible tools for Hunan Bible School students, 2014.

As the majority of Christians in China live in rural areas, many Bible students and teachers often come from poor farming families. In the 1990s and 2000s, some Bible students would sell a family buffalo or calf to pay for school fees. Hence, to be able to receive a set of Bible resources is often an affirmation of their calling and ministry.

Every year on average, UBS supports about three to four thousand students and teachers at Bible schools and training centers with a set of Bible resources through provincial Christian Councils and TSPM.

Ma Jinguang, a Bible student from Yunnan Province who received a set of Bible resources in 2012, said, "By his grace, God has chosen us, people who are of little learning and means to

Delegates from Bethesda Frankel Estate Church presenting the *Chinese Study Bible* (New Testament) to the students at the Inner Mongolia Bible School, 2018.

be his servants. So I am very thankful to the supporters of UBS for your help and support. These resources help us to know God better, grow deeper in our spiritual lives, preach, and teach more effectively to our brothers and sisters in Christ so that they may know the sovereign God, who is in control of all the heavens and the earth."

A group of Singaporean Christians from Bethesda Frankel Estate Church, led by Elder Ong Teck Chye, visiting Inner Mongolia Bible School, 2018.

Chinese Christians have come a long way from reading the Bible to becoming teachers, researchers, and scholars of the Bible. Their hunger and love for God's Word is evident in their desire to grow deeper in the word and spiritual maturity. With the aid of biblical and scholarly resources, Bible seminars, and symposiums, Bible teachers and students are mining the Bible for solid food to build and strengthen the body of Christ. Praise God that over the years Chinese Bible researchers and scholars are also gradually being raised up to lay a strong biblical foundation for the Churches in China. In the next chapter, we shall look at Bible ministry to pastors and lay preachers and how they can be supported in maintaining the health of the Churches in China.

15
Oil for the Lamps

Bible Ministry to Pastors and Lay Preachers

I will give you shepherds after my own heart, who will feed you with knowledge and understanding. —Jeremiah 3:15

The LORD is my shepherd; I shall not want.
    He makes me lie down in green pastures.
He leads me beside still waters.
    He restores my soul. —Psalm 23:1–3

Rural Chinese Christians are known for their simple faith. However, this also implies that they can easily fall prey to false teachings that sound right to their ears. In 1990, the *South China Morning Post* reported on the rise of cult groups in China and cited a tragic story of a group of twenty Christians who lost their lives when they waded into a frigid river, believing what a stranger told them—that Jesus would meet them on the other side.[1]

Along with rapid church growth came the challenge of grounding believers in biblical truths. This has become an impetus for the churches in China to strengthen the theological foundation of the pastors and lay preachers, who will then help believers distinguish between true and false doctrines. Bishop K. H. Ting described the situation in 1994 in an interview with UBS:

> Today we have at least eight thousand church buildings used for public worship. We only have 1,100 pastors, which expressed proportionally with the number of Christians is unheard of in any other place on earth. There are many tasks to perform, especially in the countryside where leadership is entirely lay. We have many difficulties there: heretical teaching … and people bringing their superstitions to church. The most important emphasis [for the church] is on leadership training both through theological training and in the training of lay people. We want to improve our theological education so that we can produce more and adequate leaders from the next generation. This is the only way for us to elevate the spirituality of [Chinese] Christians.

Since the 1990s, the churches in China have been battling the threat of heretical teachings and cult groups.

Wenzhou lay leaders training, 1998.

---
1 Wark, "China's Bible Cheats."

During my visits to China in the past decade, I continue to hear from church leaders about the threats posed by cult groups and how some of them have lost their sheep. In response, churches have conducted classes for their members to raise awareness about the activities of cult groups and to help them discern the truth. Even city churches are not spared. When my colleagues and I visited Haidian Christian Church in Beijing in 2017, we saw huge posters near the church sanctuary entrance containing messages about the tactics of cult groups and how to discern the truth. Rev. Wu Weiqing, senior pastor of the church, told us, "We have to be on the alert all the time!"

While the needs of shepherding the believers are enormous, what is equally if not more important is shepherding the shepherds. Pastors and lay preachers need to be recharged spiritually and theologically, to know that the Lord is their Shepherd. While they tend to the needs of their flocks, they must also let the Lord tend to their souls and other needs. This is something often neglected and considered a luxury in China.

The fact that church leadership development remains a critical need can be seen from what Elder Fu Xianwei said in a 2018 interview with UBS on the challenges facing the churches in China: "The main challenge is that there are many believers but not enough pastors. The rate of growth of the believers is faster, while the number of seminary graduates per year is only about one thousand or so. There are many churches without pastors. The only solution we have now is to develop and train educated people among the believers and raise up leaders who will preach and teach the word."

In this chapter, we shall look at how UBS has supported the Chinese Churches in their training and equipping of pastors and lay preachers.

Bible Seminars and Equipping Sessions for Pastors

Besides the seminaries, UBS also support pastors and preachers via CCC/TSPM to provide them with Bible seminars and equipping sessions. While the estimated national average ratio of ordained pastors to believers is 1:6,700, the actual situation on the ground varies from place to place.

Take the churches where Rev. Xu Fei and Rev. Luo Peisheng come from, for example. Both hail from Yancheng City of Jiangsu, where they have been serving as pastors for seven and eight years, respectively. Rev. Xu is one of five pastors overseeing fifty thousand believers in Xiang Shui County, while Rev. Luo is one of five pastors overseeing 100,000 believers in She Yang County. The ratio is one pastor to twenty thousand believers for Rev. Luo. One can imagine how busy these pastors must be.

Both pastors were at the inaugural pastors' Bible teaching course in 2013 held at Jiangsu Seminary, organized by Jiangsu Provincial Christian Council / TSPM and supported by UBS. A total of forty-five participants, representing fourteen counties across Jiangsu, spent one week learning from Bishop John Chew, UBS CP honorary consultant, and Canon Titus Chung, priest-in-charge of St. Andrew's Cathedral Mandarin Congregation, Singapore.

Rev. Xu said, "It is a rare luxury for us to pull ourselves away from ministry. There is always lots of work and no time to think about training or being 'shepherded,' but it is so needful that we as pastors should take a short retreat and recharge ourselves." This is the first time Rev. Xu has taken leave from ministry. Rev. Luo added, "The past few days with the two teachers have broadened my perspective. There is much to reflect on."

Lay preachers' training in Gospel Church Zhangjiajie, Hunan Province, 2014.

At the second Bible teaching course in 2016, seventy elders, pastors, and preachers attended from various parts of Jiangsu. Rev. Zhang Keyun, Jiangsu Christian Council / TSPM chairman, shared his analysis of the church scene in Jiangsu Province: "We are entering into a new phase—from an emphasis on hardware to software.[2] We need to focus on molding people and developing their talents, thus upgrading the quality of our pastors and preachers."

Praise God that through these Bible seminars, UBS could contribute toward encouraging the pastors as well as strengthening the preaching and teaching capabilities of key church leaders in various parts of China.

Bible Ministry and Support to the Lay Preachers

With the acute shortage of pastors in China, there is a special group of people helping to plug the gap—they are the lay preachers. As mentioned by Bishop Ting in the quote above, rural churches in China were entirely dependent on lay leadership. The situation is still largely so today. Praise God that there are currently about 190,000 lay preachers across China co-laboring alongside the pastors, preaching and teaching the Word of God at county and village churches and meeting points.

Fugong Bible School, Yunnan province, 2017.

Even as they serve the growing needs of the church, lay preachers themselves need ministry and help. First, many of them have only gone through basic lay leaders' training from the church and hardly any formal theological education. Hence, one key area identified by the church is Bible training. Hence, in 2016, about four hundred Lisu preachers and church leaders gathered at Fugong County in Yunnan Province for an eleven-day Bible training. UBS supported the training

---

2 "Hardware" refers to the construction of church buildings, while "software" refers to building up the spiritual life and biblical foundation of Christians and the training of pastors and preachers.

Lay preachers training in Fugong, Yunnan Province, 2015.

and sponsored a two-volume Bible reference book for all participants of the training as well as students and teachers at Nujiang Bible School, Fugong Bible School, Gongshang Bible School, and teachers at Fugong Christian Council / TSPM. Among the participants were Lisu preachers, church leaders, and Bible school students and teachers, who benefitted from the teaching sessions and Bible tools.

Ci Liheng, a Lisu lay preacher for nine years said, "It was a real blessing to soak in the Word of God, studying and learning under the guidance of experienced teachers and pastors. Their teaching and advice are invaluable to me."

During a memorable visit to Fugong County, Yunnan Province, in 2017, my colleague and I spent extended time with Lisu lay preacher Pu Zhidui, his wife, and their granddaughter. He brought us to visit churches and homes of believers in the mountains. Amid the smoke coming from the cooking pot in one of the believer's homes, we sipped tea and learned more about the situation facing lay preachers and their needs.

Lisu lay preacher Pu with his wife and granddaughter, 2017.

He told us that many lay preachers are subsistence farmers living in the villages and mountainous regions of China. They serve as volunteers and grassroots lay leaders while trying to make ends meet at home. Church members, being subsistence farmers themselves with little or no cash income, are not able to support them financially.

And the cultural perception that full-time church workers should be poor and that poverty is the mark of a true servant of God certainly did not help. Although this perception may be slowly changing, it will still take some time for it to translate into changes on the ground.

It is thus not uncommon for them to take leave from serving their churches to look for employment opportunities when the financial burden becomes too unbearable. Unfortunately, some do not return to church service again.

In response to the need, UBS has supported the churches in China by giving financial assistance to lay preachers, in a bid to save them from falling out of ministry. One of them was Preacher Mu Weixi, age thirty-three. He had faced a dilemma—he was caught between answering the call of God to preach in impoverished areas to rural Christians and being a filial son, a dutiful father, and the family's sole breadwinner. Mu admitted that he faced the temptation to seek a well-paying job in the city so that he could meet his family's physical needs, particularly when he became a father last year and his elderly parents' health started to fail. The outbreak of the COVID-19 pandemic certainly exacerbated Mu's predicament.

Thank God with financial support from UBS, things took a turn for the better. He said, "I am thankful for UBS's support. The needs of my family, including our newborn baby, can be taken care of now. This has strengthened my faith to know that God will always provide for me as I serve him faithfully. Now I can visit more brothers and sisters and travel further to preach God's Word!"

Mu Weixu, a Lisu lay preacher, Yunnan, 2020.

Bible Motorbike

How did a two-wheel vehicle come into the picture of the Bible missions in China? In 2009, a renowned Finnish missionary, scholar, and author, Rev. Risto Santala (1929–2012), was celebrating his eightieth birthday. At the party, he made a special request to all his guests—"Please give your gifts to China—in a Bible motorbike project."

Rev. Dr. Markku Kotila, CEO of the Finnish Bible Society, shared the story behind this unique request: "Rev. Santala told me that when he was serving in Israel as a missionary, his first-born son, Ismo, fell seriously ill, suffering from a kind of cancer. One day, an American missionary friend visited the family. He asked what the young boy was going to do when he grew up. The young boy said he wanted to be a missionary to China. Sadly, the young boy passed away without realizing his dream." Rev. Santala later wrote a biography of his son in 1960, his first book to be published.

Bible motorbike for lay preachers serving in rural China.

Years passed and as Rev. Santala approached his eightieth birthday, it came to him to want to fulfill his son's dream. He approached Rev. Kotila and told him about his desire. Being an avid motor biker in his younger days, Rev. Santala was eager to give the two-wheeler to needy preachers in memory of Ismo, his son.

Wee Seng was at that time traveling and came to Finland to attend Rev. Santala's birthday. When told about the idea of the motorbike, he saw that it would be a valuable and practical help to needy preachers in rural China in their preaching and teaching of the Word of God and delivery of Bibles to their congregations. The Bible motorbike project was thus conceived.

According to the China embassy website, "China has many mountains, with mountainous areas making up two-thirds of its total land area." It also has "seven of the world's 12 mountain peaks over 8,000 meters above sea level."[3] The uniqueness of China's terrain and topography

---

3 http://np.china-embassy.gov.cn/eng/China.

poses a great challenge to lay preachers. Not only are the distances great, but traversing the mountainous terrain can be life threatening. For example, preachers serving in Yunnan and Guizhou often walk for long hours, trekking up and down mountains and valleys, crossing rivers and creeks, to reach churches and meeting points. The difficulty is compounded by the extra weight of the Bibles and biblical resources they carry with them. With the Bible motorbikes, things would be radically different, as the following testimonies tell us.

Wang Hai, age twenty-nine, was one of twenty-four recipients who received a motorbike from UBS in 2012. He was a preacher and a church planter from the Miao ethnic group. Prior to getting the motorbike, Wang used to walk for days to reach a meeting point. With the motorbike, Wang was now able to shorten his journey to five hours on average. "There is a shortage of pastors and God is willing to use me. Because of UBS's donors, I now have this motorbike to get to the people in the mountains. My body may ache a little after riding long distances, but my heart is happy. There are new believers who don't have Bibles. I will use the motorbike to bring Bibles to them," said Wang.

Wen Fubin, a lay preacher from the Yi tribe in Guizhou Province, was grateful to receive a Bible motorbike in 2017. There were about nine hundred church members in his church, mainly elderly people. Hence, he had been doing a lot of regular visitations in towns and villages. "I live with my parents and struggle to make ends meet as a lay preacher. I have been praying to have a motorcycle for my visitation ministry. Thank God for his provision!"

Preacher Long Xinrong from Yunnan Province, who received a Bible motorbike in 2020, said, "With the help of the motorcycle, the time I used to cover on foot (over four hours one way) has been reduced to just one hour! This has made ministry work much more effective, as I am now able to arrange teachings and home visits with more ease, increasing my capacity to minister to his flock."

Praise God that since the start of the project, hundreds of motorbikes have been donated, going to places in China where Ismo could not go, fulfilling his dream through the ministry of Chinese lay preachers.

Bible Resources

Churches in China have also appealed for Bible resources for lay preachers. As with the seminary students and Bible teachers at Bible schools, lay preachers need Bible reference materials for their teaching and preaching ministry.

During a visit to Shandong Province in 2017, I met Zhang Qingsheng, age sixty-six, a retired physics and math teacher turned lay preacher who traveled to different rural churches about four times a week to do Bible reading and study with believers. He told me about the importance of the Bible resources to him: "People there are hungry to be fed. But sometimes they tend to read the Bible too literally and interpret it wrongly. In the rural areas, there are cult groups giving out heretical printed materials and CDs for free.

Recipients of study Bibles at a lay preachers' training in Gospel Church Zhangjiajie, Hunan, 2014.

Some only preach about grace. So, it's important that lay preachers have authorized and trusted Bible resources from which we can share and teach the believers."

Another lay preacher we met was Kong Jinxiang, age sixty, who used to look up old and worn-out sermon collections and Bible correspondence course notes to prepare for ministry. He told me he was immensely grateful when he received a set of Bible tools from his church with the support of UBS. "My church has 600–700 members, most of whom are elderly. Some of them accepted Christ without much understanding. My frequent exhortation is for them to take their faith seriously since they have chosen to believe. Receiving these Bible reference materials from UBS is like receiving precious jewels. I am very moved."

Lay preacher Kong Jinxiang with Bible resources, Shandong, 2017.

In addition, I learned from lay preacher Elder Hou Fangyu, a potato and vegetable farmer, that many of these Bible resources are only available in the bookstores of major city churches, making it harder for rural lay preachers to access them. He said, "Thank you for these precious Bible resources. I wouldn't have the means to afford them and wouldn't know where to buy them even if I had the means."

Elder Hou Fangyu with Bible resources, Shandong, 2017.

Our hearts were filled with joy upon hearing that and we asked the Lord for more open doors to bless more lay preachers with biblical resources.

Support via Publication of Bible Resources

It is fitting to end this chapter with a groundbreaking, unprecedented Bible resource published in 2017 by CCC/TSPM—the *Chinese Study Bible* (CSB). The CSB combines the Bible verses in the Chinese Union Version (CUV) with a translation and adaptation of Crossway's English Standard Version (ESV) Study Bible explanatory notes and charts. How did this publication come about?

In 2012, Elder Fu Xianwei became acquainted with the ESV Study Bible when UBS General Secretary Miller Milloy and

Biblical resources supported by UBS, including books authored by Bishop Emeritus Robert Solomon and Bishop John Chew.

Wee Seng introduced it to him during a visit to China. He was immediately taken with its rich up-to-date content, impressive graphics, and attractive layout. In view of China's dire need for

Launch of the *Chinese Study Bible*, 2017.

Bible tools, he was determined to publish a Chinese version. In response to Elder Fu's interest, a trip to the US was arranged for him to meet with Crossway to discuss the plan to translate and adapt the notes in the ESV Study Bible into Chinese.

CSB was thus the fruit of the collaborative partnership between the Chinese church, Crossway, and UBS that took five years to complete. "It is important that Christians have a deep grounding in the word. People can read but may not be able to truly understand the Scriptures. So CSB is helpful in providing more clarity and understanding as well as in defense against the influence of cult groups," said Elder Fu at the launch of the CSB (New Testament).

On the collaborative partnership, Lane Dennis, president and CEO of Crossway at the time, said, "It is a dream come true. A miracle of God's gracious provision, the fruit of a wonderful partnership that binds us as brothers and sisters in the Gospel and the publication of God's Word."

"The CSB is by far the most complete and comprehensive study Bible available in China. It provides excellent, up-to-date scholarly perspective from top-notch, reputable scholars," shared Dr. Simon Wong, UBS translation consultant of the CSB. "We had rewritten some notes that were deemed culturally sensitive and invited some Chinese seminary teachers to review it for Chinese readers, as well as work with the Crossway editors in the adaptation process."

As the existing study Bible used by the churches in China was published in the 1990s, the arrival of CSB marked a historic milestone

Dr. Lane Dennis, founder of Crossway, and Kua Wee Seng holding the CSB at APC, 2017.

in the history of the church in China. "Thank God for the *Chinese Study Bible*! It is much more detailed and comprehensive than the existing one we have," said Ji Yijun age thirty-nine, pastor of a church in Nanjing, who received a free copy of the CSB (New Testament) at a pastors' training supported by UBS.

Lay preacher Li Fanghua, age seventy-four, who leads two meeting points, shared that the CSB has helped her tremendously in shepherding the believers under her care, "The CSB has made it possible for someone like me with little formal theological education to better understand and study the Bible. The explanations are clear and concise. The illustrations further enhance my understanding. This gives me confidence to teach and preach God's Word to fellow believers."

Li Fanghua with her copy of CSB, 2022.

To date, about 115,000 copies of the CSB have been printed at APC and distributed in China, of which twenty thousand copies were given free to pastors and lay preachers for their personal and ministry use, cascading the benefits to millions of believers in their communities and congregations.

Students of Zhongnan Theological Seminary were among the recipients of the CSB, Hubei, 2023.

While the journey of helping to raise up and develop church pastors and preachers continues, it is encouraging to see the tremendous opportunities opening up across China in these past few decades to bless them through Bible-equipping seminars and other support. As a strong biblical foundation is being laid, it is exciting that some church leaders and Christians are looking to bring the values and teachings of the Bible to contribute positively to society, which we shall catch a glimpse of in the next chapter.

16
Shine like Stars

The Bible Advocacy among Leaders of Society

You must shine among them like stars lighting up the sky, as you offer them the message of life.

—Philippians 2:15b–16a GNT

But seek the welfare of the city where I have sent you into exile, and pray to the LORD on its behalf, for in its welfare you will find your welfare.

—Jeremiah 29:7

Beneficial to Society

In 1999, a group of Christians in Yunnan Province observed something in their community. They saw that people who were in the fetters of drug addiction were going in and out of rehabilitation clinics. Upon leaving the clinics, nine out of ten would return to their old habits. Families broke down. Sons followed the steps of their fathers. Moved by the sorrowful plight of these men and their families, they decided to help. Putting

City of Refuge, a Christian drug rehabilitation center in Yunnan, 2005.

together what they had, this group of Christians rented a few run-down houses and a few acres of land in a remote area in Taocheng (陶城, which means "pottery town" and is well known for a type of purple clay). They named it "City of Refuge Gospel Rehabilitation Center" (逃城福音解毒所).

Their rehabilitation therapy was simple—prayer, Bible reading, hymn singing, and farm work. There were no mandatory requirements or medications, and the drug addict was free to leave or come back. When a craving would strike, the people around him would pray, sing hymns, read the Bible to him, and accompany him until he was free from the pain. In this desolate place void of any sophisticated methods, the lives of the drug addicts were turned around and reshaped by the Grand Potter.

The success rate of this initiative was so much higher than secular therapies that more Christian drug rehab centers rooted on the principle of "not by medication nor by self-effort but solely by relying on God" (不靠药物, 不靠己力, 只靠上帝) were set up in China, catching the attention and receiving the approval of the Chinese authorities.

Wang Aiguo, deputy director general of Yunnan Provincial Religious Affairs Administration, in his paper "Christian Spiritual Therapy for Drug Rehabilitation"[1] acknowledged the work in Taocheng and the effectiveness of Christian rehab therapy: "The difference between Christian rehab and other treatment models is the emphasis on inner change and spiritual transformation from the inside out based on the teachings of the Bible and dependence on Jesus. ... It is beyond any doubt that this new comprehensive rehabilitation service is beneficial to society." The administration further affirmed the critical role of Christianity in society when it approved the establishment of the social service department by the Yunnan Christian Council / TSPM in 2006.

People gathering for Bible study, prayer, and worship at City of Refuge, 2005.

Wang Aiguo presenting his paper in 2013 at the Shanghai Academy of Social Sciences International Seminar on "The Bible and Social Service."

Thus far, we have seen how the Word of God has worked among his people in China. But the Bible is not to be confined within the walls of the church. As a library of books with different genres, the Bible offers a wealth of wisdom and counsel for human flourishing. It addresses a wide range of issues from the "creation of the world to its ultimate perfection, from the material realm to the spiritual order, from private life to public behavior, from family dynamics to social organization."[2] Since its birth, the church has been given the sacred task of unfurling for society the wisdom and salvation message found in the Bible.

As we have seen in previous chapters, since the reform era in the 1980s, the Churches in China have understandably been concerned with their survival and rebuilding. Gradually, Chinese Churches are also considering its role in society, engaging it with the Bible and contributing to it.

Praise God that various groups of Christians like those mentioned above are stepping up and seeking the "welfare of the city," sharing the goodness of Christian faith, and talking about the relevance of the Bible in their communities and spheres of influence. Creating platforms for such dialogues and sharing is important as it helps to raise the profile of the Bible and Christianity among unbelievers and leaders of society. Believers and church leaders too will greatly benefit by learning and seeing how the Bible can be relevant, applicable, and beneficial to a socialist society like China.

But how are such platforms to be created? How are the various parties going to be gathered? Will the leaders of Chinese society be interested in participating and listening to what the Bible has to offer toward human flourishing and issues facing China and the world today? How has UBS come alongside Chinese Churches in this journey?

---

1 Aiguo, "福音戒毒：云南教会参与社会服务的探索与试验" ["The Bible and Social Service"].
2 British and Foreign Bible Society, "What is the Bible?"

International Seminars on the Bible and Chinese Society

As with the setting up of the Bible printing press in Nanjing, the Lord created the platform for the treasures in his word to be shared among unbelievers and leaders in China who would otherwise not engage with the Bible. And this also started with a friendship.

Prof. Yan Kejia of SASS, 2019.

Prof. Yan Kejia, the director of the Institute of Religious Studies, Shanghai Academy of Social Sciences (SASS), was introduced to Kua Wee Seng (UBS CP director 1999–2021) by Cao Bin, Shanghai Ethnic and Religious Affairs Administration director general in 2010. With arrangements made and accompanied by Wee Seng, Prof. Yan visited the UK at the invitation of the British and Foreign Bible Society (BFBS). During Prof. Yan's visit, BFBS expressed interest in partnering with SASS to bring together three circles of people—academia, church, and government—to discuss issues relating to the Bible and society.

Prof. Yan immediately saw the potential of collaboration with Bible Societies. One of SASS's goals is to promote mutual exchanges and interaction on these issues. It was a perfect match, and the fact that it would be an international platform was a big plus. He was ready to "come on board."

In China, the study of religion as an academic discipline has been gaining momentum in recent years, with more centers and institutes for the study of religion being set up at academies and numerous top-tier Chinese universities. These institutes serve as think tanks for the Chinese government by providing valuable knowledge and rigorous research, which are used in the government's policy-making process. The Institute of Religious Studies at SASS was one such institute.

Within six months of the meeting in the UK, the inaugural SASS International Seminar came into reality in 2011. It was jointly organized by the SASS and the Center for Studies of Religion and Culture (a research arm of the Shanghai Religious Affairs Administration), with the support of BFBS and UBS. The theme, "The Role of Christianity in Modern China: The Bible in China," attracted both local and international scholars who shared research across five broad areas: the Bible and Chinese literature, the Bible and Chinese education, the Bible and Chinese society, biblical studies in China, and the Bible and the United Kingdom.

Attended by more than thirty participants, twenty from China and ten from overseas, the seminar was a significant achievement for Bible advocacy in China. This was the first time a Bible seminar with such a focus on the Bible and Chinese society had been organized. Wee Seng said, "It was a strategic initiative; a breakthrough in Bible advocacy in China!" Through Prof. Yan's willingness to partner with the Bible Societies, the Lord opened doors for his word to be advocated and promoted more broadly with influencers, opinion shapers, and leaders in China.

Papers presented by the local speakers highlighted the influence of the Bible on Chinese literature and educational studies, as well as its growing impact on community services. Prof. Chen Qijia of Renmin University said, "I have attended similar seminars in the past, but this is the first time that the focus is on the Bible. I am very encouraged by Dr. Yu Suee Yan's sharing about the Bible translation work among ethnic minorities."

Paul Wooley from BFBS, Kua Wee Seng, Prof. Yan Kejia, Bishop John Chew, and Greg Clark, CEO of the Bible Society of Australia, 2018.

By its third year, this Bible advocacy initiative was seeing further breakthroughs. First, besides academia, the seminar saw increased participation from government representatives and the Chinese Churches. This tripartite mix provided a solid and robust discussion between policymakers, academics, and practitioners. Second, there was greater participation not only from Shanghai but also from provinces like Zhejiang, Jiangsu, Fujian, and Yunnan. This was critical as it allowed participants to have a wider scope and better understanding of the Bible and its role in Chinese society.

Since 2011, UBS has continued partnering with SASS to organize these international seminars to provide biblical perspectives on themes that concern China as well as the global community. Each opportunity to highlight the relevance of the Bible to societal, national, and international issues is precious and not to be taken for granted. It is hard to imagine that Chinese academics and government officials would be keen to dialogue with international Christian researchers and scholars on the Bible and current affairs. And for this dialogue to be sustained for more than a decade, it has to be the hand of God.

BFBS CEO Dr. Paul Williams speaking at the 2016 SASS Seminar "Bible and Values."

Reflecting on the 2021 seminar, Wee Seng said, "We almost thought that this year's seminar would not happen—given the context of worsening international relations. I believe that when international relations are colder, the more we need to work toward such international dialogues to continue to bring about greater mutual understanding and learning between Chinese Christians and overseas Christians as well as between Christians and non-Christians across the globe."

Expansion in Participation and Support of Renowned Scholars

Over the years, the seminar has invited a wide range of local Chinese presenters including key leaders and scholars from the national and provincial Chinese Churches, China Academy of Social Sciences (Institute of World Religions), State Administration for Religious Affairs, various provincial Religious Affairs Administration, Shanghai Association of Ethics, top-tier universities like Beijing and Fudan, YMCA and YWCA, China Daoism Association, Shanghai Islamic Association, Institute of Chinese Marxism Studies at SASS, and Shanghai Communist Party School.

To give a taste of its international flavor, these are some of the institutes and organizations represented at the seminar (besides those from UBS): Akrofi Christaller Institute of Theology, Mission and Culture (Ghana), A Rocha International, an environment conservation organization, Natural History Museum (UK), Oxford University (UK), University of Nottingham (UK), Duke Divinity School (US), Macquarie University (Australia), Australian Catholic University, University of Bern (Switzerland), St. Paul's Theological College (Malaysia), Singapore National Education Institute, Singapore Centre for Global Missions, Diocese of Singapore, and Singapore Trinity Theological College.

Dr. Andrew Walls speaking at the 2017 SASS seminar.

Prof. Chong Chee Pang at the inaugural SASS seminar, "The Bible in China," 2011.

Dr. Robert Banks interacting with seminary students, 2017.

Bible Societies represented included BFBS, Bible Society of Australia, German Bible Society, Bible Society of Malaysia, Bible Society of Singapore, and Finnish Bible Society.

Among the many papers shared, a significant one was made by Lord Stephen Green, chairman of the Natural History Museum (UK) and former Hongkong Shanghai Banking Corporation (HSBC) chairman, titled "Mystery of the Universe" at the fifth seminar, "The Bible and Environment," in 2015. He gave the biblical account of creation and the Bible's perspective on history that gives hope and motivates action in the face of global environmental crisis.

Lord Stephen Green speaking at the SASS Seminar, "Bible and the Environment," 2015.

Well-respected theologian and writer Robert Banks, former director and dean of the Macquarie Christian Studies Institute, Macquarie University, Australia, has participated multiple times at the seminar. In 2022, he presented the paper "Biblical Clues to Developing a Church with Stronger Chinese Characteristics."

It is most encouraging to have had Bishop John Chew, UBS global council member (2013–2017) and UBS CP honorary consultant (2018–present), at the seminar from the beginning. He has been a consistent voice, demonstrating the wisdom of the Good Book in addressing the contemporary challenges discussed at the seminars. Speaking at the 2021 seminar on "The Bible and Dialogue of the Civilizations," Bishop John Chew remarked that it was "by grace that we are talking about a dialogue of the world civilizations as this is a huge progress from what Samuel Huntington purported on the clash of civilizations." He hoped that through the seminar collective wisdom could be learned, alluding to the Book of Proverbs, and that the great commandments of Jesus from Mark 12:29–33 would be given heed.

Special mention goes to Prof. Andrew Walls, Christian scholar and honorary professor at the University of Edinburgh, Richard Magnus, retired chief district judge and chancellor of the Anglican Diocese of Singapore, and Prof. Chong Chee Pang, former principal of Singapore's Trinity Theological College and UBS CP honorary consultant. They are no longer with us, but their love for the word and invaluable research on various issues raised at the seminars, like climate crisis, migration, and the contextualization of Christianity, will remain.

Retired senior judge, Richard Magnus, at the SASS seminar held online in 2021.

Participation of China's Churches and Theological Seminaries

The Protestant churches of China became an official partner of the seminar in 2019, but it had started participating even before that. At the fourth seminar in 2014 on "The Bible and Culture," Rev. Xu Xiaohong, vice chairman of the TSPM, said that the topic of "Bible and Culture" is highly significant because it plays an important role in the development of Christianity in China. "The Bible is not only a sacred text of the Christians but also an important legacy to the whole of mankind. It should also be interpreted in different cultures and religious contexts." He also highlighted that the Chinese church leadership has been working on localizing Christianity in the Chinese cultural context.

An important bridge was built as China's theological seminaries began to attend and participate in these international seminars at the invitation of SASS. Time was set aside for seminary students to have informal discussions with the speakers. "This is something strategic because such topics are rarely explored and discussed at the seminaries and churches," commented Wee Seng. "So we are very glad that since 2016, theological seminaries have begun to send their students to participate at the seminars."

Praise God that in the 2022 seminar, a record of more than 270 students and faculty of China's national, regional, and provincial seminaries attended (with some online), a huge increase from 2016. These seminaries included Nanjing Union Theological Seminary, Huadong (East China) Theological Seminary, Shandong Theological Seminary, and Jiangsu Theological Seminary.

Wu Jing, a student from Jiangsu Theological Seminary who attended the seminar on "The Bible and Shared Future for Mankind: Migration and Community" in 2018, said that the seminar had given her a new understanding of the vital relationship between religion and society. She saw how interconnected the church and society should be and that the very essence of the Christian faith, which is love, commands all believers to reach out and serve the community.

Wu Jinqian, a senior student, said of the 2021 seminar titled The Bible and Dialogue of the Civilizations, "It's wonderful that seminarians like us can attend the seminar to listen to these distinguished academics, scholars, and researchers from China and overseas. It was an eye-opening time and an intellectual enrichment opportunity for us. We are inspired to embark on our own theological journey!"

Seminarian Zhou Wenya shared how he was inspired to understand church ministries from another paradigm. "As church ministers who serve people of all walks of life, we need to expound the Bible from a broader perspective and with a more global view of harmony and coexistence in mind."

The participation of the Chinese Churches and seminaries was a breakthrough for Bible advocacy in China, especially against the backdrop of a predominant view among some Chinese Christians that the Bible should be kept within the church. However, at these seminars, seminarians and Chinese Christian leaders are discovering that the church is indeed called to share the wisdom and life that is found in the Bible with the society. They have benefitted from the seminars and dialogues about the Bible with non-Christian academics in China as well as international speakers. At the same time, they are also learning that if the Bible can make an impact in other societies overseas, so can the Bible in China!

Feedback from Chinese Academia and Government

What do the representatives from Chinese academia and government think about the seminars? What is the value of such seminars for them? Here are quotes from some of them.

Chinese Academy of Social Science, Beijing.

At the 2017 seminar on "The Bible and Sinicization of Christianity," Wang Xinhua, the deputy director general of the Shanghai Ethnic and Religious Affairs Commission, said, "It is not an easy accomplishment to sustain this international conference for seven consecutive years. We live in the age of globalization and face similar challenges in the areas of religion and society; global challenges can't be solved by a single nation but by the international community. Such conferences provide a good platform for discussion and mutual understanding on common issues."

At the 2021 hybrid seminar, Mr. Gan Chunhui, vice president of SASS, noted at the opening ceremony that it was the tenth year of the seminar and partnership, and he was glad that the pandemic did not deter SASS and its partners from continuing to meet. He highlighted the shared goal of strengthening interaction and mutual understanding across different cultural, religious, and academic backgrounds.

At the 2022 seminar, Mao Yunqi, deputy director of the Shanghai Municipal Bureau of Ethnic and Religious Affairs and director of the Center for the Studies of the Sinicization of Religions in China, highlighted that the seminar was in its eleventh year and has received increasing support from scholars and researchers who have contributed to the discussion on the sinicization of Christianity. He added, "We are especially grateful to our friends from UBS and BFBS."

That the SASS International Seminar on the Bible could be sustained was something even the Chinese organizers and leaders recognized as extraordinary, especially given the challenging situations in recent years. Prof. Yan Kejia's vision and perseverance in initiating and organizing these seminars and the strong support of the Chinese authorities, academia, and churches are not to be taken for granted. It is wonderful to see the relationships forged and the goodwill that has been engendered over the past decade. As Dr. Bernard Low, co-director (ministry) of UBS CP, said about the eleventh seminar in 2022, "This attests to our longstanding friendship and partnership with Professor Yan and SASS, which we deeply value."

Besides SASS, UBS has also partnered with the Academy of Religion at Minzu University in Beijing to organize four cross-cultural dialogues thus far, exploring the relevance of biblical texts to modern

Representatives from UBS participating at the 2023 Minzu Dialogue.

The 2022 SASS seminar was held in a hybrid format.

contexts. Another partner is the Center for the Study of Christianity at the China Academy of Social Sciences. In 2018, the International Symposium for Biblical Studies in Context was held in Beijing, attended by more than 180 academics, scholars, researchers, and church leaders.

It is exciting to know that the high-quality, rigorous research presented at the seminars have proved invaluable to the Chinese government in the process of their policymaking. Let us pray that through the seminars, more and more Christians will seek to engage their community with the Bible and create a positive tangible impact on Chinese society!

The following table shows the themes that have been discussed from 2011 to 2022 at the SASS seminar.:

Year	Theme
2011	The Bible in China
2012	The Bible and Harmonious Society
2013	The Bible and Social Service
2014	The Bible and Culture
2015	The Bible and Environment
2016	The Bible and Values
2017	The Bible and Sinicization of Christianity in China
2018	The Bible and Shared Future for Mankind: Migration and Community
2019	The Bible and Belt and Road Initiative
2021	The Bible and Dialogue of the Civilizations
2022	The Bible and Sinicization of Christianity in the New Era of China
2023	The Bible and Sinicization—Translation and Interpretation of the Bible in Today's Context

Mutual Visits and Exchanges

Overseas Visits by China Officials

Besides seminars, overseas visits by Chinese officials have helped them see how religion can play a positive role in society and how Christians, who seek the welfare of their societies, can help strengthen their social fabric and play a role in the economic and social development of China.

Since the 1990s, UBS CP has helped organize and facilitate numerous trips for government officials and academics to visit Bible Societies, churches, seminaries, and other relevant government departments and organizations overseas.

An example was when a delegation from China visited Nigeria, Mauritius, and South Africa upon joint invitation by the Global South (Anglican) Churches and UBS in 2009. The Chinese delegates were from the State Administration of Religious Affairs (SARA) of China led by Ye Xiaowen, director of SARA, and it was their first visit to these African countries. Here are some excerpts from SARA's report on the trip:

SARA minister Ye Xiaowen presenting a gift to James Catford, Group CEO of BFBS, UK, 2000.

> Christianity is developing rapidly in Africa and has become a force to be reckoned with. In the process of development, Christianity in African countries is trying to move away from the influence of Western churches and actively seeking a position and a voice in the world Christian community. ... During this visit, the delegation had extensive and in-depth exchanges and sharing with political, religious, and academic circles in the countries visited on topics such as religious issues in China and Africa, and the positive role of religion in society. ... This visit has enhanced mutual understanding and appreciation and has been very fruitful.[3]

Vice-minister of State Administration for Religious Affairs (SARA), Yang Tongxiang, introduces the director general of SARA, Guo Wei, to Rev. Dr. John Stott at All Souls Church, Langham Place, London, England, 1999.

One of the national priorities of the Chinese government has been to promote religious harmony and social stability in China. Learning what and how other countries are doing in these areas will be pertinent. Thus, it is exciting to see that through their overseas visits, Chinese officials are able to see the development of Christianity in other countries and the positive role of religion in society. It is hoped that with this knowledge and impression, the Chinese authorities will continue to pursue religious policy that is favorable toward the development of religions in China.

During these visits, Chinese officials were also introduced to Christian leaders with whom mutual understanding and relationships could be built. Some of these Christian leaders include Archbishop of Canterbury (UK) Justin Welby, Archbishop Mouneer Anis, the bishop of Egypt and presiding bishop of the Episcopal Church in Jerusalem and the Middle East, primates of the Anglican churches in Africa,* and Catholic Church leaders like the retired Archbishop of Kampala, Cardinal Emmanuel Wamala, leaders of the Catholic Church in France, leaders of the Christian Council in Norway, leaders of the Evangelical Lutheran Church of Finland.

---

3 Xue, *China Religion*.

Former Grand Mufti of Egypt, Dr. Ali Gomaa, Archbishop Mouneer of the Anglican Church of Egypt, and Bishop John Chew in Beijing, 2016.

Archbishop Justin Welby and James Catford, Group CEO of BFBS at APC, 2015.

Through these meetings and interactions, Chinese delegates gained first-hand knowledge and understanding of Christian faith, work, and practices in countries around the world. These friendships would be important in their ongoing work and ministry in China in their various offices in the government.

In addition, Chinese officials were introduced to a wide range of Bible publications, initiatives, and ministries of Bible Societies, churches, and Christian organizations. They visited prison ministries, mission schools, elder care facilities, counseling centers, and other ministries initiated by Christians like ELIS in Rome (a Catholic educational and vocational center), and the Salvation Army in New Zealand and Australia. They also visited Bible museums established by Bible Societies in the US, UK, and Germany, which showcase the foundational and instrumental role of the Bible in the development of these countries.

Elder Fu with Dr. Lane Dennis, President and CEO of Crossway, US, 2016.

Wee Seng, who has accompanied Chinese delegates on numerous trips, shared, "One of my memorable experiences was when the SARA delegation visited the Bible Society of New Zealand in 2006. During a visit to a prison, they were very impressed by a Christian prison ministry that arranged for ex-offenders to be adopted by Christian families to help them integrate back into normal life and society. They saw Christian love at work and doing good for the country as a whole."

It is noteworthy that in 2003, the Religious and Culture Publishing House, the publishing arm of the SARA, printed ten thousand copies of *Words of Jesus: Herbal Tea for the Spirit*. This booklet was a compilation of sayings of the Lord Jesus from the Gospels on different topics and aspects of life. The ten thousand copies were distributed to both Christians and non-Christians, including some government officials—an example of the goodwill that has been built and a testament of how the Lord spreads his word through unlikely channels!

Overseas Visits by Chinese Church Leaders

Overseas trips were also organized for Chinese church leaders and these exchanges helped widen the scope of Bible ministry in China. In the 1980s and 1990s, the Chinese Churches were focused on printing Bibles as their top priority. But as the church grew and expanded, the needs became more varied, and different Bible ministries, publications, and resources were needed. They were thus developing various Bible ministries for these needs.

In addition, the Chinese authorities have been encouraging religious groups in China, including Christians, to contribute to the welfare and development of society. It is thus advantageous for Chinese church leaders to go on overseas trips to learn how Christians in other countries are developing their Bible ministries, engaging with people outside the church, and serving the needs of society.

Often, it was these overseas visits that laid the ground for new Bible-related publications to be adapted by the Chinese church for China. National Chinese Protestant church leader Elder Fu Xianwei said in an interview in 2010 on the value of exchanges and meetings with Bible Societies overseas, "For the long-term, the goal [for the Chinese church] is to provide a wider range of scriptural materials and resources in different mediums … . Therefore, I am very happy that through the UBS fellowship, we have access to a range of quality Scripture materials created and produced by Bible Societies around the world."

Rev. Joseph Gu Yuese, President of Zhejiang Province Christian Council receiving a gift from Rev. Tony Yeo, Senior Pastor of Covenant Evangelical Free Church, during his visit to Singapore, 2013.

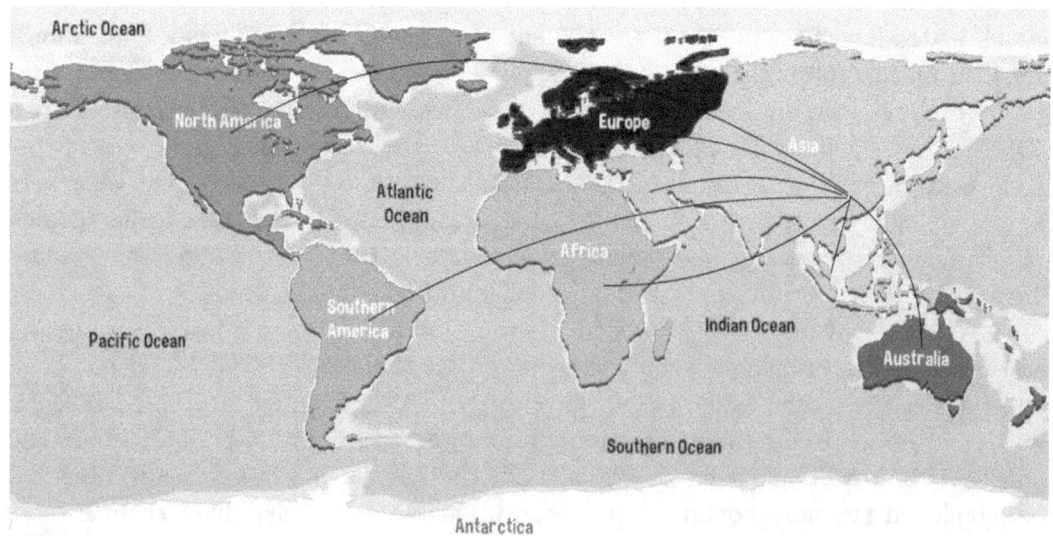

Bible Societies in Asia, Africa, North America, South America, Europe, & Australia have hosted Chinese delegates.

Examples of Bible-related publications that resulted from overseas visits include *Jesus Manga* for young adults, printed and distributed in 2015, the *Chinese Study Bible* published in 2017, a collaboration with Crossway Publishing, and the *Financial Stewardship Bible* (Chinese edition) published in 2020 in partnership with the American Bible Society. Over the years, as overseas exchanges helped Chinese government officials gain a better understanding of the Christian faith, these and other new Bible-related publications were being accepted and approved.

It is inspiring to see the UBS fellowship coming together to help Chinese officials and church leaders gain a better picture of the Christian faith around the world. As Elder Fu said aptly, "The beauty of the UBS fellowship is in its worldwide network of Bible Societies coming together in communication and partnership."

At the heart of these trips and visits is relationship building. Relationships between the Chinese government officials and the UBS fellowship as well as between the Chinese church leaders and the UBS fellowship. "It's important for the Chinese church leaders and Chinese authorities to get to know us (UBS) better. … This will help to build goodwill and trust, which are essential for our partnership in the Bible ministry in China to develop and grow," said Wee Seng.

Chinese believe it is more profitable to travel ten thousand miles than to read ten thousand books (读万卷书不如行万里路). As seen from the examples above, nothing beats visiting a place personally to see, hear, and learn for oneself. Overseas trips have promoted goodwill and opened a window for government officials and academics to see the positive contributions of the Bible and Christian faith to societies around the world and for Chinese Churches to benefit from the body of Christ through shared resources!

It is unimaginable that the Bible has gone from being banned to becoming openly discussed and appreciated in China—among people of different religious backgrounds in local communities, among Chinese scholars and academics at international seminars, and among Chinese leaders through visits out of China. Increasingly, Chinese people outside the church have gained a more positive impression of the Bible and the Christian faith in China. Praise God that over the years, through the platforms we have seen in this chapter, leaders of Chinese society have become more receptive to the contributions Chinese Christians can make to create a better and brighter future for China. Let us continue to pray for this window of opportunity to remain open and for more Chinese Christians to shine like stars in the vast skies of China.

17
In the Light of Scripture

The Bible and the Contextualization and Inculturation of Christianity in China

> Have this mind among yourselves, which is yours in Christ Jesus, who, though he was in the form of God, did not count equality with God a thing to be grasped, but emptied himself, by taking the form of a servant, being born in the likeness of men.
>
> —Philippians 2:5–7

> Christian mission is not simply about the multiplication of the church; it is about the discipling of the nations. It is about the penetration of cultures and ways of thought by the word about Christ.
>
> —Andrew Walls, missiologist and scholar of world Christianity

The old lady stands in front of the expectant congregation. She closes her eyes and starts to sing. Her low, rough voice fills the sanctuary and carries even beyond the open doors. "The Lord of Grace," she sings, "The Lord of Grace, Jesus Christ, suffered a multitude of hardships to atone for our sin, to rescue us from evil. He came down from heaven, he gave up all riches and honor he had received from his father. He left all that behind and was born more than 1,900 years ago in Bethlehem in Judea ..." The congregation in rural Shaanxi listens in rapt silence as Tao Buzhen sings a gospel song titled "The Life of Jesus." Her singing style is that of a Shaanxi folk singer and storyteller, with simple repetitive melodies. ... The language is colloquial and easy to pick up and remember even by those who are illiterate.

The above is an excerpt from a 1997 news article by Amity News Service about a Chinese believer, Tao Buzhen from Shaanxi Province, who sang Christian songs set in local folk melody. In 2017, during a visit to rural churches in Yunnan Province with colleagues from the British and Foreign Bible Society (BFBS), we had the wonderful privilege of listening to a Black Yi believer who sang, in her deep and resounding voice, a gospel hymn set to indigenous music. We, like the congregation in Tao Buzhen's church, were totally enraptured by her singing. Her rendition of the song transported us to another realm.

Black Yi believer singing a hymn, 2017.

What beautiful examples of how the Christian faith, when expressed creatively in a local culture, can capture the hearts and imagination of local people—even foreigners! Interestingly, their songs centered upon the incarnational gospel of Christ, which forms the basis of contextualization and inculturation efforts by churches all over the world.

What does it mean to contextualize or inculturate the gospel? Simply put, it is communicating and living out the Christian faith, its

A Catholic church in Dali, Yunnan, 2020.

teachings, and its practices in ways that are faithful to Scripture and meaningful to a local culture. It is helpful to remind ourselves that the Christian faith needs to be contextualized in every culture and that it's an ongoing, dynamic process for churches everywhere. As Prof. Paul Williams, chief executive of BFBS, said, "The gospel is always foreign to every

UBS leaders with Bishop Li Shan, President of CCPA at Church of Our Savior (North Church). Two Chinese pavilions (亭子) stand on both sides of the cathedral as an example of inculturation of Christianity in China, Beijing, 2023.

culture that it is in. And it must always be recontextualized for every generation."[1]

Christianity in China has been on a journey to be more contextualized since the faith first arrived in China 1,300 years ago. Great strides have been made in this journey, but many Chinese still generally perceive Christianity as foreign and Western. It has been said that "to have one more Christian is to have one less Chinese." Hence, like churches in other cultures and contexts, this journey is both important and urgent for the Churches in China.

A Christian home in rural China, 2011.

As the contextualization and inculturation of the gospel is a broad field of study, I will limit the scope to two areas: (1) the translation of the Chinese Union Version Bible in 1919 as an example of contextualization, and (2) some recent developments of the Chinese Churches in their contextualization and inculturation journey. Through both, we will also see the role played by the pioneering Bible Societies and later by the UBS fellowship in coming alongside the Chinese Churches in this important journey.

The Chinese Union Version Bible

Bible translation is often recognized as the first critical step toward the contextualization of the gospel. The message of salvation and hope needs to find a home in a people's mother tongue, expressed in words and idioms that can be easily understood, with phrases that are found and used in their everyday lives. It needs to be preached not just in the pulpit but also discussed in homes, markets, and workplaces.

Chinese Bible and Sinicization Symposium, 2019.

In China, the Word of God has found a home in the hearts of the Chinese predominantly through the Chinese Union Version (CUV). Published on April 22, 1919, in Shanghai, the CUV was the most significant Bible translation project in the history of the Chinese Protestant church, involving a team of ten missionary Bible translators, including Chinese translators and assistants.[2] Perhaps the longest Chinese Bible translation project, its making spanned three decades, from around 1890 to 1919.

During the reform era in the 1980s when churches reopened, the CUV became a key unifying factor for the Protestants in China. Former missionary H. R. Weber, who visited China in 1984, wrote, "Without this common Bible, Protestants in China would probably still be unrelated or might already again be split in separate communities." But as Chinese

---

1 As part of his paper presented at the international seminar organized by the Shanghai Academy of Social Sciences in 2017 with the support of UBS and BFBS.

2 Zetzsche, *The Bible in China*, 257.

At the centenary celebration of the CUV in Shanghai, 2019.

Christians from different theological backgrounds, denominations, and walks of life worshiped together in church and read the Bible with "an invocation of the Holy Spirit in the light of the experiences, sufferings and developments of the last 35 years,"³ they experienced a unity that was unique to them. They were now held together by the common message of the gospel found in the Bible for which they had suffered.

For over a century, it is through the CUV that millions of Chinese have come to know Christ personally and learned their language of faith. Upon it, the Chinese Churches standardize their theological language and build the foundation of their faith. As we have seen from the stories and testimonies in this book, CUV remains the beloved version cherished by the Chinese Churches and believers, who use it in their personal study of the word and corporate life in the church.

Rev. Wu Wei, president of CCC, highlighted its spiritual significance aptly when he said the CUV is a significant milestone in the development of Christianity in China, which aided the spread of the gospel. It is also an important landmark in the sinicization of Christianity in China.⁴

Through the CUV, God speaks in a voice with sounds and rhythms that the Chinese can relate to and resonate with in their hearts. To describe this feeling of closeness, the Chinese often use the phrase "亲切" (qin qie); its English equivalent I have yet to find. The first word "亲" means "dear" or "kin." The second word "切," as a noun, means "close to." Together it describes a person so kind and friendly that others feel close to them or feel dearly regarded. I imagine God bending down and drawing each Chinese person close to his heart as they read the Bible in their heart language.

At the centenary celebration of the CUV, Liu Yuanlong, leader of the Chinese Catholic Church, said that CUV, with its unique grammatical style, brings forth the warmth of the language, the texture of the words, and the rhythmic nature of the content. Chinese people can naturally, affectionately, and without any obstacles, read and listen to the word of the Lord, and be led to the joy of salvation. He also hoped that this century-old Chinese Bible would be a refueling station and a seed sower for the development of the sinicization of Christianity.⁵

---

3 Weber, "Impression on the Bible."
4 Adapted and translated from https://www.ccctspm.org/newsinfo/11574, accessed November 5, 2022.
5 Ibid.

Another significance of the CUV lies in the second word "union" (和合). By the mid-1800s, there were about twenty-seven different Bible translations done by missionaries in China from different nationalities, denominations, and mission societies. Some were done in classical Chinese, one of the earliest of which was by the first Protestant missionary Robert Morrison in 1823. Some were done in Mandarin, the vernacular of the common people (mostly in the north), like the Peking Version in 1872. Missionaries in China were using different Bible translations based on their denominations and nationalities. Attempts at producing a unified version were fraught with difficulties and stalemates due to translation and theological differences.

Gradually, a desire for a unified version of the Bible accepted by all Protestant denominations arose among the missionaries serving in China so that this would make the spread of the gospel and the nurture of Chinese Christians more effective.

But how was a unified version to be translated when there was yet to be an official national language in China? The turning point came in 1890, at the General Conference of the Protestant Missionaries in China held in Shanghai, when a formal proposal for a unified version was approved with parties agreeing to translate the Union Version of the Chinese Bible into three forms of the Chinese language—High Wenli,* Easy Wenli, and Mandarin—for different target audiences. However, by 1907, political change and cultural shifts in China led to a consensus to merge the two classical versions—High Wenli and Easy Wenli—into one, known as Wenli. The Mandarin version became what was later known as the Chinese Union Version (CUV).

In this massive project, local Chinese translators and assistants ought to be given special mention. Their contribution was remarkable, particularly in the Mandarin version, because the standard form of the language had yet to be clearly defined (especially at the beginning of the translation project). These Chinese assistants rendered critical help in finding a common form of Mandarin. One can only imagine the awesome responsibility on their shoulders. Among them were Zou Liwen, an ordained pastor who left his parish to engage in the work, Wang Yuande, an avid reader of Mandarin books and was sharp in picking out faults in sentence structures,[6] Liu Dacheng, who gave sixteen years of his life to the work, and Cheng Jingyi, who later became one of the Chinese Protestant church leaders in the early 1900s.[7]

Indeed, the critical role played by the Chinese translators was evident in what F. W. Baller, one of the missionary translators, said, "No rendering was adopted, in regard to the Chinese of it, without their agreement. Many stumbling blocks have thus been removed that would be apt to turn away an educated Chinese from reading the Scripture because the translation was foreign in its usage of language."[8]

The launch of the Mandarin Union Version (now known as CUV) could not have been at a better time. Coinciding with the publication of CUV was a watershed cultural and political movement, the May Fourth Movement (五四运动) in 1919, a massive student protest that was an impetus to the New Culture Movement (新文化运动, 1910s–1920s). It had a far-reaching impact on the country, propelling China into adopting Mandarin as the national language.

---

6 Zetzsche, *Bible in China*, 262.

7 Zetzsche, 268.

8 Zetzsche, 319.

With the New Culture Movement, the popularity and prestige of the CUV as a religious writing and literary work increased among the Chinese. Not only was it used as a model for a vernacular (白话文) translation, it was also used as a reference in literary writing for some Chinese writers. For example, Chinese school textbooks compared the creation account in Genesis using the Wenli Union Version* and CUV to teach Classical Chinese and Mandarin to school students.

According to George Mak, an award-winning scholar on Bible translation and the Chinese language, the CUV played an important role not only in spreading and standardizing Mandarin as the national language but also in forging a one-nation identity for Republican China as the country entered a new era:

> Determined to produce a Bible version targeting a national audience, these translators, who were helped by their Chinese teachers or assistants as well as their fellow missionaries from different parts of China, endeavored to translate the Bible into a kind of Mandarin that would be "everywhere current" (tongxing 通行) in China. In doing so, they set the geographical perimeter of Mandarin as a national language and attempted to create a form of Mandarin that would be acceptable to people of all social classes in China.⁹

A page from a local Chinese school textbook (国文百八课第一册) which used Bible verses from CUV.

The lasting influence of CUV on Chinese society can be seen in how a number of its phrases and idioms have been incorporated into people's daily speech. For example, gospel (福音), baptism (洗礼), an eye for an eye, a tooth for a tooth (以眼还眼，以牙还牙), just to name a few.

On the value of the CUV to Chinese culture and society, Xu Yihua, professor of the School of International Relations and Public Affairs of Fudan University and counselor of the Shanghai Municipal People's Government, said that the CUV is of great significance to the Christian church in China, but its influence extends far beyond Christianity. It can be said to be "the greatest gift and contribution that Christianity has made to Chinese culture, which is probably only rivaled by the Chinese Christian hymnal collection, 'Hymns of Universal Praise'《普天颂赞》."¹⁰

---

9   Mak, "Chinese Protestant Bible Versions and the Chinese Language."
10 Adapted and translated from https://www.ccctspm.org/newsinfo/11574 accessed on November 5, 2022.

What was the role of the Bible Societies in the translation of the CUV? The successful translation, publication, printing, and distribution of the CUV were inseparable from the crucial patronage and support of the Bible Societies—namely, BFBS, American Bible Society, and the National Bible Society of Scotland (known today as the Scottish Bible Society). The three Bible Societies covered most of the translation costs from the beginning, including the costs of reference materials, resources, and travel.

In 1913, at the request of one of the translators, C. Goodrich, and also in an effort to speed up the translation work, the Bible Societies paid for the housing accommodation and salaries of the missionary Bible translators who had been released by their mission societies to commit fully to translation work. Not only did the Bible Societies support the Bible translation, but they also printed low-cost CUV Bibles and distributed them via their extensive colportage system. By the early 1900s, there were hundreds of Chinese colporteurs who helped sell the Bibles!

Dr. Mak sharing how the CUV Bible contributed to the promotion of Mandarin as a national language in China at the CUV centenary symposium, 2019.

We should not forget the contributions of many overseas Christians and churches who gave through the Bible Societies, which made the CUV translation over the three decades (ca. 1890–1919) possible. It is inspiring to know that many Christians at that time believed in the importance of not just reading God's Word but also reading it in one's heart language and supported the Bible translation into Mandarin.

Thank God for the CUV Bible! We shall look at how the century old Chinese Bible has indeed been a "refueling station" and a "seed sower" for the sinicization of Christianity in China in the next segment.

From "Christianity in China" to "Chinese Christianity"

Those who keep up with recent news on religion in China will be familiar with the catchphrase "sinicization" (中国化), which means "to make something Chinese or with Chinese characteristics." It is in effect a national campaign affecting not just religion but also various aspects of life in China. It was first applied to religion by the current Chinese authorities in 2015.

Even though it is promoted by the Chinese authorities, the Chinese Churches have recognized that the campaign can have a positive cataclysmic effect on them. Wherever the gospel is preached, it should be communicated in ways faithful to Scripture and meaningful to the local culture.

In its five-year plan (2017–2022) for promoting the sinicization of Christianity, the Protestant churches in China were clear with the goal they aimed to achieve:

> The goal of Sinicization of Christianity is to build a church that exalts Christ and maintains unity; a church that is faithful to the biblical truths, rooted in Chinese culture, and has a contextual theological acceptance; a church that has the courage to take social responsibility and witness life through its living; a church that has communion with holy disciples in all churches around the world and makes unique contributions to the universal church, realizing the transformation from "Christianity in China" to "Chinese Christianity."

The Bible is at the heart of this transformation from "Christianity in China" to "Chinese Christianity" on two levels. First, in response to the call for the indigenization of religion, the Protestant churches have embarked on Bible revision, while the Catholic Church has embarked on Bible translation work. As we have seen in the example of the CUV, Bible translation is the cornerstone of the contextualization of the gospel; it needs to be recontextualized for every generation. To put things into perspective, there are about nine hundred English translations of the Scripture, while Chinese Protestants have largely used the same translation for over a century.[11]

Second, Chinese Churches need to develop more talent in the fields of biblical studies, Bible interpretation, and Bible translation in order to do well in their contextualization journey. This was a sentiment echoed by Rev. Chen Shenfeng of Hangzhou Sideng Church, who presented at the CUV 2019 symposium that any revision of the CUV must be built upon its existing firm foundation. He highlighted the urgent need for investing in and developing local talent in biblical studies and translation and the setup of necessary infrastructure like that of the Bible society.[12]

As mentioned above, a symposium on the "Contextualization and Indigenization of Christianity in China" was held in 2019 at the centenary of the CUV, co-organized by CCC/TSPM and UBS. It covered topics related to the CUV—ranging from its history, translation, interpretation, study, and revision to its cultural and societal impact on China—presented by leaders from the churches in China, the Bible Societies, and academia.

At the symposium, echoing the importance of collaboration as seen in the translation of the CUV, Elaine Duncan, chief executive of the Scottish Bible Society and chairman of the UBS Global Council, said, "Giving people 'the best possible Bible' is never a work done alone. The many skills, gifts, knowledge and experience that go into good Bible translation are gifts from God himself to equip His church and build His Kingdom."

Indeed, as in the past, UBS is committed to providing Bible translation expertise, resources, and consultancy support to the Chinese Churches in this journey. Over the years, teaching sessions, seminars, dialogues, and symposiums have been organized with the Churches in China on topics ranging from Bible interpretation, Bible translation, and Chinese culture to the indigenization of Christianity in China.

UBS leader Elaine Duncan at the CUV centenary symposium, 2019.

An online seminar was organized during the COVID-19 pandemic in June 2021 with the Catholic Church in China. It was attended by national leaders and Bible translation team members of the Chinese Catholic Church, Bible translation scholars from UBS as well as Bishop John Chew (honorary consultant, UBS CP), Kua Wee Seng (UBS CP director, 1999–2021) and Ignatius Lee (acting general secretary, Hong Kong Bible Society).

The Chinese Catholic Bible translation team and Bible scholars from UBS shared different aspects of Chinese Bible translation related to inculturation. They examined topics like the

---

11 American Bible Society, "Number of English Bible Translations."
12 Shenfeng, "Contextualization and Indigenization of Christianity in China."

history of the translation of the Chinese Bible as well as various translation issues related to Chinese Bible versions, including the Studium Biblicum Version and the CUV.

Bishop Shen Bin, vice president of Chinese Catholic Patriotic Association and Bishops Conference of the Catholic Church in China (CCPA and BCCCC), concluded the seminar by calling for more interaction between the Chinese Catholic Church and UBS in promoting the translation and contextualization of Scripture. UBS welcomes this and looks forward to more mutual exchanges and support between the Chinese Catholic Church and UBS in Chinese Bible translation.

Furthermore, the theme of the sinicization of Christianity was taken up in several international seminars of the Shanghai Academy of Social Sciences (SASS) organized with the support of UBS. At the 2017 seminar on "The Bible and Sinicization of Christianity," Gu Mengfei, CCC/TSPM research department director, presented the view of the Chinese church on the sinicization of Christianity. He said that it is to adhere to the basics of the faith, carry out "religious reform based on the Bible," and let Christianity "take root in the fertile soil of Chinese culture."

Such seminars are having an impact on seminary students. Han Xue, a Shandong Seminary student who attended the 2017 seminar, shared, "I used to think that Christianity and sinicization are rather incompatible. But the seminar has helped me think otherwise. Listening to the development of Christianity among the Lisu ethnic group has caused me to seriously reflect on the sinicization of Christianity in my church in Shandong."

At the 2022 SASS seminar on "The Bible and Sinicization of Christianity in the New Era of China," it was exciting to hear from Rev. Dr. Chen Yilu, executive vice president of Nanjing Union Theological Seminary, who presented on "Sow Good Seeds in Good Soil— The Practical Exploration of the Sinicization of Christianity," and Rev. Gao Ming, chairman of Shandong TSPM and president of Shandong Theological Seminary, who shared a proposal to interpret the Bible the Chinese way, "An Initial Exploration on the Chinese Way of the Interpretation of Bible—Based on Qilu Theology." Both leaders exemplify ongoing efforts by Chinese Christians to transform "Christianity in China" into "Chinese Christianity."

Dr. Lim Teck Peng (TTC), Kua Wee Seng, and Gu Mengfei (secretary general of the national TSPM), 2017.

Chen Chen, a student from Jiangsu Theological Seminary, found the seminar enlightening. "Through the discussions and dialogues on the sinicization of Christianity by experts at home and abroad, we realized that there is so much more that we can do to contextualize Christianity in China, based on the Scriptures, to various cultural forms, traditions, languages, and even different media."

The indigenization and contextualization of Christianity is more than a campaign promoted by the Chinese authorities; it is a biblical mandate. Chinese Churches are in the midst of finding and exploring ways to contextualize Christianity. There remains much ground to be covered, and they express openness and appreciation for more interactions and dialogue through seminars and symposiums. Praise God that today we hear from Chinese authorities who say, "A good Christian is also a good citizen of the country." May churches overseas and UBS continue to be faithful supporters and cheerleaders of our Chinese brothers and sisters at this critical and exciting juncture of their contextualization and inculturation journey.

On the commitment of UBS, Wee Seng said at the 2019 CUV symposium, "As always, we, the UBS fellowship, stand ready to serve, support and partner with the Churches in China in any way we are able to, by God's grace and by his provision and enabling, just as we have been blessed by the Lord to serve, support and partner with the Churches in China over the years." This was echoed by Dr. Bernard Low, co-director (ministry) of UBS CP, in 2021, "We are committed to coming alongside the Churches in China to support them as they work on developing a distinctively Chinese Christianity that is at once rooted in Scripture and two-thousand years of Christian tradition and also relevant to Chinese heritage and culture."

18
Stellar Performance

The Bible Printing Press in China: Milestones and Achievements

Look among the nations, and see;
    wonder and be astounded.
For I am doing a work in your days
    that you would not believe if told.

—Habakkuk 1:5

Then our mouth was filled with laughter,
    and our tongue with shouts of joy;
then they said among the nations,
    "The LORD has done great things for them."
The LORD has done great things for us;
    we are glad.

—Psalm 126:2–3

God's richest blessings! A mustard seed though small will grow in God's hand and time.

—Most Rev. Dr. John Chew, primate of Southeast Asia, during his visit to APC in 2011

APC aerial front view, 2008.

A view of APC factory floor, 2016.

Kua Wee Seng at APC old site with Han Shanning (R), first local general manager of APC, 1993.

As we come to a close in our journey, we are back where we first began—the printed Word of God in China and the press that intrigued me when I first visited it in 2013. Since then, I have had the opportunity to accompany several friends and colleagues from Bible Societies to visit Amity Printing Company (APC) in Nanjing. During each visit, I can see that many would marvel at the sheer size of the press and the quality and variety of Bibles produced there. Most of all, we were astounded by the mere possibility of printing Bibles in China.

According to APC's records, from 1988 to 2022, a total of 91 million Bibles were printed at the press and distributed throughout China. Take a moment to imagine the impact of God's Word on the lives of millions of Chinese. What was once thought impossible has been made possible. After a period of "bitter winter" in the 1960s to '70s when the Bible was banned, burned, and confiscated, the Churches in China have now for more than thirty years been able to consistently publish and produce Bibles at APC. Thank God that through a steady supply of Bibles from APC, millions of Chinese have had their spiritual hunger satisfied. The Lord has indeed done great things for the Christians in China! Yet, this is not to say that Bibles are plentiful in China or that the need has been met. Ninety-one million Bibles are only a tiny fraction of what is needed for China's population of 1.4 billion. If we factor in the wear and tear of Bibles printed over the years, the need is even more apparent. Henan Province alone has a population of 98 million.[1] Nonetheless, we can thank God for the 91 million Bibles that have been used in the past or are in the hands of Chinese Christians now!

Apart from China, APC has also been fulfilling the spiritual needs of people overseas. Since 1993, it has printed and distributed a total of more than 160 million Bibles for Bible Societies and other Bible agencies worldwide. This is about 60 percent of the total number of Bibles printed by APC since 1987. Today, it is the world's largest Bible printer and main global Bible supplier, producing an average of seventy Bibles per minute. In this chapter, we look at how the APC has grown over the last three decades and the work God is doing through this Bible printing press to send forth his word to the churches in China and overseas. May God bring about spiritual revivals and awakening for his glory through his word!

---

1 *Statista*, "Population in China in 2022, by Province or Region (in Million Inhabitants)."

Difficult Birth and Early Challenges

The sprawling Bible printing facility that stands today in Nanjing belies a birth that was fraught with some difficulties. After the "Memorandum of Understanding" between Amity Foundation (AF) and UBS was signed in March 1985, with UBS pledging to provide machinery, printers, and start-up costs for the press, AF had to look for a suitable local partner to comply with national regulations. Nanjing Normal University, which had a four-story printing house, was found to be suitable. Both Chinese church and UBS leaders visited the campus and met with the university's leadership to discuss the agreement. In December 1985, AF inked an agreement for joint management of Amity Press with Nanjing Normal University.

However, a few months later, Nanjing Normal University withdrew from the project after careful and extensive discussion with AF. The university found it could not meet the technical requirements of the Amity Press while maintaining its educational mission. The cancellation of the agreement was announced in August 1986. Thankfully, within a month, AF found a new partner—Jiangning Industrial Corporation, an enterprise of the Jiangning County government on the outskirts of Nanjing. A site in a developing area for industry and international trade in Jiangning County was provided for the construction of the press by the Jiangning Industrial Corporation. From this collaboration, Amity Printing Press, a purpose-built, one-story building was born in less than a year and started operating in December 1987 with machinery and equipment donated by UBS.

Signing of the Agreement on the Establishment of Amity Printing Company. UBS leader Rev. Chan Choi and vice-chairman of APC Board Chen Weizhong, June 1988.

However, halfway into the first year of operation, the printing press met with some challenges. Both parties, AF and Jiangning Industrial Corporation, found that there was a mismatch in their mission and vision, making them strange bedfellows. It had proven hard to proceed with the partnership. They then decided they had no better choice but to part ways. What was the fledgling printing press to do?

In the Lord's timing, this turn of events became a blessing in disguise. By this time, there was a Chinese government policy allowing foreign entities to enter into joint ventures with local ones. That meant AF and UBS could enter into a Chinese-foreign joint venture. This was welcomed and taken up by both parties since the benefits of such an arrangement were many, such as greater alignment in mission and vision, greater autonomy, and tax exemptions.

Six months later, in June 1988, the Amity Printing Company (APC) was registered. This move marked the beginning of a faith journey for AF and UBS, trusting God to use the press to spread his word in China. Bishop Ting reflected candidly in 1999 about entering into the joint venture with UBS, "The church in China needed Bibles and UBS was willing to help. Both sides did not know and trust each other [well] at that time. However, despite the risk involved, both sides wanted and desired to try to establish the printing work. In Jesus Christ, we became good friends."

Another challenge faced was in terms of labor. APC was furnished and fitted with state-of-the-art equipment and machinery. At that time, the press had about 250 workers, but it did not have sufficient skilled workers for proper operation and care of the equipment. During the first six months of 1988, according to a report by Peter MacInnis, general manager of APC, there were signs that the machinery was not well-maintained, and the quality of the output was found wanting. To solve these teething issues, he recommended that the press urgently hire additional highly skilled labor, conduct extensive in-service training for its workers, and have on-site visits by UBS technical advisors over a period.

Mr. Peter MacInnis (second from right), APC general manager (1989–1992), with APC staff at the commemoration of the first millionth copy of the Bible, 1989.

By God's grace, at the end of its first full year in December 1988, Amity's output reached nearly half a million Bibles. At the end of the second year, it produced about 600,000 Bibles, and in the third year in 1990, slightly more than one million Bibles. It was like watching a baby grow from a near miscarriage to a toddler trying to walk. The steady increase in annual output was a great encouragement to both the Chinese church and UBS leaders. Dr. Loh, UBS regional translation coordinator and UBS Asia Opportunity program coordinator, said in his report, just before APC celebrated the second millionth Bible in 1990, "It was good to see rows of finished Bibles stacked and lined up neatly. The Timson (web press) was rolling out signatures of the Union Version Bible. It was, in fact, printing the Psalms portion of the pocket-sized Bible in the Chinese simplified script. The Rolands (printers) were printing the new Chinese hymnals." One can imagine how his heart must have been moved by that scene, seeing that the child was developing well. What a relief to know that the initial technical challenges had been overcome and the printing equipment was in good working condition despite earlier worries.

The APC Board chaired by Rev. Rd Jen-Li Tsai, UBS Asia Pacific Regional Secretary, 1998.

Mr. Michael Perreau, UBS director general, presenting an imperial edition of the New Testament to Board Chairman of APC, Mr. Qiu Zhonghui (right), in celebration of the completion of the 200 millionth Bible by APC, 2019.

Representatives from the UBS fellowship celebrating the 200-millionth Bible printed at ACP, 2019.

At the celebration banquet hosted by Chinese church leader and founder of AF, Bishop Ting, the 2,000,001st Bible from the press was presented to Dr. John Erickson in appreciation for UBS's partnership in the joint venture. The inscription reads: "The China Christian Council has pleasure in presenting this copy of the Chinese Bible to Dr. John Erickson. We give thanks to God who makes all things possible and to our brothers and sisters in UBS for joining us in this task."

It was a significant moment for both parties to witness the miracle firsthand. The presentation of commemorative Bibles was to become a familiar but important practice as the Chinese church and UBS leaders celebrated the Bible production milestones of APC over the decades. By this practice, both parties affirm that the Bible is their common cause, and aligned in their mission and vision, they are on a common venture in faith that only God can bring about and see to its success.

At each Bible celebration at APC, the national Chinese church and UBS leaders did not fail to highlight that APC was and is a continuing miracle from God. In the words of Chinese church leader Dr. Han Wenzao at the celebration of the 10-millionth copy of the Bible printed at APC, "In 1987, nobody anticipated that we would have come to the stage of ten million Bibles by 1995. It is by God's grace and with the help of fellow Christians worldwide that this dream has become a reality."

In 2012, Mr. Michael Perreau, UBS general secretary, said at the 100-millionth Bible celebration, "Today we witnessed a miracle orchestrated by the great Designer and Architect. … APC has placed 60 million Bibles in the hands of the Christians in China and reached the world with a further 40 million copies."

In 2019, at the 200-millionth Bible celebration, Bishop John Chew, honorary consultant to UBS CP, said that it was "by the sheer Grace of God and His Living Word, that Bibles could be officially printed in China."

Reflecting on his experiences serving with UBS CP as its director (operations), Daniel Loh said in 2023, "Before joining UBS China Partnership, I had no idea what the Lord was doing in his Bible mission in China. I had read about the Amity Printing Company printing Bibles for the world but had no idea of the story behind it. I am moved and amazed at how the Lord had a plan in place to provide Bibles to millions of Christians in China. It is amazing to know that Bibles are available today in China!"

Printing Bibles to Serve the Churches in China

Since the beginning of its inception, APC's mission has been to serve the Chinese Churches by prioritizing the printing of Bibles for distribution within China. The rate of production at APC has been phenomenal. It took the press twenty-five years to print its first 100 million copies of the Bible but only seven years to complete its second 100 million copies of the Bible. Reflecting on the significance of Bible printing and distribution in China, Kua Wee Seng (UBS CP director 1999–2021) said, "Within a couple of decades of the end of the Cultural Revolution, the banned book has become one of the best-selling books in China! What is impossible with men is possible with God. The huge and widespread distribution of the Word of God has contributed to the explosive growth of the churches in China over the past decades."

Chinese Union Bibles rolling off the press, 2016.

As APC grew, the range of its products and services to the churches in China widened, keeping up with the evolving needs and interests of the Chinese people. According to a 1990 APC report, the press was producing eight different products—Bibles and New Testaments in Chinese, Lisu, Korean, Jingpo, Big Flowery Miao, and Black Yi for the Protestant churches in China. In 1994, APC expanded its domestic customer base when it received orders from the Chinese Catholic Patriotic Association and Bishops Conference of Catholic Church in China as UBS began its partnership with the national bodies of the Chinese Catholic Church. In 1995, the Braille Bible printing unit was set up in APC

Unloading Bible paper at APC, 1998.

East Lisu Bibles being printed at APC factory, 2016.

(see chapter seven for the full story). In the late 1990s, it started using domestic paper in order to cut costs and allow for more Bibles to be printed. Previously, almost all Bible paper was imported from Finland, and these imports incurred tax and duties.[2]

By 2020, APC had produced more than sixty Bible products for distribution within China. These include different versions, editions, sizes, and types of Bibles and New Testaments, hymnals, Scripture calendars, and Bible resources including devotional Bibles, study Bibles,

---

2 UBS Special Report, June 1998.

thematic Bibles, Bible dictionaries and concordances, and Braille Bibles. Besides Chinese Bibles, APC has also printed Bibles in eleven ethnic minority languages for churches in China. These eleven languages are Big Flowery Miao, West Lisu, Korean, Jingpo, Lahu, Black Yi, White Yi, Ganyi, Wa, East Lisu, and Dai.

Does this mean that the need for Bibles in China has been met? No! Despite the 94 million Bibles printed to date, some churches in China are still facing shortages of Bibles. This is due to a variety of reasons. From the visits made over the years, I have observed and also been told that because the Chinese Christians love the Word of God so much, their Bibles get worn out easily and need to be replaced. Second, they purchase Bibles not just for themselves but as gifts for their family and friends. Thirdly, due to China's graying population and by extension its Christian population, the demand for large-print Bibles by older Christians has increased. Fourthly, as Chinese Churches continue to grow, they need Bibles for new believers and seekers of the faith! Therefore, it continues to be imperative for APC to serve the Chinese Churches in their Bible needs.

Growing into a World Class Printer

By the mid-2000s, with the exponential growth of the churches in China and a growing export market, there arose a need for APC to move to a larger place. This need coincided with the authorities' development plans for the land on which APC was located. In 2006, the municipal government announced the rezoning of the area to accommodate the growing population in Nanjing City. The government offered APC another block of land in a new industrial park situated closer to the Nanjing International Airport as well as compensation of over USD$22 million for the remainder of the lease that APC had on the original site.

UBS leader Miller Milloy at APC's new site opening ceremony, 2008.

David Thorne, UBS production and supply consultant, Asia Pacific (1982–1996), UBS area secretary, Asia Pacific (1997–2012), recorded God's amazing provision in a booklet on APC:

> This was a godsend. The original factory was already proving to be too small, and the building was aging. With the compensation, accrued income and a bank loan, Amity Printing Company constructed a modern purpose-built production facility on the new site and used the opportunity to buy some more modern equipment and rebuild existing equipment during the move.

Praise God—not only are Bibles printed openly and legally, but the Bible printing press was also given the space to expand its work and reach. In 2008, APC moved from its former 36,000-square-meter site to a new 85,000-square-meter printing facility. With more modern and powerful machinery and equipment, it now has an annual capacity of 20 million Bibles. This is a twenty-fold jump compared to the beginning output of APC's operation!

In the 2010s, APC continued to keep up with new printing technologies, including installing a digital printing machine to fulfill smaller print runs in a short period of time. This will especially cater to Bible Societies printing for language groups with a small number of readers. APC began to be known as an industry expert in thin paper printing and gained recognition as a world-class printer. Before long, it was certified and awarded by the International Organization for Standardization (ISO) for quality management systems (ISO 9001 and 9002). Following that, it achieved both international and national awards for its high-quality printing service. By the mid-2010s, it took the lead in the printing industry in China, gaining the certification of "High-tech Enterprise and High-tech Product."

APC was awarded ISO 9002, 1997.

Today, APC is equipped with high-end and advanced machinery including four British-built Timson T32 high-speed web presses, nineteen single and multi-color sheet presses made by German KBA, and fifteen Italian multiplex fully automatic gathering and sewing systems, enabling it to create high-quality products. It has developed the thin paper printing technology, moving from forty-gram-thin paper in 1987 to nineteen-gram-thin paper in 2022.

Not only is APC concerned with excellence in printing, but it is also environmentally conscious. The printing press has implemented the use of sustainable materials and clean energy, paying close attention to energy conservation and reducing emissions in its operations. In 2014, it won the ISO 14000 for managing processes efficiently while reducing its adverse impact on the environment.

APC continues to improve on its thin paper printing technology.

In 2016, APC started its solar energy project, which produces up to 20–30 percent of its energy usage. APC is also increasing its usage of paper that is certified by the Forest Stewardship Council (FSC). FSC-certified paper is paper that has been harvested in a responsible manner. FSC standards ensure that both the environment and communities are protected during the process. APC obtained the chain of custody certification from FSC in 2018, showing its high commitment to forest-friendly sourcing.

Despite the rising costs of printing due to the significant investments required for using clean energy and "green" materials, APC CEO Luke Liu said that the company is committed to sustainable development and protecting the environment. APC is today one of the leading examples in energy conservation and emissions reduction in the printing industry in China.

In addition, APC was recognized for being a caring employer. It won the Printing Industry Best Employer Award for six consecutive years for its staff welfare and providing a fair and safe working environment.

China–The World's Bible Exporter

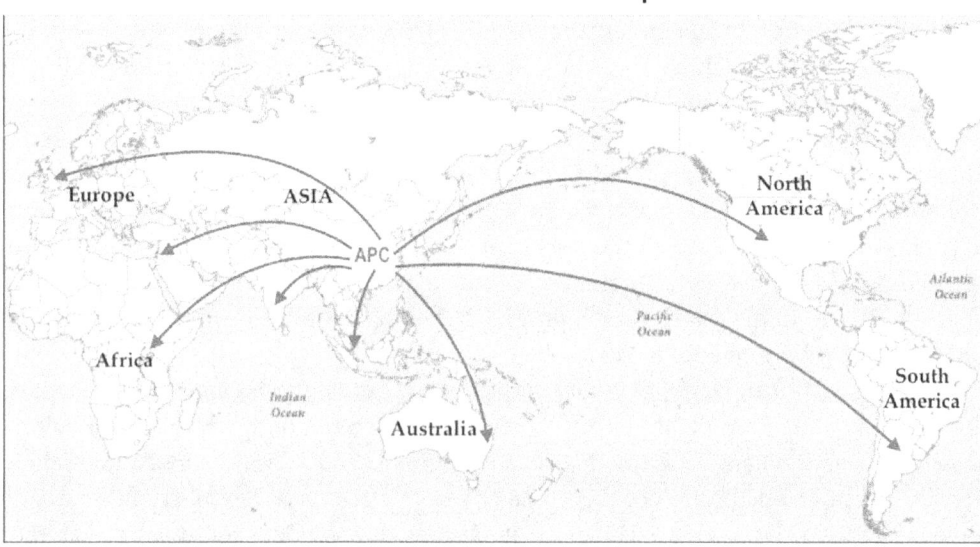

The global reach of APC export.

The stellar performance of APC has made China the world's largest Bible printer and exporter today. Not every Bible printed at APC is for the domestic market. By late 2023, it had printed 162 million Bibles in more than two hundred languages for more than 160 countries and regions. This constitutes about 60 percent of the total number of Bibles printed by APC since 1987. How did APC's export journey begin?

APC's first export job started in 1993 when the Bible Society of India ordered twenty thousand full-colored children's Bibles. This grew to 4.5 million in 2004 as Bibles were exported to Bible Societies, including those in Africa, UK, Hong Kong, Thailand, the Philippines, and Japan, as well as for Gideons and other publishers.

At the thanksgiving service in 2004, David Thorne recalled, "During those years (early 1990s), there was a dream. I remember on many occasions that Mr. Han Shanning (general manager of APC) would say to me, 'David, when can we do export work?' And I would say to Shanning, 'I don't think we are ready yet?' But today, as I looked through the Bibles that we can get in the gift pack, I looked at this with my technical eyes and I will be pleased to buy these in the bookstore in Australia."

David Thorne speaking at the 4.5 million export celebration, 2004.

In time, APC was able to develop and print more than five hundred different Bible products for more than 140 countries and regions in more than 190 languages. Apart from the more common Western languages such as English, Spanish, and German, there are also editions in African languages such as Swahili, Amharic, and Oromo. It is astounding that since 1993, more than 160 million Bibles have gone out from China, where Bibles were once banned, to different parts of the world!

At the 100-millionth Bible celebration in 2012, Qiu Zhonghui, board chairman of AF and APC, affirmed APC's commitment to serving the Bible mission, "All of APC's achievements today would not have been possible had it not been the friendship and support offered by the United Bible Societies. In the initial years of APC, UBS stepped in to provide us with timely and much-needed help—this we will not forget. Now APC hopes to reciprocate this gesture of friendship by printing more Bibles for the Bible Societies."

One example was the landmark *African Women Devotional Bible* for the African churches, printed and distributed in 2021 by APC. It was the first of its kind and the result of a beautiful collaborative effort spanning four years, involving more than 280 women writers across Africa and twenty-five Bible Societies in the continent. To enhance reader experience, APC used the latest gilding and engraving technology to produce a high-quality product for this first full-color Bible. Notably, this was the first high-end technology in Bible printing used successfully by APC for the Bible Societies in Africa.

The *African Women Devotional Bible* comes in five binding styles and four different cover colors, moving away from the traditional black cover. The cover design was created by Amity's research and development department, featuring daffodils and African stripes and bright, bold colors. At the online dedication of the *African Women Devotional Bible* held on International Women's Day 2021, Dr. Barine Kirimi, UBS publishing development coordinator, and Thomas Tharao, Bible Society of Kenya operations manager, expressed their gratitude for the tremendous support from APC.

The spiritual significance of Bible export by APC was captured aptly by the Most Rev. Albert Chama, primate of Central Africa, during his visit in 2011, "The printing factory has inspired me that evangelism and the spread of the Word of God is visible by the printed Word of God. The Bible changes the world. Therefore, it is my prayer that the Good Lord will continue to provide all that is needed in the production of Bibles as a means of reaching many globally with the Word of God."

George Yeo (center), former foreign affairs minister of Singapore visiting APC, 2014.

See, the Child Has Grown

To better coordinate the Bible production for the African churches, APC set up an Africa Service Center in Ethiopia in 2015 and Amity Kenya Office in 2019. As demand for Bibles in Africa grew, APC decided to establish a branch in Addis Ababa to print Bibles for African Bible Societies and other publishers. The groundbreaking ceremony was held in 2020. Construction has been delayed due

Ground preparation for APC branch at Ethiopia, 2020.

APC CEO Luke Liu and the management team, 2019.

to the COVID-19 pandemic but the APC leadership is committed to see to its completion. The child has grown and is now even reproducing itself.

It was also able to withstand the storms of life. In 2022, despite the economic downturn as a result of the COVID-19 pandemic and intermittent lockdowns in China, APC broke its own record and reached its highest annual output in history at 16 million copies of full Bibles! Imagine blessing 16 million people around the world with the Word of God during the stressful period of the pandemic.

To provide better quality and more diversified printing and binding processes and speedier delivery for its partners, APC started to build a second factory building in April 2023 in Nanjing, due to be completed in April 2024. This second factory building will add another 37,000 square meters to the current space and will house a digital printing center, research and development center, Bible museum, chapel, auditorium, additional production, and warehousing space.

The Word of God is unstoppable. A fledgling press has grown into the world's largest Bible printing press today. From this press, God has sent forth his word to the nations. From this press, his light shines, his truth is proclaimed, his salvation message is heard. Despite a difficult birth, the press was established in one of the world's most unlikely places. And it has thrived and flourished, grown and matured. A beautiful chapter has been written by those who have come before us. Some might ask, "So, what's next?" Here's an apt reply from Wee Seng, "May we look to the same Sovereign Lord and act with the same faith and courage of the pioneers to forge ahead and write the next chapter of the Bible mission in China."

Epilogue
Light unto the Nations

The Unstoppable Word of God in and beyond China

I am the LORD; I have called you in righteousness;
   I will take you by the hand and keep you;
I will give you as a covenant for the people,
   a light for the nations.
—Isaiah 42:6

The process of researching and writing the story of the Bible in China has been both exhausting and exhilarating. I feel as if I've trekked through the mountains, taking in all the sights and sounds, making sense of them all, and trying to keep on track. My objective has been to connect the dots and understand the significance of the existence of a Bible press in China and the spread and impact of God's Word in China today. And I have been awed by the wondrous work of God.

Yet, the story of the Bible in China is not something distant that the Lord is doing. He is also doing work within me through this book project. And I believe in you too as you read it. I sense him impressing upon my heart some messages that inspire me in my walk with him, both in life and ministry. I would like to close this book by sharing them with you.

Nothing Is Impossible for God (Luke 1:37)

We have had a glimpse of one of the greatest revivals in Christian history, we have been privy to an indigenous Bible movement in China. The Chinese church and the Chinese Bible have not only resurrected post-Cultural Revolution but also thrived and flourished. Forty years ago, scarcely anyone would have imagined China would be home to one of the world's fastest-growing churches and the world's largest Bible printer and exporter. Within a couple of decades, the Bible has gone from a banned book to a bestseller in China. It can be bought at an affordable price in all the provinces, both rural and urban. It is being read and taught openly in churches and parishes. The word of the Lord has spread and gone out to the poor, the blind, ethnic minority groups, young and old, men and women, families, the hurting, laity and clergy, and leaders and opinion shapers of society and communities. All of this is happening in a country with the world's largest and most powerful atheistic government. Clearly, the Lord has done the impossible, and his word is unstoppable.

His invitation to me: Are you willing to trust me for the impossibles in your life and ministry?

The Word of God Is Living, and Its Impact Is Real (Heb 4:12)

Over the years, I have had the privilege to interview Chinese Christians about the impact of God's Word in their lives. Their stories echo past testimonies collected by former UBS staff. Many testify that they encounter God through his written word and they have been changed when the word is read on its terms as God's revelation.[1] Each of their stories testifies to the divine encounter with the Lord of the universe through his word. Their testimonies bring me to an undeniable truth—God speaks to human hearts through his word revealed in the Bible. The Holy Scripture teaches, rebukes, corrects, trains a person in righteousness (2 Tim 3:16), leads a person to the truth (Ps 119:9–10), and brings joy and delight (Jer 15:16). Millions of Chinese Christians have tasted and ingested the word and found divine guidance, satisfaction, and blessings the world cannot give. To all ministers of the word: don't give up preaching and teaching. To all believers: don't stop reading the word.

His invitation to me: Do you experience the reality of the power of my word in your daily life even as you write and read about it in the lives of others? Don't miss out on the greatest blessing of knowing me from the pages of my word.

God Is Not Done Yet; His Light Will Shine Yet Brighter (Isa 42:6)

The hope and prayer of many Christians around the world is to see Chinese Churches increasingly contributing to the global body of Christ, to world missions and evangelization. As they continue to dig deep into the word and lay a strong foundation through their obedience to the Lord, may God's Word go beyond China, not just through APC's exporting of Bibles but also through Chinese Christians. Compared to the heyday of the past few decades, one may say the current religious regulatory climate in China is colder. But let us continue to have faith in the Lord whose ways are beyond our imagination and will prevail. Already we know that Chinese Christians are serving cross-culturally in different parts of the world today. In the Lord's timing, may the churches in China become a bright light unto the nations, an unstoppable harvest force of the Lord, to the glory of God.

His invitation to all of us who are concerned about the churches in China: Are you willing to come alongside and participate, in whatever capacity, in the next chapter of the story of my work through my word in China?

---

1 Peterson, *Eat This Book*.

Appendix
A Timeline of Bible Missions in China

The Pioneer Era (7th Century–1911)	
635	Missionaries from the Church of the East (Syrian Church) engaged in Bible translation at Chang'an (present day Xian).
1294	John of Montecorvino, a Franciscan missionary monk, translated the New Testament and Psalms into the Mongolian language, which was then the lingua franca of the Yuan Dynasty.
1582	Jesuit missionary Matteo Ricci and his team translated Bible stories and Gospel readings for liturgical use.
1707	Jean Basset, a French missionary of the Missions Etrangères de Paris, with the assistance of local converts translated part of the New Testament into Chinese. Their work became the basis of Robert Morrison's translation.
1807	Arrival of Robert Morrison, the first Protestant missionary to China. He was sent by the London Missions Society.
1811	First grant from British and Foreign Bible Society (BFBS) given to Robert Morrison for his Chinese Bible translation work.
1813	William Milnes, second Protestant missionary to China, joined Morrison in the Bible translation work.
1822	Completion of Morrison's Bible translation. The Chinese Bibles were printed in Malacca in 1823.
1833	First grant from American Bible Society (ABS) for Bible distribution in China.
1844	Emperor Daogaung issues the edict of "toleration of the religion of the Lord of Heaven." Prior to this, there was a restriction in the distribution of Christian literature.
1853	At BFBS Jubilee, the *Chinese Million New Testament Fund* was set up.
1863	BFBS sets up its first China Agency in Shanghai to coordinate its Bible mission in China mainly in Bible translation, publication and distribution. Develops an extensive colportage system for Scripture circulation.
1863	National Bible Society of Scotland (NBSS) appoints its first Bible agent in China.
1874	A private school for the blind opens with the support of NBSS.
1876	ABS sets up its first China Agency.
1890	General Conference of the Protestant Missionary Conference held in Shanghai. Bible Societies (BFBS, ABS, NBSS) support the decision for unified versions of the Chinese Bible, including the Mandarin Union Version (later known as the Chinese Union Version).
1899	Boxer Rebellion in China. Anti Foreign uprising. Bible Societies work severely interrupted and Scripture circulation dropped as colportage ceased in many areas.
1905	BFBS reports that it has 300 colporteurs working with 180 missionaries representing 32 missions societies in China.
1911	Collapse of the Chinese Empire. Sun Yat-sen was declared president of provisional government, the first Chinese Republic.

During the Two World Wars (1914–1976)	
1914	Beginning of World War I.
1916	ABS reports Scripture circulation reaching its peak with more than 2 million volumes of Scripture being distributed by colporteurs.
1918	End of World War I.
1919	Completion of Chinese Union Version, the de facto authorized version in use by the Churches in China.
1921	Founding of the Chinese Communist Party.
1920s	BFBS and ABS begin joint work at the subagency level.
1929	The Great Depression hits. ABS reports an all-time high in a single year with a total of more than 5 million volumes of Scripture distributed in China.
1930s	The Scripture was available in more than 30 Chinese dialects and ethnic minority languages in China.
1933	The Centennial of ABS work in China was celebrated in Nanking.
1937	BFBS & ABS draft constitution for the establishment of China Bible House. China Bible House opens in Shanghai (3 Hong Kong Street). Integration of China agencies of BFBS and ABS.
1937	Sino-Japanese War starts.
1937-1950	China Bible House plays an important role in the translation, publication and distribution of the Bible in China enduring through the ravages of the Sino-Japanese War (1937) and World War II (1939–1945). It also held a Colporteurs' Training Conference.
1939	World War II starts.
1939	China Bible House distributes Scriptures in 39 dialects and 30 other languages.
1945	World War II ends.
1945	NBSS joins BFBS and ABS in the work of China Bible House.
1946	Founding of the United Bible Societies (UBS) by around a dozen Bible Societies to strengthen Bible ministry around the world.
1949	China Bible House elected to membership in the United Bible Societies.
Late 1940s	China Bible House became more nationalized with the management coming under local Chinese.
1949	The Chinese Communist Party came to power under Mao Zedong. The People's Republic of China is founded.
1950	China Bible House ceases ties with UBS. Bible Societies set up emergency offices in Hong Kong.
1954	Three Self Patriotic Movement (TSPM) National Committee was established, emphasizing on self-governing, self-supporting and self-propagation of the Churches in China.
1959	Official closure of the China Bible House at Shanghai.

1966	Beginning of Cultural Revolution. Political and cultural purges take place. Old customs and traditions are attacked. Churches closed. Pastors and preachers sent to labour camps, farms and factories. Bibles banned, burned and confiscated.
1968	Publication of the Chinese Catholic Bible in Hong Kong (also known as the Studium Biblicum Version).
1976	Mao Zedong passes away. End of Cultural Revolution.

A Bible Press for China! (1978–1987)

1978	Deng Xiaoping announces Reform and Opening up policy. China welcomes foreign businesses and investments.
1979	Deng Xiaoping visits the US. The first Chinese leader to do so since the founding of the PRC in 1949.
1979	Bai Nian (Century) Church in Ningpo is the first church to re-open.
1979	First contact between Chinese Church leaders and UBS leaders.
1983	First contact between Catholic Bishop Aloysius Jin of the Diocese of Shanghai and UBS leaders.
1985	UBS leaders Drs Chan Young Choi and I-Jin Loh visited Nanjing during which the possibility of setting up a printing press was first brought up and request for Bible paper made by Chinese Church leaders.
1985	Chinese Church leaders Bishop K. H. Ting and Dr. Han Wenzao set up the Amity Foundation, a social welfare organization.
1985	Bishop Ting (on behalf of Amity Foundation) and Rev. Payne (on behalf of UBS) signed "A Memorandum of Understanding" in Hong Kong announcing the intention to establish a printing press in Nanjing which would give priority to the production of Bibles and Testaments." Donation of first hundred metric ton of Bible paper from UBS to CCC/TSPM.
1985	Bishop Aloysius Jin completed the Chinese translation of the four Gospels of the Jerusalem New Testament and printed them with UBS's support.
1986	Formal announcement of the UBS "Bible Press for China" project launched and fundraising for the press begins.
1986	Jiangning Industrial Corporation selected to be the new partner, and a cooperative joint venture agreement was signed between it and the Amity Foundation.
1986	The foundation stone laid for the Amity Press. General Secretaries and fundraisers from 10 UBS member societies present for the ceremony.
1987	The printing equipment was officially presented to the Amity foundation.
1987	15 Sept. First full day of Bible production at the Press. 14 Oct. First Bible to roll off the press at Amity.
1987	5 Dec. The Amity Printing Press officially dedicated and inaugurated.

\multicolumn{2}{c}{**A New Era of Bible Missions in China (1990s-2000s)**}
1988	Amity Printing Company formed as a joint venture between Amity foundation and UBS.
1989	Launch of the CUV Simplified Script with horizontal typesetting.
1989	One millionth Bible printed at APC.
1994	First batch of Chinese Catholic Bibles (Studium Biblicum Version) printed at Amity Press with the support of UBS.
1994	Launch of The New Jerusalem New Testament, a Chinese translation by Bishop Aloysius Jin.
1995	Braille Bible printing unit set up at Amity Printing Company.
1998	First official meeting with ethnic minority churches at the national level on Bible Translation for ethnic minority Christians in China.
1999	First batch of three Chinese Postgraduate students supported by UBS to study Biblical Exegesis and Translation.
2000s	Beginning of partnership between Chinese Churches and UBS in the printing and distribution of Scripture booklets, Gospel portions, Scripture for the young, and Scripture literacy classes.
2001	First Bible distribution van donated by UBS to Bible distribution centers.
2004	First Bible Ministry Exhibition by CCC/TSPM in Hong Kong with the theme "A Lamp to My Feet, A Light to My Path."
2006 & 2011	Bible Ministry Exhibition in the USA. "A Lamp to My Feet, A Light to My Path" (2006), "Thy Word is Truth" (2011).
2007	Bible Ministry Exhibition in Germany. "A Lamp to My Feet, A Light to My Path."
2008	Protestant Churches in China printed and distributed 50,000 free copies of Chinese-English Four Gospel Portion, and 10,000 copies of Chinese-English Bible (CUV/ESV) at the Beijing Olympic Village chapel and churches with UBS support.
	The Catholic Church in China printed and distributed 30,000 free copies of Chinese-English Diglot NT (SBV/NRSV) at the Beijing Olympic Village chapel and churches with UBS support.
2009	Printing and distribution of one million copies of the Scripture by the Catholic Church of China, a Bible project co-funded by Taizé Community and UBS.
2009	Launch of East Lisu New Testament with UBS support—first ethnic minority language to be translated and printed since 1949 with official approval.
2009	Launch of the Big Flowery Miao Bible.
2011	First Bible in China seminar, an annual seminar on Bible Advocacy in China.
2012	Celebrating the printing of the 100 millionth copy of the Bible by Amity Printing Company.
2012	Opening of Bible Resource Center at Nanjing Union Theological Seminary.
2012	First Old Testament Seminar conducted for Chinese Bible teachers with the support of UBS.
2014	Opening of Bible Resource Center at National Seminary of Catholic Church in China.
2015	Launch of the West Lisu Annotated Bible and White Yi New Testament.

2015	Thirtieth anniversary of Bible ministry partnership between the Protestant Churches in China and UBS.
2015	Twentieth anniversary of Bible ministry partnership between the Catholic Church in China and UBS.
2016	Launch of the Wa Bible, Black Yi Bible and East Lisu Bible.
2017	Launch of the Chinese Study Bible (with notes translated and adapted from the English Standard Version Study Bible).
2018	Fiftieth Anniversary of the Studium Biblicum Bible (Chinese Catholic Bible).
2019	Hundredth Anniversary of the Chinese Union Version Bible (Chinese Protestant Bible).
2019	Celebrating the printing of the 200 millionth copy of the Bible by Amity Printing Company.
2019	Amity Printing Company set up an Amity Office in Kenya to better serve the African Churches.
2020	Amity Printing Company held groundbreaking ceremony in Addis Ababa, Ethiopia in preparation for construction of a printing branch.
2023	Amity Printing Company held groundbreaking ceremony in Nanjing, China in preparation for construction of second factory building.
2023	Launch of the CUV/Greek/ESV Triglot New Testament.
2023	Launch of the Ganyi/Chinese Diglot Bible.

Acknowledgments

I am deeply indebted to Kua Wee Seng, my former director at UBS CP, mentor and friend who taught me that writers are like worship leaders, they invite people to sing praises to God. He was not only the first to encourage me to embark on this writing project but also provided tireless and patient support since day one, granting me countless interviews, reading the manuscript and giving me his comments and input. Without his guidance and wise counsel, I would not have had the confidence nor the tenacity to complete this book.

I am also grateful to the UBS leadership and colleagues for their support, and the UBS CP leadership and team who gave me time to focus on writing. I will not forget how they journeyed with me and prayed almost every week for the writing project and especially when we were looking for a suitable publisher. Special thanks to Angela Teo who read the manuscript, to Yeo Tan Tan, Pamela Choo, Jenise Lee, and May Ang for contributing stories and testimonies to the archive of UBS CP of which many were being used and adapted for the book, and to Chris Quek for helping with the publishing process and providing IT support for me.

My gratitude also goes to an important team of people at William Carey Publishing who believed that the story in this book needs to be told. They have worked hard to get the book out. I want to thank publishing manager Vivian Doub for her patience and kind help when we needed to make changes to the working document, copyeditor Madison Cannon, who made sure that my ideas are clear to the readers, senior editor Melissa Hicks, and designer Mike Riester who conceptualized the book cover to effectively convey the message within and for handling all the photographs. It was a great pleasure working with them.

I am humbled by the endorsements given by esteemed church leaders, experts on China and accomplished scholars and authors. I thank them for their kindness and grace.

Most photographs featured in this book are from the UBS multimedia database. Credit goes to the American Bible Society, British Bible Society, Finnish Bible Society, Norway Bible Society for contributing generously to the treasure trove over the decades. Special thanks to photographers Clare Kendall, Dag Smemo, Hans Johan Sagrusten, Maurice Harvey, Andrea Rhodes, Jared Wong, Jimmy Lam, Deborah Yuen, and Andrew Hood for sharing their wonderful gifts with us. I am also grateful to OMF International, Maryknoll Mission Archives and School of Oriental and African Studies (UOL) for granting free use of their photographs and their archivists who responded swiftly to all emails.

Lastly, I want to thank friends from church for praying during the entire writing process, sharing the ups and downs of the project, and Susan Lim, my mum who lovingly prepares hot meals to nourish both my body and soul.

Praise be to God!

About UBS

United Bible Societies (UBS) is a global Fellowship of around 150 Bible Societies working in more than 240 countries and territories. Founded in 1946, the mission of UBS is to make the Bible available and accessible to everyone who wants it, and to help people engage with its message in meaningful and relevant ways. Its headquarters is located in Swindon, England. (https://unitedbiblesocieties.org/)

United Bible Societies China Partnership (UBS CP) was established by UBS to serve and support the Churches in China on behalf of the Fellowship. Since 1985, besides Bible printing and distribution, UBS CP has expanded its support of the Chinese Churches to include areas like Bible translation, publication, engagement, equipping, discipleship and advocacy. Its office is located in Singapore. (https://ubscp.org/)

Bibliography

The Abundant Life. Shanghai: China Christian Council / TSPM, 2015.

American Bible Society. "Number of English Bible Translations." *American Bible Society* (news), December 2, 2009. https://news.americanbible.org/article/number-of-english-translations-of-the-bible.

Argall, Kris. "The Woman Who Brought the Bible to Blind Chinese Children." *Eternity.* February 7, 2018. https://www.eternitynews.com.au/world/the-woman-who-brought-the-bible-to-blind-chinese-children/.

British and Foreign Bible Society. "What Is the Bible?" *International Bible Advocacy Centre.* Accessed November 2, 2022. https://www.bibleadvocacy.org/the-bible/.

Broomhall, Marshall. *The Bible in China.* London: China Inland Mission, 1934. https://missiology.org.uk/pdf/e-books/broomhall-m/bible-in-china_broomhall.pdf.

Chao Wang. "Christian Missionaries, Blind Converts, and Braille Literacy in China (1874–1911)" (paper, University of Chicago, Chicago, IL, February 9, 2018). https://voices.uchicago.edu/disabilitystudies/2018/01/29/29-chao-wang-christian-missionaries-blind-converts-and-braille-literacy-in-china-1874-1911/.

Chen, Shenfeng. "Contextualization and Indigenization of Christianity in China" (presented at the Centenary of the CUV seminar, 2019).

China News and Church Report quoting State Statistics Bureau Survey, 1992 (CNCR 2026).

Doyle, G. Wright. "William Milne," *Biographical Dictionary of Chinese Christianity.* Accessed November 2, 2022. https://bdcconline.net/en/stories/milne-william.

Du, Peng. *Hundred Years of Harmony, Eternal Light Shining.* China Christian Council / TSPM website, January 16, 2019. https://www.ccctspm.org/newsinfo/11574.

Feng, Shuxian. "To Strengthen Mental Resilience: Stay Mentally Healthy." *China Christian Council / National Committee of Three-Self Patriotic Movement of the Protestant Churches in China,* trans. Bei Feng, November 16, 2022. https://en.ccctspm.org/faithinfo/15839.

Gan, Nectar. "China Has 8 Million Blind People, but Only 200 Guide Dogs." *CNN.* November 24, 2020. https://edition.cnn.com/2020/11/23/china/china-guide-dogs-intl-dst-hnk/index.html.

Hallihan, C. P. "Robert Morrison, Bible Translator of China, 1782–1834." *Quarterly Record* 585 (2008): 11–28. https://cdn.ymaws.com/www.tbsbibles.org/resource/collection/331DF25E-7DDA-42C8-840A-C12967EDA8F0/Robert-Morrison-of-China.pdf.

Hattaway, Paul. *Guizhou: The Precious Province.* London: SPCK, 2018.

"History of Early Christianity in China." http://www.orthodox.cn/localchurch/jingjiao.

Lewis, C. S. *An Experiment in Criticism.* Cambridge: Cambridge University Press, 1965.

Lewis, M. Paul, Gary F. Simons, and Charles D. Fennig (eds.). *Ethnologue: Languages of the World,* 18th edition. Dallas, Texas: SIL International, 2015. Online version: http://www.ethnologue.com.

Li Xiang, Jia Hua, Dong Li-fang, Wang Bai-suo, Chang Wen-hui, Ren Qiang, Zhang Lu, Cui Meng, and Xing Ai-hua, "Reported HIV/AIDS Cases in Shaanxi Province, 1992–2010," *Disease Surveillance* 26, no. 8 (2011): 620–22, http://www.jbjc.org/article/doi/10.3784/j.issn.1003-9961.2011.08.011?pageType=en.

Li, Xing. "Making Life Easier for the Disabled." *China Daily,* April 21, 2007. https://www.chinadaily.com.cn/opinion/2007-04/21/content_856357.htm.

MacInnis, Donald E. "William H. Murray," *Biographical Dictionary of Chinese Christianity.* Accessed November 2, 2022. http://bdcconline.net/en/stories/murray-william.

Mai, Jun. "Why China's Floods This Year Are Different from 1998 Catastrophic Disaster that Killed 3000." *South China Morning Post*, July 6, 2016.

"Main Mountain Range." *Embassy of the People's Republic of China in Nepal*. October 2004. http://np.china-embassy.gov.cn/eng/ChinaABC/dl/200410/t20041027_1998292.htm.

Mak, George Kam Wah. Lunchtime Talk on China Bible House.

Mak, George Kam Wah. "Chinese Protestant Bible Versions and the Chinese Language." In *The Oxford Handbook of the Bible in China*, edited by K. K. Yeo. New York: Oxford University Press, 2021. https://doi.org/10.1093/oxfordhb/9780190909796.013.14.

McConnell, Walter. "God's Mission to the Lisu." *Mission Round Table* 14, no. 1 (2019): 24–34. https://omf.org/gods-mission-to-the-lisu/#_ednref20.

Miles, M. "Blind and Sighted Pioneer Teachers in 19th Century China and India." Revised Ed. Accessed November 2, 2022. https://www.independentliving.org/files/miles201104Pioneer-Teach-Blind_v2.pdf.

Moffett, Samuel Hugh. "John of Montecorvino." *Biographical Dictionary of Chinese Christianity*. Accessed November 2, 2022. http://bdcconline.net/en/stories/john-of-montecorvino.

Nida, Eugene Albert. *The Book of a Thousand Tongues*. New York: United Bible Societies, 1972.

People Group Profiles. *Asia Harvest*. Accessed on November 2, 2022. https://www.asiaharvest.org/people-group-profiles#china-part-1.

Peterson, Eugene H. *Eat This Book: A Conversation in the Art of Spiritual Reading*. Grand Rapids: Eerdmans, 2009.

"Pray for: People's Republic of China. Key Stats." *Operation World*. 2010. https://operationworld.org/locations/china-peoples-republic.

Statista. "Population in China in 2022, by Province or Region (in Million Inhabitants)." October 2023. https://www.statista.com/statistics/279013/population-in-china-by-region/.

Sweeny, Sandra Silver. "The Nestorian Stele Content." *Early Church History*. Accessed November 2, 2022. https://earlychurchhistory.org/christian-symbols/the-nestorian-stele-content.

The Lancet. "Mental Health after China's Prolonged Lockdowns." *The Lancet* 399, June 11, 2022. https://doi.org/10.1016/S0140-6736(22)01051-0.

The Lancet. "Mental Health in China: What Will Be Achieved by 2020?" *The Lancet* 385. June 27, 2015. https://doi.org/10.1016/S0140-6736(15)61146-1.

Wang, Aiguo. "福音戒毒：云南教会参与社会服务的探索与试验" ["The Bible and Social Service"] (seminar paper presented at the Shanghai Academy of Social Sciences, 2013). http://www.pacilution.com/ShowArticle.asp?ArticleID=1444.

Wark, Andrew. "China's Bible Cheats." *South China Morning Post*, August 8, 1992.

World Health Organisation. "Depressive Disorder." March, 31, 2023. https://www.who.int/news-room/fact-sheets/detail/depression#:~:text=An%20estimated%203.8%25%20of%20the,among%20women%20than%20among%20men.

Xue, Chunmei. *China Religion*. State Administration Religious Affairs publication, 2009.

Zetzsche, Jost Oliver. *The Bible in China: The History of the Union Version or the Culmination of Protestant Missionary Bible Translation in China*. Sankt Augustin: Monumenta Serica Institute, 1999.

From United Bible Societies Archives (some are unpublished reports)

American Bible Society, "ABS in China 1931–1966." ABS History, Distribution Abroad, 1966.

Amity News Service, 1992 to 2000.

Amity News Service, May 8, 1993.

British and Foreign Bible Society Annual Report, 1895.

British and Foreign Bible Society Report, "After a Hundred Years," 1905.

Cann, Kathleen. "Bible Work In China: Inception to 1959." United Bible Societies Background Paper prepared for UBS executive committee. November 1991.

"China Church Conference Hears of Rapid Growth," *UBS World Report 320,* May 1997.

"Christianity in Beijing." *UBS World Report 312*, September 1996.

Documents shared by China Christian Council / TSPM.

Erickson, John. "The UBS, China and Chinese Scripture." 1984.

Erickson, John. "Presentation to UBS Executive Council in Vienna." 1985.

"First Opportunity 21 'Gospel Wagon' Takes Scriptures to Rural Churches." *UBS World Report 361*, October 2001.

Han, Wenzao. "How Bountiful Is God's Grace—A Report on the Publication of the Bible in Simplified Script." *Tian Feng*, June 1990.

Lan, Xin. "The Story of One Bible." *Amity News Service*, 1998. Translated from *Tian Feng* magazine.

Loh, I-Jin. "Bible Work in China since 1979." 1994.

Loh I-Jin. "Brief Chronology of the Amity Printing Press Project." 1989.

Loh, I-Jin. "Report on Asia Opportunity Programs." *UBS Asia Opportunity News Update, No. 8*, February 1990.

Loh, I-Jin. *UBS Asia Opportunity News Update, No. 2*, 1989.

Pike, Errol. "Bible Challenge in China." *UBS Special Report*, June 1998.

Qiu, Cun Kiu. "An Encounter at a Bible Distribution Center." *USB Asia Opportunity News Update No. 5*, September 1993.

Selected Annual Reports of ABS and BFBS.

"Singing in a Cesspool." *UBS World Report 347*, 2000. Adapted from an article by Dan Wooding, a British journalist working with ASSIST Communications.

Stories and Testimonies included in this book can be found in www.ubscp.org.sg.

"The Time Is Ripe for Building Chinese Theology," *Amity News Service*, 1999.

UBS Asia Opportunity News Updates No. 1–105 (1989 to 1998), Asia Pacific Regional Center.

UBS China Partnership Reports and News Update 2005 to 2023.

UBS World Reports 1998 to 2008.

"Vivid Picture of Need for Bibles in Rural China." *UBS World Report 345*, October 2000.

Weber, H. R. "Impression on the Bible and Church Life in New China Feb 18–29." 1984.

Wickeri, Philip. "Interview with Bishop Shen Yifan." *Amity News Service*. April 15, 1993.

Yick, Bing. "One Bible and the Growth of a Church." *UBS Asia Opportunity News Update, No. 60*, June 1, 1994.

Index

A

Abundant Grace, The 133
Abundant Life, The 133–34
American Bible Society vi, 4–5, 8–10, 28, 43, 79, 101, 118, 120, 147, 149, 187, 195–96, 213, 221, 223
Amity Foundation 28–31, 37, 80, 201, 215
Amity Printing Company xi, xiii, 37, 200–01, 203
Amity Printing Press 30, 201
Anhui 39, 42, 48, 66–68, 74, 127–28, 158

B

Beijing xix, 2, 11, 26, 28, 38, 51, 56, 73, 78–79, 83, 87, 117–19, 161, 166, 179, 182, 185, 216, 223
Bible
    advocacy xix, 62, 177–78, 181
    distribution xvii, 20, 38–42, 44, 46–50, 54–55, 61, 66, 95, 213, 216
    distribution van xvii, 46–47, 216
    equipping 62
    medical van 62
    motorbike 111, 169–70
    paper 29, 38, 42, 53, 204, 215
    printing iii, xi, xiii, xvii, 13, 20, 28–29, 37, 53–54, 77, 82, 94, 148, 177, 200–01, 204–05, 208–09
    Resource Center 216
    resource room 161
    resources 53, 108–09, 138–39, 141, 148, 156, 162–63, 170–71, 204
    seminar 159, 164, 166–67, 177
    training xix
Big Flowery Miao xviii, 92, 96–98, 101–02, 105, 108, 204–05, 216
Black Yi 90, 92, 94, 97–98, 104–05, 107–08, 189, 204–05, 217
Black Yi Bible 97, 105, 108, 217
Braille Bible ix, xiii, 77, 79–87, 204–05, 216
Braille, Louis 77
British and Foreign Bible Society (BFBS) 2, 119, 177, 189, 213

C

Chew, John (bishop) i, 166, 171, 178, 180, 185, 196, 203
China Academy of Social Sciences 179
China Christian Council/TSPM 45
Chinese Union Version xiii, 5, 27, 34, 171, 191, 193, 213–14, 217
Chongqing 69, 73, 125–26, 128–30, 139
Crossway vi, 119, 172, 185, 187

D

discipleship ix, 125, 132–33

E

East Gates Ministries International 42
East Lisu xviii, 92, 97–99, 102–09, 204–05, 216–17
East Lisu Bible 97, 99, 102–05, 107–09, 204, 217
Ethnic minority 108, 110, 140

F

Financial Stewardship Bible xviii, 187
Fugong Bible School 167–68
Fujian 2, 40, 44–45, 67, 69, 71, 132, 178

G

Gansu 57–58, 60, 131, 133–34
Ganyi xviii, 93, 97–98, 103, 106, 205
Gospel booklets 113–14, 121, 123
Guizhou 90–92, 96, 162, 170, 221
Guizhou Bible School 162

H

Hebei 41, 56, 60, 136–37, 139, 141
Heilongjiang 159
Henan 20, 23, 39–40, 44, 46, 48–49, 70–71, 83, 114–15, 117, 121, 128, 130–31, 138–40, 163, 200
Hubei 71, 150–51, 173
Hunan 11, 21, 49, 75, 126–27, 139–42, 163, 167, 170

I

Inner Mongolian 108

J

Jesus Manga 187
Jiangsu 39–40, 46–47, 66–67, 71, 75, 94, 119–22, 128–29, 135–36, 139, 155, 166–67, 178, 181, 197
Jiangxi 44
Jingpo 94–96, 108, 204–05
Jingpo Bible 95–96, 108

L

Lahu 17, 94–95, 106, 108–10, 142, 205
Lahu Bible 94–95, 108, 110
large print Bibles 132
lay preachers 111, 136, 151, 156–57, 163, 165, 167–68, 170, 173
Liaoning 17, 40, 47–48, 50, 85, 162
Loh, I-Jin 28, 53

M

Metcalf, George 99, 104
Milloy, Miller 53, 171, 205
Minzu University 182
Morrison, Robert 2–4, 193, 213, 221

N

Nanjing Union Theological Seminary 216
National Bible Society of Scotland 195
National Seminary of Catholic Church 160

P

pastors ix, 165–66, 215
Perreau, Michael 202–03
Pictorial Bible Stories xviii, 116, 135, 138–41

S

Samuel Pollard 91–92, 94
Scripture literacy ix, 109, 125, 128, 132
Scripture portions 9–10, 62, 113–14, 116, 119, 12–23
Shaanxi 1, 42, 51, 61, 115–16, 127–32, 135, 139, 141, 159, 189, 221
Shandong 25, 49, 51–52, 57–58, 60–61, 69, 120, 125, 128, 133, 136, 158–59, 161, 170–71, 181, 197
Shandong Theological Seminary 158–59
Shanghai xix, 5–7, 9–0, 16, 35, 38, 52–53, 56–57, 69, 176–80, 182, 191, 194, 197, 213–15, 222
Shanghai Academy of Social Sciences 176–77, 191, 197
Sichuan 47, 54–55, 57, 59–61, 123, 155, 158, 161

T

Ting, K. H. 27–29, 32, 53, 68, 142, 165, 167, 201, 203
Triglot New Testament 217
Trinity Theological College 158, 179–80
Tsai, Jen-Li 72, 202

W

Wa 94, 103–08, 217
Wa Bible 103–08, 217
Wang Aiguo 94, 98, 176
Wang Zhiming 15, 97
Wenzao, Dr. Han 215
West Lisu xviii, 93, 98, 105, 108–11, 205, 216
West Lisu Annotated Bible 108
White Yi 105, 108, 110–11, 216
White Yi New Testament 105
women vii, 6–7, 12, 76, 101, 106, 117, 126, 131, 158, 208, 211

X

Xianwei, Elder Fu 118–19, 166, 171, 186
Xinjiang 41, 48

Y

Yunnan xviii, 15, 17, 23, 41, 48, 72, 86, 89–90, 92–99, 102–08, 110, 115, 139–40, 142–43, 149–51, 153, 157, 163, 167–70, 175–76, 178, 189–90
Yunnan Theological Seminary 98

Z

Zhejiang 14, 17, 20, 39, 68, 70, 141, 178, 186
Zhongnan Theological Seminary 173

visit us at missionbooks.org

Supracultural Gospel: Bridging East and West
Mary Lou Codman-Wilson and Alex Zhou

Drs. Mary Lou Codman-Wilson and Alex Zhou dialogue about Alex's experience becoming a believer in the US and his struggle to share his faith when he returned to China. They model a process of examining our cultural worldview to overcome the tensions associated with living out our faith in a context dominated by different religious or secular systems.

Supracultural Gospel presents seven principles to adapt the gospel to bridge East and West; essential attitudes and practices of emotionally healthy and spiritually discerning discipleship; and key gospel concepts in non-Western terms, while retaining biblical accuracy.

Heading Home with Jesus: Preparing Christian Students to Follow Christ in China

Debbie D. Philip

Thousands of Chinese students visit our churches and join Christian activities. Many even say they have become Christians while abroad. However, many fall away from their faith after they return to China. Debbie Philip has visited hundreds of returnees. She offers a new perspective for understanding what happens when Chinese students encounter Christians abroad and what needs to happen if they are to continue following Christ after returning home. The life stories, illustrations, and suggestions in this book will help you understand and support Chinese returnees better as they prepare to go home.

www.ingramcontent.com/pod-product-compliance
Lightning Source LLC
Chambersburg PA
CBHW080323080526

44585CB00021B/2448